A YOUNG GIRL READING
Jean-Honoré Fragonard
National Gallery of Art, Washington, D.C.
Gift of Mrs. Mellon Bruce
in memory of her father, Andrew W. Mellon

THE
SOCIAL AUDIT
FOR
MANAGEMENT

THE
SOCIAL AUDIT
FOR
MANAGEMENT

Clark C. Abt

amacom

A Division of American Management Associations

Library of Congress Cataloging in Publication Data

Abt, Clark C
    The social audit for management.

    Bibliography: p.
    Includes index.
    1. Industry--Social aspects. I. Title.
HD60.A27   658.4'08   76-30674
ISBN 0-8144-5384-8

First Printing

Preface

THIS book presents one of the more optimistic and ambitious views of social accounting. It is intended for the reader who wants to know about the measurement of corporate and organizational social performance—why such measurements are needed, how they can be done, and what kinds of problems typically are encountered and how to deal with them. In particular, I hope that the book will be helpful as a rough guide to action for corporate executives and government officials. No detailed knowledge of social science, econometrics, or accounting is required to understand the material, even though most of the concepts discussed are related to one or more of these fields.

The text is based on lectures at graduate schools of business (University of California at Berkeley, Catholic University of America, Columbia University, Harvard University, Massachusetts Institute of Technology, New York University), briefings to business executives and boards of directors of large corporations concerned with social responsibility, and reports to government officials involved in social programs and regulation of industry.

Much of the research upon which the book rests was conducted over the last five years. Ever since Congressman Thomas P. O'Neill, Jr., read our initial proposal for an annual social audit into the *Congressional Record* in 1970, we have been developing the concept and its applications further. There have been efforts to make it more consistent and accurate—which led to additional complexity—and to apply it to real business decisions—which simplified the concept and made it more practical.

Looking back at these five years of research, implementation, and evaluation, I feel that the concepts of social performance measurement and social audit have become much more widely accepted; the awe and disbelief that greeted initial efforts for these "quantifications of concern" (to use the late Eli Goldston's phrase) have died down considerably. Unlike in 1970 or 1971, most large corporations today make a definite effort to report on their social performance at least in their annual reports. At the same time, our most ambitious hopes for widespread implementation of the entire concept, with the scope, detail, and precision urged in this book, have not yet been realized, even though the federal government has adopted a number of components of social auditing, in the form of legal requirements for annual reports on corporate performance in the areas of occupational health and safety, equal employment opportunity, environmental impact, product safety, and truthfulness in financial reporting and product descriptions.

Many of my colleagues in the social sciences, business, and government have made valuable contributions both to the development of the concepts of social audits and to the technical discussions in this book. At Abt Associates Inc., the major contributions to the continuing development of the social audit were made by Peter Merrill, Chris Hamilton, Peter Miller, Donald Muse, Neal Perry, Louis Phillips, and Walter Stellwagen. In industry, the late Eli Goldston, former president of Eastern Gas & Fuel Associates, Bruce Henderson, president of the Boston Consulting Group, and Dean LeBaron, president of Batterymarch Financial Management Corporation, were the most creative contributors to the continuing debate on the possibilities and limitations of social performance measurement in industry. In the academic community, professors Robert Ackerman, Melvin Anshen, Raymond Bauer, Daniel Bell, Neil Churchill, and Prakash Sethi have contributed the most in the way of constructive criticisms that have stimulated me to respond with further developments of the concepts. I particularly want to thank my assistants Perenna Fleming, Dolores Sullivan, and Marianne Rusk for their support in editing and producing the manuscript.

Clark C. Abt

Cambridge, Massachusetts
November 1976

Contents

1

Corporate Social Responsibility

THE widespread concern over social responsibility in the decisions of corporations has its origins in at least two disturbing aspects of contemporary American society. The first is a general awareness of the grave social problems we face and the inadequacy of the attempts to deal with these problems by individual citizens and by governments at all levels. Since our social problems are not being solved by government organizations, what other large organizations can be mobilized to deal with them? Will the answer be the private corporations? Many government officials, leaders of industry, and individual citizens are now calling on the corporations, great and small, to help with social problem solving.

The second major source of concern as to the social responsibility of corporations is anxiety about the survival of our system of private capitalism and constitutional government. The decline in the prestige of business careers, particularly among the youth of the country, and in the public respect for industry threatens the overall confidence of our economy in its own survival in its present form. Public pressures not only from radical and youth groups but increasingly from the large centrist segments of society represented by consumer and labor and church groups, are questioning the right of corporations to act in any way other than with social responsibility.

To Whom Are Corporations Responsible?

The five publics affected by the activities of corporations are the owners, the customers, the employees, residents in the corporations' local neighborhoods, and the general public. All five of these publics are concerned, in different ways, with the inadequacy of current governmental social problem solving and with the survival of the corporation as a socioeconomic entity.

The *owners* of the corporations are concerned as individuals about the inadequacy of current efforts to solve social problems because the quality and security of their lives are threatened. As owners or shareholders, they are concerned about the increasing inefficiency and reduced productivity of their enterprises which stem from unsolved social problems. Social problems raise the costs of doing business, thus reducing earnings for shareholders. Crime raises insurance rates and operating costs. Drug abuse raises labor costs by increasing the costs of recruitment and decreasing the productivity of labor. Social and racial conflicts increase the costs of labor and of personnel management. Environmental pollution raises production costs because of demands for more pollution-free technology. Altogether, unsolved social problems reduce profits.

Owners of corporations are also concerned about the survival of the corporation as an economic form. With costs increasing and profits declining as a result of social problems, and with growing demands for public intervention in the management of corporations to assure their social responsibility, the corporation as an organizational form is threatened with extinction—either through unprofitability leading to bankruptcy, or through absorption into the government by increasing regulation. With the socialization of industry, the game of picking the winners will be all over for shareholders. There will then be only one game in town (the government's), and winning or losing in this game will be mainly a political problem limited to fewer individuals. Ironically, the net effect of an egalitarian-striving socialism will be a new elitism with a higher and narrower pyramid of power than the one we now have under liberal capitalism.

The *customers* of the corporations are concerned about unsolved social problems because they fear a decline in the quality and availability of goods and services. As the costs of doing business are driven up by social problems, many of these costs are passed on to the consumer in the form of higher prices or lower quality or both. Furthermore, as government regulation increases, the availability of a variety of goods and services declines; with the corporations totally under government operation, the variety, quality, and availability of products and services would be typical of that under most government monopolies. In consumer goods and services, those have never been very good.

Employees are concerned about the major social problems of poverty, crime, drug abuse, race conflict, social injustice, and environmental pollution, because these problems directly affect the quality and security of their lives. At the same time, employees are concerned with the survival of the corporation, not necessarily because they love it so well, but because they fear the insecurity of seeking their economic incomes—and perhaps their psychic incomes— elsewhere. Where else is there to go for gainful employment, except the government, the educational institutions, and firms owned by individuals? The government and educational institutions together can offer only some 30 percent of the jobs needed, and individual proprietorships are difficult and very risky. If corporations were to cease their existence, even the shift to socialist all-government employment would mean many changes and the disruption of many vocations and careers, not to mention the many new constraints that would then be imposed on employees by an all-powerful employer.

The *residents* of the local environments of corporations are concerned about the corporation's attitude toward social problems, partly because they are also members of the other three publics— employees, owners, and consumers—but also because the effects of corporate activities spill over onto their own lives and properties. The small householder living near a chemical plant suffers directly from the plant's neglect of such social issues as pollution, unemployment, health, and housing. Furthermore, if local corporations become unprofitable and go out of business, the entire community tax base will suffer, with attendant decline in municipal services.

Finally, the *general public* is concerned about the solution of social problems with the participation of industry because it sees little hope of the government's doing the job alone, and because of a general concern with the stability, survival, and growth of the country's traditional economic system.

Changing Attitudes Toward Corporations

To understand what has caused the current widespread interest in the social audit, it is useful to consider several recent social, economic, technological, and political trends that have contributed to the public concern about industry's social performance. These include automation, intensive industrialization and its undesirable side effects on the environment, the unanticipated social costs imposed by certain technological advances, and counterproductive effects on systems resulting from technological advances in subsystems.

Automation has had two dominant socioeconomic impacts: mass distribution of cheap automobiles, radios, and television sets, and a decline in worker job satisfaction. The great increase in automobile use has resulted in much air pollution as well as a reduction in average transit speeds due to traffic jams. Widespread diffusion of communications technology has provided mass publics with views of life styles that encourage demands for greater participation in a higher quality of life.

Industrialization has created environmental pollution on a dangerous scale, now widely perceived by the public. Technological advances thought to be beneficial have had surprising negative effects, as for example the water-polluting consequences of intensive nitrate-fertilizer agriculture, the ecologically unbalancing effects of certain pesticides, the genetically damaging effects of radiation and drugs such as thalidomide, and the structural damage caused by the sonic booms of supersonic aircraft.

Since the first atomic bombs, people have in fact begun to question whether science and technology do more good than harm. Technologically based industry is often perceived as ruthlessly unconcerned with the human costs of technological advances, and as these costs have become more dramatically apparent, public pressure for socially oriented technology assessments has mounted.

At the same time, social, economic, and political changes have accelerated the public concern about industry's social performance. In the last decade, youth, women, minorities, and other previously powerless social groups have emerged as major political forces, rebelling against authoritarian institutions and challenging the legitimacy of large business organizations as well as governments. The political ideal of democratic participation, diffused globally by advanced technology in transportation and communication, has generated expectations of affluence and personal rights that have risen faster than the ability of governments and industries to satisfy them. The resulting gap between expectations (fed by the political promises of elected politicians) and their realization is the basis of much public frustration with all major institutions, and with big business in particular.

At the same time that these negative side effects of industrialization were being felt and resented by the public, technology also developed new decision-making techniques and stimulated the development of social sciences that gave promise of correcting the undesirable side effects. Industrial engineering led to systems engineering, systems analysis, and operations research. Macroeconomics, microeconomics, operations research, and the behavioral sciences that were developed as management sciences led to new capabilities in economic planning and evaluation.

Thus at the same time that technology has generated obnoxious side effects, it has also been the source of some rational decision-making techniques that offer hope of controlling the monster. Most of the educated public has never really abandoned science as mankind's salvation—only an unbridled technology that is insensitive to human values. The demand is in fact growing for analytical methods to control industrial technology for human purposes.

The corporate social responsibility "movement" in the United States—if it can be called that—represents an informal, loose coalition of groups with a number of related concerns: environmental preservation (conservationists), equal employment opportunity (minorities and women), consumer protection (Ralph Nader, consumer groups, and others), employment security and quality of work (unions), keeping industrial enterprise free of government controls (management and investors), the responsiveness of private and public institutions to social needs (government officials and socially concerned citizens), and the application of efficient decision-making methods to the many socio-political-economic trade-offs required by the inevitable conflicts among all these legitimate interests (economists and social scientists).

In the late 1960s, a system of "social indicators" and an annual national social report were proposed by Raymond Bauer, Mancur Olson, Walter Mondale, and others. The social indicators idea was initially a response to the problems of poverty, health, and racial inequality, and thus seemed more relevant to the concerns of government than to those of industry, but by the early 1970s, several developments focused attention on the performance of private industry.

First, environmental pollution reached such a degree of public visibility and annoyance that the environmental issue became widely salient; the principal polluters were private industries or their products. Second, Ralph Nader and others successfully dramatized the consumer frauds and antisocial actions of certain private industries and achieved widespread public support for consumer movements in the United States. Third, class action suits involving equal employment opportunity were brought by women and minority groups, resulting in many millions of dollars in damages being paid by such prominent companies as AT&T, General Motors, and General Electric. Fourth, the women's liberation movement in the United States threatened expensive readjustments in wages for many United States industries that had previously exploited cheap female labor (telephone, insurance, textiles, electronics). Fifth, the general disenchantment with all major institutions and all traditional authority occasioned by the disasters of the Vietnam war combined with the other dissatisfactions to generate a widespread climate of distrust for big business. Sixth, the flight of small investors from the New York stock markets as a result of "insider" deals among big businesses and large institutional investors, and the collapse of the 1960s bull market, further deepened public suspicions concerning the degree to which business and industry operate in the public interest. And seventh, enlightened business leaders everywhere, but particularly in the United States and Japan (where the social pressures are greatest, although different), have begun to understand that corporate social responsibility is no longer merely a charitable activity, but very possibly a decisive condition of organizational survival.

Reflecting public pressures, new regulatory agencies have emerged since 1960, such as the Occupational Safety and Health Administration (OSHA), the Consumer Product Safety Commission (CPSC), the Environmental Protection Agency (EPA), the National Commission on Water Quality (NCWQ), and the Equal Employment Opportunity Commission (EEOC), and such social action agencies as the Office of Economic Opportunity (OEO).

Threatened by consumer boycotts, government fines and regulations, employee legal action and punitive damage suits, investor disenchantment, and community opposition to new plants or even to ongoing operations (see examples in Appendix A), many corporate managements began in the early 1970s to accept some of their social responsibilities as routine operating costs of doing business, like any other factors of production, such as the costs of labor or capital (see examples in Appendix B). With effective social performance now regarded as seriously as financial performance as a requirement for survival, business leaders and managers began to find a need to measure their social performance, not only to defend themselves against dangerous public criticism, legal actions, and threats of government intervention, but also to provide a rational basis for allocating their social investments.

The full application of corporate social performance measurement may not occur until the 1980s, but even in the early 1970s many corporations—approximately 25 percent of those in Japan and the United States—felt the need to make a report on their social performance along with their annual financial report to the stockholders. The pressure for social accounting has recently been much increased by the world energy crisis. The energy shortages imposed in Japan, Europe, and America by the Arab oil boycott increased the economic pressure to withdraw environmental controls on the more polluting fuels. This has sharpened the conflicts among the constituencies of corporations—owners, employees, consumers, communities, and general public—requiring both careful decisions concerning the trade-offs involved and better communication of the reasons for management decisions.

In any financial crisis, financial accounting tends to be taken very seriously. In the current social crisis for business and industry, social accounting is also likely to be taken very seriously. There are impediments to the prompt application of social audits: first, certain unresolved and misunderstood theoretical problems, which are discussed in this book, and second, the time required for the diffusion of the new social accounting concepts to managers who are not yet educated in their use. However, a few of the university graduate schools of business management are now beginning to offer courses in the measurement of social performance and a few social research organizations now offer management training in social audits. Adoption of the social measurement approach will be gradual and may require many years, but it has definitely begun.

Definitions of Corporate Social Responsibility

Given the widely felt need for social responsibility in private corporations, how is such responsibility defined? Is it the responsibility of corporations to solve all of society's social problems left unsolved by government? Or merely to try to do so? Or merely to try to solve some of the problems? Which ones? How much?

Milton Friedman, the University of Chicago economist, would define the social responsibility of the private corporation to be the making of money, or profit. The Dreyfus Third Century Fund feels that to be socially responsible, companies should observe legal constraints with respect to employment practices, marketing, environment, health, and safety.

Since definitions of social responsibility vary, it may be useful to mention first the areas in which there is wide agreement, and then the areas about which agreement is less universal. For example, there is wide agreement that corporations should refrain from capital crimes; there would be agreement of a lesser degree as to the need for veracity in advertising; and there would be low agreement about the social desirability of doing business with nondemocratic governments or selling antipersonnel weapons to the Department of Defense.

Until the government further defines corporate social responsibility through legislation and enforcement, it will have to remain a matter for industry and individual companies to define for themselves. Within the constraints of law and public opinion, the type and amount of corporate social responsibility a company should have will be determined by its owners, managers, and operators. However, this does not eliminate the need for some kind of widely acceptable definition. If a company is to apply objective measures to its social performance, as in the case of a social audit, it is necessary to set standards which are widely accepted and hence widely applicable.

Level of Agreement

On the basis of this writer's experience with corporate managements, it can be said that there is widespread agreement (among all or most industries in all or most areas), or "core consensus," that corporations are responsible for the following:

1. Obeying major laws, particularly where the law also has widely accepted moral sanctions associated with it, such as laws against murder, enslavement, and larceny.

2. Humane treatment of employees, usually but not always enforced by law.
3. Honest, truthful, and fair dealings with other enterprises, consumers, and employees.
4. Truthful financial reporting.
5. Respect for the intent as well as the letter of contracts, in providing a reasonable quality and quantity of product or services for the price negotiated.
6. Providing—or at least attempting to provide—a fair return on investment to shareholders through profits.
7. Equal employment opportunity for entry level jobs only.

There is majority agreement (among most industries in most locations) that corporate responsibility includes these points:

8. Internal accounting and capital budgeting of all major expenditures, including those for social benefits.
9. Obeying *all* laws, including those weakly enforced, restricting pollution or unsafe practices and products, establishing minimum wages, and so on.
10. Complete truthfulness in advertising.
11. Nonharmfulness of products and services.
12. Nonharmfulness of production processes to local communities in which they are situated.
13. Employee benefits that assure family health, security, and welfare at least as long as a person is employed, and afterward if his/her employment ends with retirement.
14. Modest contributions to local charitable causes in kind or in cash, to the extent that these do not reduce after-tax earnings by more than 2 percent.
15. Equal employment opportunity for all races and both sexes *at all levels.*
16. Some sort of recording of social responsibility actions (such as the EEO-1 form) and disclosure of these to shareholders in at least a qualitative form.

There is minority agreement (among most industries in only some locations, or among only some industries in most locations) on the following points:

17. Active efforts to achieve equal employment opportunities, both racial and sexual, at all levels, including the officer level, regardless of difficulty and costs.

18. Actively improving the local environment of the company, by reducing pollution and by other actions.
19. Actively working to improve the quality of life of employees, consumers, and local residents by whatever means are consistent with company requirements for financial performance.
20. Actively pursuing improved social justice and quality of life for all by direct actions concerning customers, suppliers, lessees, and any other groups that are affected directly by the company.
21. Measuring, recording, and publicly disseminating detailed descriptions of social benefits and costs and social assets and liabilities generated by the company, on a regular, periodic, quantitative, and objective basis, as is done in annual financial reports.

These three levels of corporate social responsibility correspond approximately to those outlined by Eleanor Sheldon of the Russell Sage Foundation: first (and widely agreed to) that "business has the responsibility to make a profit while dealing fairly and honestly"; second (and probably agreed to by the majority) that "business has a responsibility to society with respect to its employees and products, and a responsibility to mirror the ideals and values of the society within its own microcosm"; and third, that "it is a primary obligation of business to use its power to promote social ends perceived as moral." Since the levels of acceptance tend to move up with time, we may expect all 21 requirements to be in the "widely accepted" category in a few years.

To some extent the degrees of responsibility for actions are independent of the degrees of responsibility for measuring and recording them. It is quite conceivable that a company would elect to be rather activist in its definition of its social responsibility, but eschew complex audits for measuring the results of its efforts. One can easily imagine an old-fashioned "benevolent despot" entrepreneur dispensing with measures of social performance and insisting that his own judgment of what pays off socially will suffice. On the other hand, a thorough and cautious modern manager trained in management sciences might elect to execute a most comprehensive and detailed program for measuring social performance—not because of any penchant for liberalism, but for the sake of optimizing his capital budgeting by getting more social responsibility payoff for less investment.

Corporations—and the reader—can make their own decisions as to what degree of corporate social responsibility is appropriate. My own view is that the first 16 points in the list ought to be the bare minimum standard. Beyond that irreducible core, companies should be encouraged to accept as much corporate social responsibility as they feel they wish to accept seriously, and to execute the appropriate actions. Corporations still have the option of anticipating—and hence rendering unnecessary—further government regulation in these areas.

In all cases, whatever a company's commitment to various degrees of corporate social responsibility, it would seem simply good management sense to develop a concise statement of the company's social objectives (even if they are only to make money while "staying legal"), and then annually measure and record the estimated progress toward these objectives. For the most conservative companies, this might be little more than the annual financial audit and annual report, plus a statement specifically disavowing any social objectives for the company other than profit generated by legal means. In other cases, stockholders and employees might feel that their corporate social responsibility extends considerably further, perhaps to include all 21 points described above. It is not necessarily true that the larger and more comprehensive definition of corporate social responsibility threatens the financial responsibility or profitability of a company. On the contrary, there can be powerful correlations between good social performance and good financial performance.

It may be helpful to give a few examples of corporate social responsibility, because definitions of social responsibility can differ. For example, responsibility for human treatment is a concept whose execution depends on the definition of "humane." Agricultural concerns may honestly believe that a $50 a week wage for an agricultural worker with a family of ten to support is humane, particularly when they contribute "free" temporary housing (possibly in shacks with outhouses and no running water). Industrial corporations may consider it humane to terminate employees in their late fifties, just short of their achieving pension rights. Service firms may consider it humane to lay off women who become pregnant, and to refuse to pay medical benefits or provide continued employment to unmarried women who become pregnant. In each of these cases and similar ones, however, the general public would not for the most part consider the actions humane. Public response to company actions, if measured, can help to correct an inadequate definition of "humanity" on the part of the company.

Responsibility for attempting to provide a fair return on investment to shareholders would seem too obvious to mention. Yet many small shareholders may invest in a company—for instance, a high technology "growth" company—on the assumption that the management is dedicated to creating a competitive return on investment, when in actuality the management is chiefly dedicated to achieving quick capital gains for its own holdings by promoting the future potential of a still untested concept or product. This has happened with many high technology companies in recent times. If a company consistently fails to provide a reasonable return on investment year after year, and does not give persuasive reasons, then an audit— even a purely social audit—might discount the net social worth of the enterprise by some amount representing the "opportunity cost" of capital to those investors who were mistakenly led to anticipate a reasonable return on their investment.

The responsibility for truthful financial reporting is a subject unto itself, but despite the best efforts of generally honest and skilled public accountants, much financial reporting is not precisely truthful and some is intentionally misleading. A company that overstates its earnings and thus stimulates stock price increases or investments that later turn sour might be charged with a social cost of the loss of credibility in its statements, as well as the "opportunity cost" to investors of the capital they would have otherwise invested elsewhere. This is a difficult cost to compute, but merely an effort to estimate it might deter some of the more flagrant "take the money and run" kinds of financial reporting.

As for internal accounting and capital budgeting for major social benefit expenditures, many large companies devote considerable resources to socially directed activities, ranging from employee benefits to contributions to local charities, without budgeting and accounting for these expenditures at a level of accuracy and detail consistent with their accounting for other expenses. A company might allocate 2 percent of its earnings to charitable purposes, but then give much less attention to budgeting and accounting this amount than to a similar amount expended for plant, equipment, or labor— as if expenditures for social purposes should be measured only by their inputs (costs), not also by their outputs (benefits generated). This practice seemingly assumes that social investments have no measurable output, and indeed, where social investments are treated in such a cursory manner, the efficiency of the investment in producing socially desirable results is likely to be low.

The responsibility for obeying all laws, however inconvenient or poorly enforced, is a surprisingly difficult one for many large corporations to accept in practice. Laws against water and air pollution are regularly broken by major chemical, oil, and power companies, who then pay modest fines for the privilege of breaking the law. Corporate scofflaws include agribusinesses that consistently break laws governing working conditions, and consumer products manufacturers that repeatedly break laws concerned with truthful advertising and adequate testing of products, laws against political contributions and bribes, laws against collusion in pricing, and so on. Since the penalties and fines for the breaking of most of these laws have not been set high enough to represent the real cost to the public of their infringement (nor a balance to the perceived economic benefit to the company), many companies find it cheaper to continue breaking the laws and paying the fines. A social audit of these companies might list as a liability—or social cost—the difference between the amount of the fine and the actual cost to the public of the violation.

Future Requirements of Social Responsibility

Corporate social responsibility is required by law in the form of FDA, EEO, EPA, OSHA, FCC, and other federal and state regulations, by public and consumer opinion, by employee opinion, and by stockholders to the extent that it affects profits (which it does). According to a majority of executive opinion in large corporations (see George Steiner's survey of 284 large corporations described below), the requirements for corporate social responsibility will be increasingly enforced in future, both by government regulation and by organized consumer and employee action. The requirements will encompass the planning of corporate actions that have social impact, documenting and measuring the costs and benefits (inputs and outputs) of such actions, and the actual implementation of such actions at operating levels, including the procedures and incentives required to make the actions effective.

Since not all of these requirements can be met within the current operational or conceptual capability of many corporations, investment in some research and development in this area seems essential for them. This R&D investment can be justified by the probable increases in productivity as a result of socially responsible actions, by a reduction in the risk of adverse opinion and consequent adverse actions by the public, consumers, employees, stockholders, and local and national government; and a greater feeling of participation in the major social problem-solving of the times on the part of management.

While it is true that most organizational reforms, including those in public institutions, are initiated by outside pressures and by the lower echelons of the organizational hierarchy, rational social policy requires the attention of top and middle management. In the face of competing demands for time and resources, no important new activity is likely to be implemented in any corporation unless it receives impetus from top management and unless top management follows up to make sure that lower levels of management actually execute the new policy. It is top management that must integrate the pressures for corporate social reform and social performance measurement with the traditional demands for economic performance and devise a plan for action.

Corporate management can establish priorities among the different corporate constituencies—employees, stockholders, consumers, neighboring communities, and the general public—by determining the number of people affected in each constituency and the extent to which they are affected. These must then be balanced against the basic survival conditions of the organization, economic and operational.

The following list of social performance activities is derived from a survey of the efforts of 284 major United States corporations to develop measures of their social performance.* The activities are listed in the order ranked by the respondents. Some suggested measurements of the success of these activities are given in the right-hand column.

---

* Conducted by John J. Corson and George A. Steiner, *Measuring Business's Social Performance: The Corporate Social Audit* (New York: Committee for Economic Development, 1974).

CORPORATE ACTIVITY	RECOMMENDED MEASUREMENTS
1. Ensuring employment and advancement for minorities.	Comparison this year versus last year of percentage of minorities and women who were: Employed overall Employed at various levels of company hierarchy Newly hired Promoted versus overall company average Paid less or more than position average, compared with non-minority employees.
2. Increasing productivity in the private sector of the economy.	Revenue per employee this year versus last year. Company revenue per payroll dollar. Company net earnings on assets.
3. Improving the innovativeness and performance of business management.	Number of innovations proposed and adopted, with estimated productivity increase. Number of products or new services initiated. Number of new employee benefits added. Number of satisfactory organizational changes instituted.
4. Improvement of work/career opportunities.	Upward mobility of employees, as measured by percentage of promotions and skill upgradings per year. Responses to sample survey of employees concerning attitudes toward work/career opportunities. Turnover rates. Ratio between applications and resignations.
5. Installation of modern pollution abatement equipment.	Absolute and relative reduction of air or water pollution as a result of equipment installation, compared with government standards. Improvement in availability of recreational or other facilities (such as a river) as a result of pollution abatement, in terms of number of people now able to use the facility who couldn't use it before. Reduction in incidents of respiratory illness related to air pollution. Reduction in perceived unsatisfactory

CORPORATE ACTIVITY

RECOMMENDED MEASUREMENTS
air quality: its frequency and extensiveness as determined by survey of affected population and of its movements in response.

6. Facilitating equality of results by continued training and other special programs (civil rights and equal opportunity).

Percentage of promotion and pay increases for minorities and women compared with majority employees. Percentage of promotions of minorities and women employees versus majority employees. Fulfilled opportunities in job enrichment and job transfer, for minorities and women, compared with those for majority employees.

7. Supporting fiscal and monetary policies for steady economic growth.

Percentage of goods and services for which prices were not increased or increased less than industry average (compared with national average for similar goods and services that had price increases) as measure of cooperation with anti-inflation efforts. Support of international trade policies as measured by percentage of goods and services exported and imported, in relation to national policies. Conservation of working capital as measured by ratio of overall revenue to working capital employed. Increased labor intensiveness in times of high unemployment, increased labor-saving changes in times (or places) of labor shortage.

8. Direct financial aids to schools, including scholarships, grants, and tuition refunds.
(Note that in Steiner's survey, this is given—as are some other activities—in terms of inputs rather than in desired outputs and impacts. The presumed goal of this activity is improvement in the educational level of the public and improved access to higher education by minorities and women.)

Increase in number of minority and women students at educational institutions supported by the company, as a direct result of support supplied. Increase in number of women and minorities and other graduates from institutions supported by the company, resulting from its support.

CORPORATE ACTIVITY

RECOMMENDED MEASUREMENTS

9. Engineering new facilities for minimum environmental effects. (Again this is an input rather than an output.)

Efficiency in energy consumption by new facility compared with national norms and company facilities built previously. Reduction of effluent pollution in new facility, both absolutely and relatively. Degree to which environmental standards are met, compared with the degree to which they are met by previously built facilities and by comparable industry as a whole.

10. Active recruitment of the disadvantaged. (Again, an input rather than an output.)

Improvement in percentage of disadvantaged employees hired (presumably drawn mainly from ethnic minorities, women, and the handicapped) versus nondisadvantaged, with "disadvantaged" being defined as those having annual incomes below the poverty line of $5,000 a year.

11. Encouraging adoption of open-housing ordinances.

Actual percentage of housing in neighboring communities required to operate under open-housing ordinances as a result of company efforts.

12. Preserving animal life and the ecology of forests and comparable areas.

Change in incidence of small-bird counts (usually a direct measure of the ecological health of an area). Percentage of land in company's area maintained in natural state as estimated by conservationists.

13. Helping secure government financial support for local and state arts councils and National Endowment for the Arts.

Increase in local and state artistic and cultural activities as a direct result of company efforts, in numbers of concerts given, number of art shows held, number of plays produced, and total audiences served per year.

14. Designing and running new hospitals, new clinics, and extended-care facilities.

Number of additional patient days supplied as a direct result of company activities. Number of hospital beds made available as a result of company activities. Increase in per-

Corporate Activity	Recommended Measurements
	centage of local low-income population having access to medical treatment as a result of company activities.
15. Augmenting the supply of replenishable resources, such as trees, with more productive species.	Number of trees planted. Increase in total acreage of replanted areas.
16. Designing programs to enhance the effectiveness of the civil service.	Hours of executive service supplied *pro bono* to government services. Improvements in management, reductions in costs, increases in total service hours and/or numbers of people served as a result of company activities.
17. Building plants and sales offices in ghettos.	Change in the percentage of plants and offices built in low-income urban areas versus other areas. Total amount of floor space built in ghetto areas. Total number of employees operating plants and offices in ghetto areas.
18. Provisions of day-care centers for children of working mothers.	Absolute capacity to provide day care to children at company locations and in neighboring localities. Percentage of the demand for day-care center slots that is satisfied as a result of company activities. Child days of day care supplied per year. Savings to employees as a result of below-market costs.
19. Restoring aesthetically depleted properties such as strip mines.	Percentage of aesthetically obnoxious acreage that has been restored. Reduction in number and size of aesthetically obnoxious areas. Perceived change in aesthetic worth of areas affected by company actions, as determined by survey.
20. Running schools and school systems and establishing new schools.	Additional number of pupil days supplied. Increase in number of students finishing grade, and reduction in dropout rates. Gains in achievement scores and college placements. Number of new schools established. Number of new student slots created. Number of new teachers supplied.

It should be noted that all the measurements suggested above are fairly simple quantitative measures of the social outputs or impacts of various socially relevant corporate actions. In the social audit approach proposed in this book, all of these quantitative measures can be converted to dollar values that are mutually commensurable, by determining the market worth of these various quantitative achievements to the populations affected, and then translating that unit market worth into a total aggregate market worth. This means that it is possible to make explicit quantitative trade-offs among these different types of benefits and to develop an optimal mix of resource allocations for the company's portfolio of socially relevant actions, either to maximize the social productivity of a fixed level of social investment, or to minimize the investment required to achieve a fixed level of social productivity.

In the course of the following chapters I shall refer on occasion to the experience of my own work and that of my associates. I do this for two reasons. First, it is the experience I know best, and in a field which fosters some disagreement among reasonable men, it is probably best to stick to what one knows. Second, though I have taken some pains to be cognizant of other work in the field, I obviously cannot know it as well as mine. If I am thus able to communicate to the reader my own sense of the concreteness and practicality of the social audit, the reader will be better served than by a more generalized discussion.

2

Measuring Social Performance: Methods and Criteria

THE mission of the social audit is to provide more objective, accurate, and comprehensive information about an organization's social performance than is usually compiled. The primary audience for this information is management, which can act on it in many ways. Management need not necessarily publish the information on the corporation's social performance that is provided by a social audit, beyond what is already legally required for compliance with EEO, environmental impact, FDA, OSHA, and other government regulations. Nor need it take any action based on the information if it finds the information reassuring.

When ideological and public relations considerations are put aside, probably the most fundamental question responsible executives have about corporate social responsibility activities is: "Is this a good investment?" The answer to the question is not simple, because the "this" consists of highly diverse corporate actions with social impacts, the range and variability of which are great.

20

How We Measure: Techniques and Concepts

The direct financial costs of social actions can usually be computed by any trained financial manager, but the valuation of the social costs and benefits—and even the determination of what those costs and benefits might be—is usually very difficult for corporation executives who are not trained in the social sciences. The social audit is an application of some of the most advanced techniques developed by scientists experienced in the field of social programs.

Available Data: Public Studies

To begin with, there is a substantial body of socioeconomic impact theory, practical experience, and data concerning the relative effectiveness of various social responsibility projects. Most of this theory and these data have been developed in connection with federal government social action programs and their planning and evaluation. The many federally supported cost-effectiveness analyses of programs in health, education, welfare, employment, housing, transportation, and economic development provide a data base for the evaluation of comparable social responsibility projects by corporations.

For example, the rate of return on human capital from investment in education has been theoretically and empirically determined by Gary Becker of the University of Chicago * in a study that provides some general data on rates of return from different levels of education. The comparative cost-effectiveness of various urban economic development attempts has been studied, and there are studies available of the economic productivity of hospitals, housing projects, and transportation systems.

A common methodology of socioeconomic impact analysis runs through most of these public studies. Total benefits are estimated in money terms, total costs are subtracted from total benefits, and a net benefit or benefit/cost ratio is estimated for comparison with other programs. Assuming that a corporations's social actions can achieve rough comparability with the efficiencies typically achieved in the public programs, such benefit/cost estimates provide data for determining the best mix of corporate actions, given a company's known capabilities and the level of investment it desires.

* *Human Capital* (New York: Columbia University Press, 1964).

"Market Worth"

The other major method of determining the worth of social investments is to determine the "market worth" of the expected benefits to the population affected. For example, a purely financial measurement applied to fair employment practices may enormously understate their social worth to the people concerned. Alternatively, the fiscal value of retirement benefits may greatly overstate their social worth as perceived by a young employee population. Such measurements can save money by indicating where benefits not desired can be reduced and where modestly funded but highly desired benefits can yield disproportionately high gains in productivity.

Social audits make extensive use of "market worth" in assesssing social benefits and social cost. The worth of social actions to the people affected by them is in my opinion the most meaningful measure of their effectiveness. It provides a standard unit of measurement (dollars) and eliminates the need for weighting or for indirect computation.

A major theoretical advantage is that differences among individuals in their opinion of social costs and benefits, and differences between the opinions of individuals affected and those of the social auditor, are eliminated as a problem. The social auditor's responsibility is simply to measure the central tendency of the market worth of a given social benefit or cost to the individuals affected, and specifically not to intrude the social auditor's own estimation of the "true" or ultimate social worth of the particular action.

The concept of market worth for estimating the money equivalent of social costs and benefits generated by corporations is clearly founded on the concept of consumer sovereignty. We assume that consumer preferences are sovereign in the market of social goods and services, just as they are in the market for economic goods and services.

Consider an example of the specific steps in the cost/benefit quantification process. First, the estimated impact of a particular corporate action is identified in terms of what particular populations or constituencies are affected. Second, a determination is made by means of sample surveys or interviews or analogy to similar experiences in the past as to whether the particular socially significant action is perceived as a benefit or a cost by the populations affected. The next problem is to determine the *degree* or *amount* of benefit or cost as perceived by the population affected. This is determined on the basis of an average unit cost or unit benefit in money terms per person affected, by methods already discussed or to be discussed below. Then that unit cost or benefit is multiplied by the total number of people affected to arrive at a total benefit/cost measurement.

Thus the unit social benefit or cost of a particular corporation's action or process is determined by estimating its average monetized market worth to the individuals affected. This market worth should be determined on the basis of analogies to identical or highly similar social actions that do have a specific price or cost attributed to them by consumers or, when such prices have not been established, by the method of "shadow pricing."

"Shadow Prices" and "Opportunity Costs"

"Shadow pricing" is extensively used in the social audit. A somewhat imprecise economic definition of a shadow price is "a value which is not derived from the market." For example, the shadow price of an input in a firm's production process would be the value of the input to the firm, as opposed to the market price which the firm paid for that input.

In this sense the shadow price concept is almost identical to another concept important in the social audit: the concept of "opportunity cost." Shadow pricing is a means of measuring the "opportunity cost" * and is used extensively in the application of a social audit.

"Consumer Surplus"

The major measure used in social audits to estimate the net social benefit to consumers of a company's product or services is the "consumer surplus." The consumer surplus is defined as the area under the demand curve and above the selling price line when the demand curve is plotted as a function of price on the ordinate and of quantity on the abscissa (Figure 1). It is the difference, or "surplus," between what a consumer would be willing to pay for a given economic good and the actual price charged.

---

* "Opportunity cost" is the cost of what must be sacrificed in order to provide the resources to produce an item. "To use a popular wartime example, devoting more resources to the production of guns means using fewer resources to produce butter. The social cost of guns is the amount of butter foregone." (Charles E. Ferguson, *Microeconomic Theory,* Homewood, Illinois: R. D. Irwin, 1972, p. 208.)

The concept is significant because it expresses the idea that economy in production through economy of scale, technological improvement, and efficient organization creates a social benefit for the consumer by lowering the price he has to pay for a desired good, making the price less than what he would be willing to pay. Robert Solow of the Massachusetts Institute of Technology and others have suggested that this is probably as good a measure as any of the social worth of a given product or service.

In a sense, the concept of the consumer surplus aggregates the "multiplier effects" of a given product or service by multiplying the social benefits for the individual consumer beyond the "social opportunity cost" he has expended in purchasing the product or service. There are of course other ways of determining indirect additional ("multiplier") effects, but these are complex and costly to execute, so that where consumer demand data are available for demand as a function of price, the "consumer surplus" concept provides a theoretically simpler and sometimes more efficient means of measuring the social benefit generated by specific products and services in terms of economic values.

"Consumer surplus" is not the only measure of the social value of a product or service to a consumer; there are additional factors to

Figure 1. Derivation of consumer surplus from demand curves.

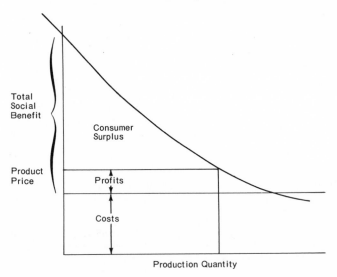

be considered. For example, it is conceivable that a new type of drug might create a fairly substantial consumer surplus by curing the common cold at a price substantially lower than what consumers are willing to pay for it. But the drug might also create toxic side effects in a significant percentage of the persons using it, with enough debilitating consequences to be measured economically in terms of lost working days. In such a case the "consumer surplus" (net social benefit to the consumer) would have to be reduced by subtracting from it the social cost of the unhealthful side effects to produce a *net* social benefit (or cost) to the consumer of the particular product.

In cases where demand curves are not available for a particular product or service—perhaps because it is monopolistically supplied, or its supply is government-regulated, or it is a relatively new or unique product—the consumer surplus concept can still be applied to determine the net social worth of a product to consumers by combining it with shadow pricing. For example, if consumers are obtaining electricity from a monopoly supplier and consuming it more or less independently of the price charged (inelasticity of demand), then a way of determining the consumer surplus in the supply of electric power to a large consumer would be to estimate what it will cost that consumer to generate his own electricity if the normal supply does not expand to satisfy his needs. Here the cost to build and fuel an electric motor generator for the new plant would determine the alternative costs of electric power if it were not available from the power company. The difference between the high cost of self-generated electricity and that supplied by the power company (which would usually cost less) would then be the "consumer surplus" to the new user of utility-supplied electric power. Since no alternative actually exists, but is only postulated in order to determine what its cost might be, the price of the alternative source is essentially a "shadow price," and here the difference between the shadow price and the actual price is the consumer surplus.

In summary: The concept of consumer surplus is important in the corporate social audit by providing one way of determining the net social benefits to consumers of products or services. The consumer surplus may be expressed in the conventional use of the term as the area under the demand curve and above the price volume line, or it can be determined by the price difference between actual sources of supply and shadow-priced alternative sources. If neither of these relatively simple approaches suffices, the consumer surplus can be determined by identifying and adding the direct and indirect effects estimated through detailed analysis of the relevant processes of production and consumption.

In all cases, however, the essential idea remains of a social benefit accruing to consumers from the economies they realize by being able to purchase a good for less than they are willing to pay for it. Although the specific technique for computing these values may differ according to the circumstances of the particular company and the type of data available, the concept is a highly significant one for the social audit.

"Externalities"

Corporate social responsibility involves many activities that the economist describes as consisting of "externalities"—functionally internal but financially externalized costs and benefits that are not "captured" by the standard financial accounts or financial audits of the business enterprise. However, the social audit assumes that all social benefits and costs have economic values that can be expressed in monetized, quantitative terms. A principal objective of the social audit is to measure and internalize, or capture, these externalities.

One of the principal problems in measurement is to identify the externalities which result from the company's own actions and to separate them from the costs and benefits which originate from other causes: the spillovers, or side effects, or externalities of other actions which "contaminate" the effects of the company's own social action.

For example, if a company puts a plant into a town with high unemployment and unemployment drops by more than the added employment offered by the new plant, is this a secondary effect, attributable to the greater expenditures of the newly employed, or is it the consequence of independent, parallel activities by other organizations or forces? It is not always easy or practicable to disaggregate the consequences or social impacts of a given social action from other "external" causes.

This is a complex problem common to much of social science research and evaluation. The usual procedure is to trace the effect of a social program's *input* (the resources devoted to it), follow it through the *process* (in which the input is applied to the problem), then to the project *output* (the specific actions which result), and finally to the *impact* of these actions on the variables which the program was intended to change.

To illustrate: A company might create an *input* by providing child care to all its female employees with preschool children, investing the capital and human resources to operate a day-care center on its premises. The *process* would be the actual operation of the day-care center. The *output* would be so many hours of child care, and the intended *impact* would be improved quality of life and higher productivity among female employees. Yet such an improvement in quality of life or productivity might take place for a quite independent reason, or might not even take place, in the net, because the hoped-for improvements might be canceled out by concurrent negative factors.

The theoretical approaches to the problem of tracing causal chains in complex, interdependent systems (such as most socioeconomic systems) are either statistical or microanalytical. Given an appropriately controlled experimental design, we can apply statistical methods in an attempt to disaggregate the impacts of experimental variables from those of other variables, provided that we have statistically significant numbers of similar cases. We do not always have such data, however, and the analysis is usually costly. Alternatively, we can analyze the apparent causal chains in minute detail but this too can be difficult and costly.

If the costs and difficulties of statistically valid controlled experiments are excessive for most industry situations, industrial firms and smaller government units can use the data available from the large-scale social and economic impact research done by the federal government—over seven billion dollars' worth in the last decade—and draw whatever useful analogies are possible between the social actions contemplated by the organization and those already studied by the federal government.*

Social Audit and Economic Theory

The earliest known attempt to quantify in economic terms the benefits of social actions is probably Sir William Petty's calculation † of the return on investment of moving the London population out-

---

* For a summary of the federal research and an evaluation of its usefulness, see *Toward the Benefit/Cost Evaluation of Government Applied Social Research* by the author (Abt Associates Inc., 1976).

† *Political Arithmetick, Or a Discourse Concerning the Extent and Value of Lands, People, Buildings, Etc.* (London: Robert Clavel, 1699.)

side the city during a plague epidemic. He computed the benefit/cost ratio of this action, the benefits of immigration and migration, and the worth of lives saved thanks to medical care.

In a relatively obscure passage in his classic book, *An Inquiry into the Nature and the Causes of the Wealth of Nations* (published in 1776), Adam Smith discusses the cost to society from the abuses of justice. Smith cautions his sovereign not to assert that the cost of justice is only the pecuniary cost of administering justice. Rather, he says, it is the nonpecuniary cost to society of administering justice, in addition to the direct expenditures on justice. In modern terminology we might say that the total cost of a given activity is the sum of the direct cost plus the "social opportunity cost."

The work of John Stuart Mill on the labor theory of value illustrates further the relationship between the social audit and the work of the classical economists. Mill's conclusion that workers do not reap the benefit of their labor completely can be interpreted as early recognition of the existence of "nontraded services." However, no explicit treatment of social costs and externalities was presented by classical writers.

A neo-classical author whose work has had significant impact on the development of the theoretical basis of the social audit is Alfred Marshall, in his *Principles of Economics* (1890). Although not necessarily the inventor of any novel concepts, Marshall rigorously discussed and developed the theory of microeconomics (the economics of the individual firm) and the concepts of "consumer surplus" and "externalities."

A. C. Pigou * made the first attempt to resolve the externality problem through a system of corrective taxes and subsidies. Pigouian principles have recently gained prominence as a possible approach to the solution of the pollution problem. These principles are also useful in developing the methods of the social audit.

Measuring Costs and Benefits: Examples

A typical corporate action having significant social impacts might be the building of a new factory. Let us assume that for economic reasons the new factory is to be built near a public park and

---

* *Economics of Welfare*, 4th ed. (London: Macmillan & Co., 1950.)

that the factory employs chemical processes that give off a bad odor. The following estimates would be taken by a social auditor, in sequence: First, the population affected by the company action would be determined. This would include all the individuals living in the neighborhood of the new factory who are subject to the bad smell and all the individuals from the neighborhood or elsewhere who are accustomed to using the park that is now affected by the bad smell. The next problem is to determine whether the social impacts of the smell on this population are positive or negative. On the basis of simple analogy with past experience, it can immediately be determined that bad smells are overwhelmingly regarded as a social cost rather than a social benefit. The question then is to determine the monetized market-equivalent social cost per person affected so that it can be multiplied by the total number of people affected to yield the total social cost.

The average unit social cost of the bad smell to those community individuals and park users affected can be determined by what the market worth of a *non*-bad-smelling air supply is to them. Since people do not generally pay explicit prices for good-smelling air, we will have to resort to the method of shadow pricing to determine what they are willing to spend for good-smelling air. In this particular case, that can be determined by a comparison of the market price of land or real estate for otherwise comparable neighborhoods where the only difference among them is the olfactory quality of the air. The differences in rental rates and land prices yield the market worth of the good-smelling air. This average unit market worth of the good-smelling air can then be multiplied by the number of people affected by the bad-smelling air to determine the shadow price of the social cost imposed on them by the location of the bad-smelling factory.

This is not yet the *total* social cost of the bad-smelling factory because there are probably numbers of users of the park who now suffer a social cost because of the bad smell but live far enough away from the park not to be affected by the social cost imposed on rentals or land values. For these individuals, the shadow price of the social cost of the bad smell can be determined by the cost to them of achieving a previously attainable quality of park use before the factory created the bad smell. In other words, the social cost of the bad smell to the nonresident park users is the additional cost they have to spend to regain the quality of park use that they had before the factory was built. This can be computed by determining the average unit cost to the park user of traveling to another, probably more distant park equivalent in other qualities and without the bad smell. One can determine this by estimating the average travel time and travel cost for the nonresidents to reach another park of similar quality. Their average wage rate, multiplied by the average difference in their travel time to get to the two different parks, multiplied by the number of people thus affected, yields the shadow price of the total social cost of the bad-smelling factory to nonresident park users. This, added to the social cost to the resident park users, constitutes the major or "primary" or "direct" social cost of the bad-smelling factory to park users.

The placement of a factory is a socially significant action. The *physical* result in this hypothetical (but typical) case is smell and air pollution. The *psychological* result is that the people who live in the neighborhood are immediately opposed, first because they anticipate that they will not like the physical effect, and then because they suffer direct unpleasant effects. The *behavioral* result is that some of them move away because they are angry and they don't like the physical effect. The *economic* result of their moving away is a drop in land value and land price, and that drop in land price totaled for all the people affected is the *monetary impact* or *social cost* of that social action. One could add the cost of lost trade by local merchants whose out-of-area customers are driven away by the bad smell.

In every case imaginable, either the direct market price of a particular social benefit or cost can be determined (for example, the prices actually paid for health benefits, for additional safety features, or for additional recreational advantages), or where there is no market price involved, the market worth can be determined by shadow pricing.

Another example might be that of a company that takes a socially significant action in installing antipollution equipment in one of its plants located near a residential area. The company's "input" consists of putting in stack-gas scrubbers and can be measured by the cost of their installation. The physical change that results (cleaner air and better health) and the anticipation of it also brings about a psychological change in the people affected. They like what is happening. As a result of that psychological change, there is an "output" in the form of a change in their behavior. More people move into the area now or fewer people move out—they "vote with their feet." The *impact* of that behavioral change on the part of the population affected is an economic change: The market value of the real estate in the area goes up. We can measure that impact very easily by doing just a simple survey of real estate values.

Thus (Figure 2) we trace the result of a socially significant action via the psychological changes in the people affected, and then their behavioral changes as a result of those psychological changes, down to the economic changes which result from their behavioral changes. All these changes can be measured by the proven, ordinary survey methods of social science—measuring *impact* or *ouputs,* not inputs.

Here are some typical questions and replies on the social audit approach, as they occurred in a management training seminar for Japanese executives.*

Figure 2. How all impacts of socially significant actions are measured.

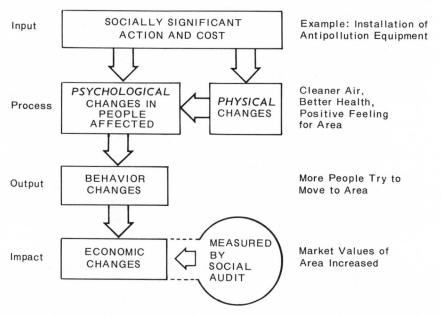

* Other questions that were discussed in the exchange between the author and the Japanese businessmen cover a wide range of issues and are reported in Appendix D.

Question: How can you be really sure, in the case of the increased real estate value, that it is definitely related to the decrease in pollution?

Answer: By doing a controlled sampling—that is, we look at another comparable area which doesn't have the decreased pollution to see how general economic forces have changed the real estate values there. That's the control group. To get comparability and ensure that extraneous factors aren't influencing it, we need a comparison with a similar population, a similar environment, where the particular social action does not take place.

Question: How do you determine which corporate constituencies value which social benefits?

Answer: We divide up the various constituencies of an organization into different groups, some of which overlap, and we determine the worth to each from what an opinion survey of representatives says is most important to them. We do this with employees and stockholders and all the different constituencies. A simple sample survey asks, "What items do you think are most important?" and "What market value do you attribute to those items?" There is some overlap between a community population and employee population and a stockholder population. Those overlaps are treatable by separating the individuals in both groups into one group or the other, to avoid double counting.

Question: Doesn't this whole theory assume that we are presenting a political document rather than a financial statement?

Answer: Yes and no. To the extent that a financial statement is a political document, yes. To the extent that a financial statement is a statement of an approximation of the truth of the financial status of an organization, and that statement of truth may be used for political purposes, the social statement is also an estimate of the truth of the social situation of an organization that may or may not be used for political purposes. Financial statements, when they look good, are used for political purposes—for example, to motivate stockholder support of management. Social statements will also be used for political purposes if they look good. It is the virtue of public accounting and government auditing that one has to produce reports that are fair statements of the realities whether they look good or not, and whether they are politically useful or not. When they don't look good, they may not be politically useful (at least to most managements—some may find it useful to justify otherwise unpopular social investments they believe are essential for survival). We advocate the use of social performance statements whether they look good or not, in the hope that the use of such statements will motivate productive social investments because people prefer to "look good."

Question: Are we not just measuring short-term financial benefits? We're not measuring the long-term harm or reduction in harm done by reduction of air pollution or water pollution.

Answer: That's not correct. When doing a social audit for an electric power company in Japan (a billion dollar a year operation), there was precisely this problem. It was necessary to quantify the social benefit to the general public of a significant reduction in air pollution. The problem was to balance the direct financial cost of putting in stack-gas scrubbers against the social benefit achieved. We know from various studies that the annual cost of air pollution in the United States is roughly $4 billion, as of 1972.* The $4 billion comprises the cost of man-hours lost from work as a result of various pulmonary and respiratory ailments brought on by air pollution, additional medical costs, and so forth.†

Extrapolated to Japan, on the assumption that Japan has about half the population and half the GNP of the United States, it was assumed that the annual cost in Japan is about $2 billion. Assuming that the percentage of air pollution created by the Japanese power company can be estimated on the basis of its percentage of the total effluent in Japan, then one can determine that percentage cost on a prorated basis. It turned out to be about $20 million. The ratio of the company's contribution to air pollution to the total amount was assumed to be the ratio of the social cost of the respiratory diseases that it created to the total national cost. Thus for about $2 million or $3 million investment in stack-gas scrubbers—assuming they eliminated most of the harmful emission—an annual social benefit of about $20 million could be created—a very high return—nearly 10:1—on social investment. It offers an argument to the government to provide tax incentives because the government is saving itself productivity losses and health costs far in excess of the amount invested by the company in reducing air pollution.

* For 1976, the correct figure is probably $5 billion. (Robert Dorfman, personal communication, August 1976.)

† Robert Dorfman and Nancy S. Dorfman, eds., *Economics of the Environment* (New York: W. W. Norton, 1972).

Question: Wouldn't companies rather have the government pay for it?

Answer: There is always competition for social investment—a negative competition—between private industry and the government, with each side hoping the other will pick up the tab. Government can provide incentives, direct and indirect—tax incentives, regulatory incentives—to urge private industry to share some of the costs in return for reducing other costs. In addition, there is the informal incentive of public opinion and the favorable change in consumer opinion. Unfavorable public opinion costs a lot of money and sometimes it costs as much as bankruptcy.

Question: This problem of pollution—there is a big problem where the unit one is studying is contributing to an overall problem in perhaps a minor way. How can you actually establish a benefit if it doesn't decrease the problem to where you can deal with it?

Answer: By prorating. The problem is similar to that of unallocated and allocable overhead. This is a social overhead. Prorate the social overhead on the basis of proportional revenues or proportional effluent flow or whatever quantity it is that is relevant. Unless there is a significant number of contributors to pollution participating, you may not reduce the level to any real benefit. That's why in the long run either strong public opinion or government action has to provide a fair standard for all industries. Otherwise, some of the most socially irresponsible industries can take advantage of the social responsibility of their competitors and, transiently, look as if they are performing better financially.

Criteria in Designing Measurements

For efficient design of the instruments and procedures used to measure corporate social responsibility—by social audits and perhaps by other means as well—the measurements must be:

Useful as a guide to decisions by managers (to do certain things or not to do them), by employees (to accept or reject jobs), by consumers (to buy or not to buy products), by owners (to buy or sell the stock), by reformers (to attack or defend the company), by legislators (to pass or not to pass legislation to control the company, or possibly even to eliminate some controls).

Objective.
Reliable and repeatable.
Widely accepted.
Responsive to a range of social concerns.
Feasible.
Quantitative.
Fully exploitive of the available potential for action.
Offering maximum information (with minimum admixture of
  "public relations").
Effective in institutionalizing social concerns in the corporation.
Transparent in their assumptions and estimates (so a user can
  make his own judgments).
Based on full use of expert, disinterested opinion.
Simple enough to be widely understood.

The measurements themselves, to be *useful,* must deal directly
with the issues which concern the various groups involved with the
company. Thus the variables to be included in any useful social audit
(perhaps determined by opinion surveys) might include:

For *managers,* the total budget and the allocation of it among
  different programs of social responsibility, as well as the policies and procedures to be applied.
For *employees,* the quality of life, the quality of work, the possibilities of advancement, and fairness on the job.
For *consumers,* the quality and efficiency of the products or services sold, compared to those of competing products, and the
  reliability and veracity of the information about them.
For *owners* (stockholders), the overall prospects of the company
  in terms of expected future earnings, risk, and growth as honestly reported.
For *reformers,* the responsiveness of the company to changing
  standards and its willingness to respond to new social needs.
For *legislators,* the ability of the company to respond to public
  needs without the need for regulatory legislation.

For measurements of social performance to be *objective,* they
must be verifiable by disinterested parties, and not devised simply as
a way of showing the company in a favorable light. To be *reliable* and
repeatable, the measures should be sufficiently universal to be applicable to widely different companies and provide meaningful information in all cases.

Wide acceptance of social performance measurement is essential to their being widely used, and hence effective. Their acceptance requires that the measurements relate to widely accepted concerns and be based on widely accepted principles.

Responsiveness to a wide range of social concerns is essential if measures of social performance are to be taken seriously by all groups significantly involved. Thus social performance measures that deal only with environmental issues, for example, but not with equality of employment opportunity will not win the acceptance of many of the minority members and women among the clientele or employees of the company. The criterion here is that *all* possible major social concerns be addressed. Since social problems change in their relative saliency with time, the issues to be addressed must change with the times.

Feasibility has operational, financial, political, and technical components. The implementation of a given set of social performance measurements must be possible without major disruption of the organization. It must cost some amount less than what can be readily afforded to take social measurements and what the individuals affected would regard as a reasonable amount to pay for information. It must be possible to make the social performance measurements without so offending various affected groups as to render the exercise counterproductive. Finally, the measurements must be implementable, using the latest techniques in social science for surveys, measurements, and the drawing of conclusions.

Social performance measures must be *quantitative* in order to provide a net result of benefits and costs and of assets and liabilities (and capable of being *replicated*, as a basis of comparison for the same organization over periods of time as well as for different organizations). To appreciate the effect of purely qualitative measures of social performance, it is only necessary to imagine the usefulness of an annual financial report stated in purely qualitative terms. For example, "This year we increased our income faster than our expenditures, so that net income was greater than last year."

The social performance measures should fully exploit the available *potential for action* on the part of the corporation by addressing specifically those areas under its most direct control: hiring, personnel, administration, production, advertising, procurement and purchasing, marketing, investment, location, research and development, and the like. Any medium-size or large company makes an enormous number of decisions concerning where and from whom it buys what, what it does with what it buys (including labor and capital equipment), and whom it sells it to and how. All these decisions should be reviewed for the quality of their responsiveness to social issues and hence the quality of the social performance involved in these decisions.

The criterion of offering *maximum public information with a minimum of unfavorable public reaction* is essentially one of making honest statements rather than boasting. If social actions are heavily exploited for their public relations value, not only will they tend to be heavily discounted by those most concerned but they may also be poorly chosen. Sometimes the most socially productive decisions are not particularly productive of publicity.

Effectiveness in institutionalizing social concerns in the corporation is required to ensure continuity of the social performance effort. Unless the company's social concerns are institutionalized, social performance efforts and measurements of them will tend to be one-shot efforts without consistent, long-term follow-up. Furthermore, the various levels of management in a company are unlikely to give serious attention to directives on social performance (and its measurement) if these directives are not formalized in organizational terms. The survival and growth of corporate social responsibility efforts require their formalization and some sort of institutionalized, repeatable procedure.

Since the assumptions and estimates in any social audit are bound to be subject to change because the state of the art is rapidly growing and since different perspectives yield somewhat different estimates of social costs and social utilities, it is essential for the sake of objectivity and widespread acceptability that any assumptions and estimates be absolutely *transparent* and clearly expressed. Only in this way can the user of the social performance measures either accept the assumptions of the measurer or supply his own interpretations based on the facts offered him.

The full use of available *expert, disinterested opinion* is a step toward the overall professionalization, legitimization, and widespread acceptance of social performance measures and audits. Unless full use is made of the available techniques and the skills of measurement experts, the effort can be criticized as not using all the tools available. Furthermore, the measurement of many of the social variables involved is difficult even for experts, although the layman may think otherwise (everyone is an expert on education, family health, working conditions, and the like). Expert opinion and the use of professional methods help to set objective scientific standards in information gathering and to ensure that the information and its logic will be scientifically comparable (statistical logic is the same everywhere).

Finally, the measures of corporate social performance must be *simple enough to be widely understood,* or they will simply not be used. One of the virtues of generally accepted accounting principles is that the fundamentals can be mastered in a few hours of diligent study (even though the proper application of all the procedures involved may take years to master). If social auditing becomes too complex, it might quickly become an academic curiosity.

An example of a good simple measure of social performance in a field that is of widespread concern is the percentage of minorities and women employed at all levels. This is direct, concrete, familiar, and simple. However, if expressed in terms of the variation of the Lorenz curve of participation by minorities and women in a particular type of industry and at particular levels of activity, the measure would be too abstract, unfamiliar, indirect, and complex.

In product safety and its social impact on consumers, a direct, simple measure would be the absolute and percentage number of accidents from year to year in the use of a company's products or services. For the purposes of the social audit, it is not immediately necessary to measure the statistical incidence of different types of accidents, weighted by their cost to the individuals affected and by the indirect effects of such costs on the society at large—even though such information might be useful to management in other contexts.

Levels of Precision in Measurement

Given these criteria, what sorts and degrees of measurement of corporate social responsibility can be developed? The first step (Figure 3) would appear to be a simple qualitative statement of the significant social costs and benefits perceived and a qualitative estimate of the degree to which these desired social benefits have been achieved and at what social costs. For the company which assumes only the core group of social responsibilities, the simple qualitative statement of its aims in social performance are: (1) make a profit and (2) stay legal. The simplest measurement of the achievement of these goals would be the binary determination of whether profit had in-

Figure 3. Levels of precision in social measurement.

Type	Advantages	Limitations	Current User
Level 1 *Qualitative Checklists* Lists of socially significant actions	Simplicity; focuses attention	· Misleading · Compares items of very different magnitudes · No results · No targets	Scovill Manufacturing Company
Level 2 *Listing Inputs Only* Costs of social programs	Supplies budget data for significant actions	· Analyzes inputs only, not outputs or impacts · Contains no efficiency measure, thus no basis for optimization	· Aetna Life & Casualty · Dow Chemical
Level 3 *Assigning Performance Goals* Measurements of project performance	Estimates degree of goal achievements	· Incommensurable project measurements · Incomplete coverage	· Bank of America · Eastern Fuel and Gas
Level 4 *Benefit/Cost Estimates* Benefit/cost ratios measured in money units	Provides quantitative ROI estimates to allow optimal choice	· Not comprehensive · Not integrated with financial accounts	U.S. Government
Level 5 *Integrated Social/Financial Audits* Social audit (impacts measured by standard accounting procedures)	Integration with financial accounts	· Requires data collection and analysis comparable to financial audit	· Japan Ministry of Finance · Abt Associates Inc. · R. G. Barry Co.

deed been generated and whether the enterprise had indeed operated legally.

Qualitative Checklists

Beyond this simplest kind of check on achievement, it is possible to make lists of specific social objectives, such as equal opportunity and maintenance of local environmental standards, and to estimate whether any progress toward them—or a little, substantial, or complete progress—has been made. This is the *checklist* approach, and it is a useful, quick, and simple beginning. It also serves a kind of "consciousness raising" function for executives who employ it, thus tending to mobilize their commitment to exploring more sophisticated and precise measures.

The major limitation of the qualitative checklist—no matter how comprehensive, detailed, and elaborate it is, and no matter how many dimensions of it are expressed in some matrix—is that there is no logical way of determining whether or not there is any *net* social benefit resulting from the company's social performance. One can make a long list of "good" things the company has done and a short list of the "bad" things, and make it look as if one has done more good than bad. There is no measurement of the different quantities involved, or any allowance for the fact that they may have very different weights. The checklist is thus used mainly as a public relations device and certainly is no great aid to management decisions in capital budgeting or other resource allocation.

Listing Inputs Only

The next level is to summarize expenditures. Here at least we have budget data that will provide some basis for management decision. The trouble is that expenditures measure only the inputs to social activities and not the outputs; there's no measure of efficiency or effectiveness. And the mere fact that a company is spending a lot on social action programs doesn't mean it is getting its money's worth and that the whole program is worthwhile. While this approach gives some attention to budgets, it offers no measure of relative cost-effectiveness and offers no basis for optimizing investment.

Assigning Performance Goals

The third level of sophistication is that at which social projects are assigned specific performance criteria, such as EEO goals of 20 percent minority participation at all levels, or environmental goals of 50 percent reduction of air pollution by the plant, and so forth. The advantage of this approach is that it encourages management by objectives and sets specific goals against which achievement can be measured. The limitations are that the company can't compare the social worth of different social projects. How much is a 10 percent improvement in air pollution worth compared to x amount of improvement in reducing sex discrimination or in increasing employee benefits? These quantities are incommensurable unless they are reduced to common terms, such as dollars.

Benefit/Cost Estimates

The fourth level, often used by the government in making selections among competing projects, is the benefit/cost approach, where benefit/cost ratios or cost/effectiveness ratios of different projects are estimated. The advantages here are that we can get a return-on-investment estimate to allow optimal choice. The limitation is that it's still not integrated with the financial accounts. And so we cannot make trade-offs between social and financial investments.

Integrated Social/Financial Audits

The highest level of sophistication is that at which the social benefit/cost approach is integrated with financial accounts and financial statements. Here we can make direct trade-offs between social and financial investment and social and financial returns and maximize both.

Risk/Benefit versus Benefit/Cost

Benefit/cost evaluation of alternative social programs implies that one can establish a real or shadow price for the various programs. In cases where the social costs are probabilistic and where the risks cannot be so clearly related to price, a risk/benefit analysis may reveal possible courses of action more lucidly than a cost/benefit analysis. Particularly where the risks are to life and health, experience often shows that these dominate other social costs.

How much is it worth to reduce the risk of accident by 50 percent? Or how much in extra benefits do you have to pay if you double the risk of accident by 100 percent? In the 1960s, Chauncey

Starr of the Edison Electric Institute did a very interesting survey *
of people's attitudes about how much additional dollar benefit they
felt they were owed in order to take increasing risks of death or, correspondingly, how much money a given decrease in risk was worth
to them—the market worth of differential risk. (Interestingly
enough, people are willing to accept a much higher degree of *voluntary* risk such as that from skiing or sky-diving or private flying than
of *involuntary* risks from, for example, industrial accidents.) The
relationship Starr found was that the amount of benefit required to
compensate for increased risk went up as the cube of the risk—that
is, if one doubles the amount of risk of death, one has to offer people eight times as much compensation to accept this doubled risk.
This offers a concrete and quantitative way of determining how
much increased risk is worth how much increased benefit or, alternatively, how much decreased risk is worth how much dollar benefit.
Thus one can deal with probabilistic changes in social benefits and
social costs as well as purely deterministic ones.

Such analysis would be useful in managing physical security
forces in local municipal government—police, fire, health protection,
and so forth. One can relate the reduction of risk quantitatively to
the market worth of the attendant benefit and then allocate resources to provide the greatest possible value to the consuming public in terms of service.

The matter is complicated by the fact that the exponential relationship between risk and its perceived social cost (or worth) is not
likely to remain the same at extremes of the range and for different
groups of individuals. Thus the willingness to sacrifice other social
goods to reduce a high risk of death may be much more highly exponential for the individuals concerned than for those not at risk.
Conversely, for a modest risk to health, such as the risk of a broken
arm or leg, the social cost may be rather low as perceived by youthful and energetic populations, as is demonstrated continually by the
popularity of hazardous body contact sports such as football and
hockey.

The issue of risk/benefit analysis is an important one, particularly for technological changes that appear superficially to offer high
benefit/cost ratios but may threaten a high ratio of risks to benefits.
Examples abound, ranging from thalidomide and other drugs to

* "Social Benefit versus Technological Risk," *Science,* September 1969.

chemical fertilizers and pesticides that subtly change the ecological balance of the environment negatively over the long term, while initially and superficially offering positive net social benefits. A recent example was the banning of a food substance by the U.S. Food and Drug Administration on the basis of its potential carcinogenic effects as indicated by tests using concentrated doses on laboratory animals. In their defense, the manufacturers of these chemicals argued that any very intense concentrations of most chemicals are carcinogenic, and the same chemicals in modest concentrations are benign in their impacts on humans. Therefore, the manufacturers considered the ban as a case of eliminating a minute social risk at a high social cost to the public. Yet if one were to ask parents of small children whether they would entertain even a minute risk of poisoning their children as a result of using a chemical additive that they could readily avoid at some modest economic cost, one suspects that most of them would happily avoid that risk. Part of the reason for this is that small risks of catastrophic events are terribly difficult to estimate in terms of their real-life impacts, so that a natural and perhaps sensibly conservative response on the part of socially responsible individuals is to assume that a small risk of a catastrophic event may be understated and that social responsibility in such situations requires the avoidance of the low probability event as if it might be of substantially higher probability.

3

Using the
Social Balance Sheet

THE basic purpose of a business corporation is to maximize the financial return earned on its financial investment, plus the amount of social return on its social investment. To make rational investment decisions in the social area it is necessary to know what the social returns are, and if we are to assess them by the same measures as for financial investment, these must be expressed in dollar terms. Social accounts and social audits do not necessarily suggest that a company should put more money into social action; they may argue for putting in less. On the other hand, spending nothing on social investments does not necessarily minimize costs; not doing anything may result in social problems that are more expensive than the investment would be. Audits are likely to help the company to invest more *efficiently* in the social area.

We can assume that management usually wants to behave in a socially responsible way—not because it's altruistic, not because it's interested mainly in public relations, but because in the long run (I think) most mature managements realize that socially responsible behavior is one of the conditions of operating effectively in a pluralistic society in which public opinion and the expression of public opinion through legislation and government regulation hold the ultimate power.

However, finances constrain social investment. We can't do everything we want in any field; we have limited resources; we have to make choices. We can't give the stockholders a fair return on investment and at the same time spend all the money a business generates on projects with social impact. There has to be some balancing of competing interests.

If a corporation invests all its surplus or working capital in social projects and then goes out of business because it can no longer afford to keep its doors open, it has created more social costs than benefits: It has sacrificed jobs, it has ended its contribution to public activities through the payment of taxes, and it has created more harm than good. On the other hand, if the corporation generates a lot of profit for its investors but does nothing that is socially responsible, makes a mess in its community and in dealing with its people, its environment, and its consumers, the company is essentially exploiting a large group of people in order to enrich a small group. That also represents a high social cost.

The problem, therefore, is to distribute scarce social and financial resources among competing interests with increased efficiency. We can do this by measuring the social performance, as well as the financial performance, on a systematic and periodic basis, by studying the results in the form of balance sheets and income statements, and by analyzing the marginal productivity of each component and investing more in the increasingly productive and less in the decreasingly productive ones.

Social Accounts versus Financial Accounts: How They Compare

Social and financial balance sheets and income statements are comparable. The social balance sheet presents social assets, such as organization, research, and taxes paid, and social liabilities, such as employee commitments, organizational liabilities, environmental degradation, and consumption of public services paid for by taxes. The net of the two is society's equity.

The social income statement is an annual flow statement in which social benefits to employees, communities, consumers, and the general public are added, and social costs to each constituency are subtracted, to determine a net social income on an annual basis.

The net social income does not necessarily flow into society's equity on the social balance sheet the way financial income flows into retained earnings on financial balance sheets because there is no way of storing it. Social income is assumed to be distributed as it's created. One way of storing it would be as goodwill, but it seems clearer to think of social income as being distributed as rapidly as it is produced to all those participating in it. Thus society's equity is mainly the result of the net difference between social assets and social liabilities.

There are many similarities between social and financial audits. Both are comprehensive evaluations of performance. Both are formal examinations and verifications of accounts. They're both available for internal and external audit. They both result in annual and often monthly reports, and accounts are established according to formal principles. The operating or income statement gives annual changes and the balance sheets show cumulative results to date. Expenses equal the lesser of cost or market prices. They are both quantitative in money terms. They both have year-to-year comparability and company-to-company comparability. Both can be used by management in decision making, can be private or public, can be integrated (one with the other), and cost about the same.

A technical difference is that in financial statements the value of money is its value at the time it is spent or received, while in social audits, we prefer to measure *future* returns as well as current expenditures, both in terms of equivalent present-value dollars.* That is because from an income statement point of view, a company may bear all the costs of a social investment in the first year but get few of the returns until subsequent years. Thus anything that doesn't return on investment within a year artificially tends to show up as not being worth the investment.

Perhaps the most important difference is that there are formal financial principles embodied in generally accepted accounting prac-

* By present value, we mean the worth today of future benefits (or costs) discounted by an appropriate discount rate (usually the average current commercial interest rate), given by

$$\Sigma \frac{\text{Annual worth}}{(1 + \text{Discount rate})^n}$$

where n = number of years of benefit (or cost). At a discount rate of 8 percent, for example, a dollar of social benefit created next year is worth only 92¢ this year.

tices, but we do not yet have formal principles for social accounting which are generally agreed on. In arriving at generally accepted standards, the role of government auditors at the municipal, state, and federal levels will be crucial. They are already enforcing some social accounts in the form of equal employment opportunity and environmental impact statements and other practices of good management. Gradually, through government procurement regulations and other codifications, these will be standardized. (Government now spends more than a third of the GNP.) This will eventually lead to standardization of social accounting principles as well.

How Social Balance Sheets Are Used

Financial balance sheets express the cumulative financial status of an organization in terms of assets, liabilities, equity, and retained earnings. Assets are what is owned by the organization, or owed to it—such as cash deposits and receivables—and liabilities are what the organization owes to others.

Financial balance sheets are used by management to evaluate four major aspects of an organization:

- Overall *resources*—their *scale* and their *worth* (expressed as net worth or book value);
- Cumulative net *productivity* (sometimes expressed as retained earnings plus cumulative dividend distributions divided by assets or return on assets);
- *Flexibility* or *liquidity* of resources (expressed as current ratio— ratio of current assets to current liabilities—or quick cash ratio);
- *Efficiency* in the use of resources (expressed as return on assets or return on investment) or the net productivity per unit worth.

These characteristics provide important information for the comparative assessments of different companies by investment and commercial bankers, merger-acquisition specialists, and private investors. When used to express the cumulative financial status of several subsidiary corporations or divisions of a larger corporation, they provide the parent management with a rational basis for efficient allocation of resources among them. Balance sheets show some of the resources accumulated by and available to a corporation; income statements indicate the ability of management to apply the resources productively.

Social balance sheets also express the scale worth of resources and their productivity, flexibility, and efficiency—but deal with social assets and liabilities rather than financial. (A social investment is defined as any investment of either financial or social assets that has significant social impacts.) Social balance sheets offer aid to management concerning important policy questions, such as:

> What is the relative scale and worth of two different social assets or social liabilities?
> What is the relative productivity of different social investments?
> How relevant to major social needs is a given social investment likely to be in the future, given its flexibility (liquidity) today?
> How efficient are different social investments in multiplying the social and financial assets invested in them?

As for the *scale* and *worth* of social investments, the answer to the first question can yield data for policy recommendations concerning the resources required and the resources available for different types of social projects. For example, a river pollution abatement program requires a much larger commitment than do most production safety programs.

Analysis of *productivity* can lead to policy recommendations concerning the likely degree of social impact per unit of resources invested. For example, health and education programs may promise a relatively higher "social income" than welfare programs.

Flexibility of resources indicates their capacity to adopt to changing social needs; for example, the capacity to liquidate a now irrelevant social investment in a tuberculosis sanitorium and reallocate the assets to deal with a currently more significant social problem such as alcoholism.

Measuring the *efficiency* of social investments leads to policy recommendations concerning ways to maximize the total social and financial return from alternative mixes of social and financial investments. This can be done by standard mathematical optimization techniques * or the simpler rough equalization or balancing of

---

* Optimization means the seeking of the optimum alternative solution to a problem. Typical mathematical methods such as linear and dynamic programming can be found in any standard operations research textbook.

marginal returns once the relative efficiencies of different social investments are obtained from social balance sheet items reflecting their cumulative returns on investment. Typically, a chief executive might ask: "How can we obtain greater social performance within the same social investment budget?" or "If we increased our social investment budget 10 percent, are there any efficiencies of scale we could exploit to obtain a 20 percent increase in social performance?" These questions could be answered with the aid of social balance sheets of actual and projected social investments.

Application of social balance sheets to management policy decisions begins with simple identification of the relative magnitudes of various problems and can extend either to partial or to comprehensive "satisficing" * of company goals or to the most sophisticated mix of policy recommdations. The simplest applications can be made by merely comparing the line item quantities in a social balance sheet; the most sophisticated require application of optimization methods.

Ratio Analysis of Social Performance Statements

Twelve major measures are conventionally employed in the ratio analysis of financial statements:

1. Current assets to current debt (solvency).
2. Net profits to net sales (profitability).
3. Net profits to tangible net worth ("ultimate" profitability).
4. Net profits to net working capital (financing capacity).
5. Net sales to tangible net worth (turnover rate of invested capital, or capital use efficiency).
6. Net sales to net working capital (working capital use efficiency).
7. Collection period (collectibility or assurance of receivables, or one measure of risk).
8. Fixed assets to tangible net worth (liquidity or flexibility of capital investment).
9. Current debt to tangible net worth (leverage, or risk pressure on earnings for debt service).

* "Satisficing" means satisfying a given requirement only to the level of that requirement and no further, as opposed to "optimizing." See discussion of profits, Chapter 9.

10. Total debt to tangible net worth (leverage, risk, and independence—when over 100 percent, creditors have a call on more of the assets of the business than the owners have).
11. Funded debts to working capital (risk).
12. Contribution (total revenue less total costs).

We can make analogies to each of these ratios in the social accounting field, as follows:

1. The ratio of "current social assets to current social liabilities" might be used as a measure of social "solvency," indicating the quality and solidity of a company's social performance to date.

2. The social audit analog of "net profits to net sales" would be "net social income on total social benefits" since the total social benefits on the social income statement are analogous to sales or revenues on the financial statements. This being an important yardstick of financial profitability in any one reporting period, it can also be used as a measure of social return in any one reporting period and provides information on social efficiency that is similar to benefit/cost ratios.

3. The measure of "ultimate" financial profitability being "net profits to tangible net worth," the cumulative measure of social performance can be regarded as the ratio of net social income to social net worth. The financial ratio generally calls for a rating of at least 10 percent net profits to tangible net worth as a desirable minimum for providing dividends and growth financing. For social performance statements, no such minimum has been identified as yet since the measure of a "social dividend" is still undefined and since the standard of investment of social income for future social growth still remains to be developed.

4. The financial ratio of "net profits to net working capital" represents the reserves available for financing day-to-day operations and inventory and receivables; it is thus a measure of the self-financing capacity of the business. The social analog would be net social income to net social assets. Since the denominator for the social analog (net social assets) is difficult to determine at this time, the ratio is not particularly useful in analyzing the social balance sheet.

5-6. The ratio of "net sales to tangible net worth" is a measure of relative turnover of invested capital and indicates something about the efficiency of this capital's use. The social audit analog to net sales is social benefits, and the social analog to tangible net worth is either zero (if one interprets the word "tangible" very strictly) or the accumulated social income and social investment of the company. Since social audit theory has not yet defined a standard way in which social assets can be treated as social capital to be reinvested to produce social income, but instead converts social assets to financial ones that can then be reinvested in either social or financial or combined programs, this ratio is not yet particularly useful for social performance evaluation. For similar reasons the same is true of the sixth ratio, "net sales to net working capital."

7. The "collection period" indicates the collectibility of receivables and gives some indication of the probability of collection itself, thus providing a measure of risk. Since there is no direct analog in the social audit to receivables, the collection period is not a particularly applicable ratio for social audits.

8. The ratio of "fixed assets to tangible net worth" offers some indication of the liquidity and hence the flexibility of investment in a company. This could be useful in social performance ratio analyses because it might provide an indication of the probable responsiveness of an organization to changing social needs. For example, if a power company has a very high ratio of fixed "social assets," such as pollution abatement facilities, in comparison to its overall social net worth, it may lack the flexibility of resource allocation needed to respond to changes in social needs, for example, from environmental preservation to fuel conservation. For purposes of the social audit, this ratio might be better named the ratio of fixed social investments to "total socially available resources" or to "potential maximum rate of response to social change."

9–10. The ratio of "current debt to tangible net worth" is an indication of leverage and risk, as is also the ratio of "total debt to tangible net worth." Both those ratios when translated into social audit terms give some indication of the ratio of the total net social obligations of the company (corresponding to "current and total debt") to the total company social resources available to respond to these obligations (corresponding to "financial tangible net worth"). If this ratio gets too high, as in the case of the financial ratio, there is a risk that the company will not be able to meet its social obligations fast enough to satisfy its social "creditors," who may then take away some of the company's independence by possibly "calling" some of the social "debt" by imposing specific legal requirements and operational constraints. Furthermore, a high ratio of social obligations to socially available resources indicates that the company is doing something wrong in its operations by incurring social obligations which are too large when compared with its capacity to meet them. It thus strongly suggests either a lack of intent to meet social obligations or a lack of awareness of the extent to which they exist. In either case such a state of affairs, when it becomes known, is likely to invite government regulatory action and consumer and community protest, in extreme cases accelerating the path to "social bankruptcy," which has associated with it a definite risk of financial bankruptcy as well.

11. The ratio of "funded debts to working capital" is difficult to apply to social performance statements because, as stated previously, the concept of working capital is difficult to translate into social performance terms. To the extent that this ratio is used as some measure of liquidity and risk, the previous ratios of social audit analogies can provide this information in social performance measurement.

12. The financial "contribution" of any division or operation of a company is usually measured by the difference between its total revenues and total costs. (It sometimes provides its most meaningful efficiency information as regards profitability alone because the standard "profitability"—margin on billings—need not take into account the contributions to the overhead pool made by any particular set of profit-making revenues.) Its social performance analog would be total social benefits less total social costs. To the extent that the social contribution ratio can be determined differentially for different divisions or operations of a company, the relative social contribution to overall social performance can be estimated for the different units. This estimate can be useful in devising incentives to managers to achieve effective social performance, establishing rewards which correspond to their contributions in the social area as well as in the financial.

Integrating Social and Financial Statements

An ultimate aim in measuring a company's social performance is to integrate the measurements with the financial statements. This is currently still beyond the state of the art but several companies are working on methods for doing it.

There is obvious reason for integrating financial and social measurements; mutual inputs and trade-offs in the two types of gains and losses *do* interact in company decision making. However, high costs are currently associated with the integration of financial and social data. Because public accountants do not yet recognize social audits (they are not opposed to them, but are undecided and uncertain) they will not certify an integrated statement embodying both a financial and a social audit. If a company wants to integrate its financial and social reporting, the options are either to integrate them and sacrifice the certification of the statement by public accountants—a serious risk, likely to affect stock market confidence—or, on the other hand, to publish *both* the conventional certified financial statement and an integrated but uncertified statement accounting for both financial and social performance. This latter course obviously incurs additional analytical and printing costs and throws some doubt on the credibility of the integrated statement.

These latter costs are bearable. In money terms, the extra analysis and printing might cost at most a few tens of thousands of dollars. The greater difficulty—and for those who do not know how to approach it, the greater analytical cost—is in the theory and practice of actually integrating the financial and social performance statements.

The financial and social reports of my own company illustrate some of the theoretical and practical difficulties of integration that remain to be solved. Many of them involve gaps and overlaps of social and financial categories; these might result in double counts or noncounts of some items if the two statements were integrated. For example, what we list as "social benefits to staff" includes career advancement in terms of added earning power but the financial income statement carries only the total costs of staff as direct and indirect costs, not the incremental increase. A partial overlap also exists between "overtime worked but not paid" (a social cost to the staff) and the financial benefit of this in terms of higher quality, reduced selling costs, and thus reduced overhead and higher profit. The problem with sorting out this overtime effect is that it is only one of many contributions to profit—the familiar "spillover" or "externalities" problem. Some possible approaches include entering the equivalent salary cost for overtime work not paid under overhead, recomputing profit, and then estimating that the difference between the actual profit and this lesser profit is the financial benefit balancing the staff social cost. Another approach, more complex and sophisticated, would be to relate individual productivity to overtime,

Table 1a. Financial benefits and costs deriving from social benefits created by corporate decisions.

Social Benefits	Corresponding Financial Benefits	Corresponding Financial Costs
To employees Employee fringe benefits	Increased morale, leading to higher productivity and reduced turnover and training costs	Overhead costs
Career advancement (salary increases merited by increases in responsibility and/or productivity)	Increased productivity per payroll unit	Increased direct labor costs per capita
Quality of working space and environment	Increased working efficiency and morale, raising per capita productivity and reducing recruitment and turnover costs	Increased overhead cost of facilities
	Increased market value of property beyond cost (in some cases)	
To local community Taxes paid	Community services not required to be bought by company	Cost of taxes paid
Environmental improvements	Decreased recruiting and selling costs	Costs of improvements
	Community goodwill	
Local tax worth of net jobs created	Increased labor capacity, reducing selling and sometimes production costs	Increased contingent liability of unemployment insurance and employee termination costs (if over-staffed)
To consumers Added value of services and products supplied to clients, beyond their market price ("consumer surplus")	Reduced sales costs and increased future revenues (customer goodwill) and reputation and associated reduced cost of recruitment	Opportunity costs of providing consumer surplus
To general public Federal and state taxes paid	Cost of tax-paid services less than if purchased privately because of economies of scale	Federal and state services (e.g., law enforcement, public health, education) not required to be bought by company
Knowledge created	Cost of producing knowledge not paid for by clients offset by efficiency increases from applications	Increased technical efficiency and competitiveness; thus reduced sales and production costs
Tax worth of jobs created	Same as local community	Same as local community

which is not necessarily a monotonic function. Then a staff survey could determine individual productivity increases as a result of the efficiency-weighted unpaid overtime. This would probably produce more accurate results at somewhat higher costs than the linear extrapolation of labor productivity mentioned first.

Various social actions and their corresponding financial costs and benefits are listed in Table 1(a) and (b).

As can be seen, every social benefit and cost has associated with it financial benefits and costs, and vice versa. Some of the relationships are shown in the table. In a social audit they would have to be quantified to determine the *net* financial impact of a particular social benefit or cost, and vice versa. For example, computation would be needed to show how much the short-term increase in financial profit resulting from the decrease in labor costs due to overtime worked but not paid exceeds the present value of the long-term cost of this activity in employee turnover, exhaustion, and the like.

Another problem to be resolved in the integration of the financial and social performance audits is the possible difference between the cost and the market worth of various social benefits. This would vary among benefits and would have to be determined by consumer surveys.

To use an example familiar to me, the balance sheet and income statement of Abt Associates Inc. in a recent year showed a large difference between financial book value, market value (which was three times as large), and "society's equity" or "social net worth" (six times as large as the book value). The difference between book and market value is "goodwill," a term that in this case probably represents the market's discounted present value of future earnings. The difference between the market value and the "social" value of the company must be attributed to social benefits generated by the company but not "captured" and hence not contributing to its market value.

Incentives to Integrate Social Audits
with Financial Audits

This raises a critical question: If the social net worth detected by a social audit exceeds company market value and that excess consists of social benefits not captured by the company, then why generate those social benefits and why measure them (from a self-interested

Table 1b. Financial benefits and costs deriving from social costs created by corporate decisions.

Social Costs	Corresponding Financial Benefits	Corresponding Financial Costs
To employees Layoffs and involuntary terminations	Reduction of surplus or inefficient labor, reducing overhead costs of production	Decreased perceived employment security resulting in decreased morale, labor productivity Loss of training investment
Overtime worked but not paid	Decreased short-term labor costs resulting in increased profits	Increased long-term labor costs from increased turnover and replacement cost
Inequality of opportunity	Decreased short-term labor costs (from what they would be in an "equal pay for equal work" market)	Increased labor costs from employee dissatisfaction and turnover, legal costs, possible loss of government contracts and associated increased selling costs
To local community Local services used	Saving of costs of services that would otherwise have to be supplied by company	Costs of taxes paid to support services
Environmental pollution	Saving of costs of pollution-reducing devices and processes	Hostile community reaction, possibly resulting in legal costs, higher recruiting costs, and fines raising production costs
To consumer Opportunity costs to consumers of unsatisfactory services and/or products purchased, resources wasted in producing unbought goods	Revenues and associated profits for goods sold, "educational value" of having produced unbought goods for better future investment decisions	Loss of client goodwill, resulting in increased sales costs and reduced future revenues, increased recruiting costs from loss of reputation, increased cost of capital to compensate for higher risks
To general public State and federal services consumed	Savings of costs of services that would otherwise have to be supplied by company	Costs of taxes paid
Public (environmental) resources consumed	Savings of costs of "free" resources that would otherwise have to be purchased	In the long run, perverse incentive for quick and wasteful exhaustion of "free" resources, raising resource costs

corporate viewpoint)? What is the purpose of generating and revealing this previously hidden asset of social "consumer surplus," which is unrecognized by the market valuation?

First, the corporation's incentive for generating social worth is the strengthened justification of the real worth of "goodwill," which otherwise is often only an accounting plug. Social worth helps to justify on a realistic basis the difference between book and market value, and conceivably could be legitimately used to justify an *increased* difference between the two.

Second, a major incentive for the financial expression and integration of the social audit is the justification of a corporation's capitalization of current costs expended for social benefits in the public interest, which are expected to yield both social and financial returns in the future. The net effect of such a procedure could be to increase earnings per share because of the capitalization of social costs or, alternatively, to permit increased social expenditures without damage to earnings.

One major social effect of such a financially integrated social audit is therefore to decrease the apparent financial cost of the corporation's social responsibility activities, without reducing its short-term profitability and indeed in most cases actually increasing its long-term financial profitability.

To be absolutely clear, it should be emphasized that the capitalization of current social action costs is not a shabby cover-up of current losses nor a delay in recognizing current costs in order to avoid bottom-line decreases. On the contrary, the financially integrated social audit mobilizes the profit incentives of corporations for their own interest *and* that of the public.

If the social investments were *not* made, we would probably recommend a writing off of some of the goodwill of a company because the social net worth of the company would probably be below its market worth, reflecting an increase of contingent social liabilities. For example, if each of two chemical companies executed a financially integrated social audit, the company neglecting to invest in pollution abatement and equal employment opportunity would actually be storing up future troubles for itself, to the detriment of its "real" goodwill. The socially responsible chemical company, using the financially integrated social audit, could and would invest in depollution and equal employment opportunity without reduction of current profits (because of the financial returns on its social in-

vestments: fines and legal actions avoided and reduced costs of recruiting and sales).

The following are some typical social responsibility expenses
that could be capitalized under a financially integrated social audit.

Capital costs:
> Research and development to improve product/service value
> and safety.
> Depollution equipment.
> Less polluting, less noisy, or safer equipment.
> Safety equipment.
> Health-supporting equipment and facilities.
> Environmental improvements.
> Facilities improvements (quality of working life).

Operating costs:
> Minority recruitment and training.
> Adjustments in salary for equal employment opportunity
> reasons (insurance companies, banks, employment of under-
> paid women).
> Employee fringe benefits.
> Contributions to knowledge.
> Any unusual losses on minority loan programs and suppliers.

Social Bankruptcy

Bankruptcy—the bane of business life—is an inability to meet
the liabilities a business has incurred. Financial bankruptcy occurs
when a firm's liabilities exceed its assets, and its creditors are unwilling to extend further credit. The metaphor of "moral" bankruptcy is
applied to individuals or institutions that have exhausted their
"moral" capital, having run out of moral assets, so to speak, in paying for their moral liabilities. "Social bankruptcy" is a term that can
be used either metaphorically or literally, but here we propose to use
it literally.

If a firm's social liabilities exceed its social assets, and the lenders
of social assets are unwilling to extend further credit, the firm is
socially bankrupt. This may not be immediately apparent, because
social solvency is not yet commonly measured as is financial solvency.
However, just as firms that do not keep financial accounts can still go
bankrupt—and indeed are more likely to do so—so also can firms

that do not keep social accounts go socially bankrupt and indeed are more likely to do so than those which maintain social accounts.

What happens when a firm becomes socially bankrupt? Does it go into a kind of social receivership? What are the sources of "social credit" that refuse to extend further credit? Is social bankruptcy related to financial bankruptcy?

When a firm goes socially bankrupt, its social assets cannot cover its social liabilities, and the excess of the liabilities over the assets becomes stable and apparent. This is what happens when public opinion turns against a firm for creating such social liabilities as consumer fraud, employee abuse, environmental depredations, or other moral offenses to a degree unmitigated by any positive economic or social contribution to society.

A socially bankrupt firm may go into the equivalent of social receivership if it becomes more intensely regulated by the public's agent, the government, or if its ownership is actually transferred to the public. The sources of social credit that may be first exhausted in such circumstances are, first, a favorable public opinion and, then, the formal and informal licenses to do business, which are granted by the public through its agent, the government.

Social bankruptcy is related to financial bankruptcy by the same types of relationships that connect social relations with financial activities. For example, loyalty and cohesiveness in a work force (created by a certain set of social relationships and leading to high productivity) can have specific financial value; if those social relationships are disrupted, the financial value will be reduced correspondingly. The obverse can also happen: Since most effective social relationships require some investment of financial resources, a reduction of the financial investment in social relationships can affect the relationships themselves. Each of these factors in business success depends on the other.

4

Social Audits in Management Decisions

SOCIAL audits were devised to provide evaluative data to executives to help them make better decisions about social policies and programs in their organizations. This discussion is intended to clarify some of the practical applications of social audits to corporate decisions. If these applications become better understood, it is hoped that social audits will become the management tool they deserve to be, rather than another weapon in the battle of words about social responsibility.

The social audit can contribute to the effectiveness of decisions about general corporate strategy ("What business are we in?"), corporate finance, capital budgeting, marketing and distribution, production, facilities and equipment, personnel and labor relations, product development and engineering, research, diversification, mergers and acquisitions, and almost any other organizational decision that involves investment or operating actions affecting people and their welfare.

Without the inputs from social audits, management decisions

are based on a combination of quantitative economic data and qualitative, usually subjective, estimates of social impacts. (Complete neglect of the social impacts of a management decision is also a qualitative estimate by default, implying that there is no impact worth worrying about.) Where social impacts are a significant aspect of the issue being decided, as is the case with all decisions affecting the environment, the community, consumers, workers, and the general public, management decisions made without social audit inputs are less likely to be good ones, except by luck, because the social component of the issues will not receive the quantitative analysis needed to integrate it with the economic component. Such decisions will tend to be narrowly "financial," overlooking the sometimes enormous contingent liabilities associated with high social costs.

Social Audits in Decision Making

Table 2 shows 20 kinds of management decisions made more effectively with the use of social audits. (Some specific examples will follow.) The decisions are divided among those clearly involving issues of corporate social responsibility and therefore obviously better made with the information from a social audit—such as decisions directly affecting the employees, consumers, and the environment—and those not so obviously involving social issues. One or more of six major management divisions is checked if it is strongly involved in these decisions: Chief Executive Officer, Finance, Personnel, Production, Marketing, and R&D.

Charitable Donations
Probably the first area in which social audits or similar evaluations are naively sought to provide an aid to decision making is that of corporate charitable giving. Underlying this is the erroneous assumption that external social problems are the main opportunity for the company to exercise social responsibility. The basic questions usually asked are how much to give and to whom. Industry averages run from zero to 5 percent of annual after-tax earnings. In the larger, billion-dollar corporations, that percentage can amount to several million dollars per year. The activity has not been notable for the maximum application of business intelligence; one suspects that the decision to give large sums to any plausible set of conventionally

Table 2. Twenty management decisions made more effectively with social audits, and the functions they affect.

	Chief Executive	Finance	Personnel	Production	Marketing	R&D
Obvious						
1. Corporate charitable giving	x				x	
2. Equal employment policy	x		x	x		
3. Employee benefits	x	x	x			
4. Product safety			x	x	x	x
5. Plant safety				x		x
6. Antipollution measures	x	x		x		x
7. Plant site selection	x	x	x	x	x	x
8. Advertising content and ethics	x				x	
9. Community relations	x		x			
10. Foreign operations	x	x	x	x	x	x
Not-so-obvious						
11. Financial reporting	x	x				
12. Executive recruitment	x		x			x
13. Supplier selection		x	x	x		x
14. New products development	x	x		x	x	x
15. Labor-management relations			x			
16. Government relations		x			x	x
17. Sources and type of financing	x	x				
18. Selection of markets	x	x			x	x
19. Long-range planning	x	x	x		x	x
20. Administrative procedures	x	x	x	x		x
Total functions affected	15 75%	13 65%	12 60%	10 50%	10 50%	13 65%

worthy charities seems to satisfy the deciding officers that they are achieving their ethical and public-image aims. However, these officers could hardly be rated for their performance in charitable investments in the way they'd be rated for their performance in business investments, and their often sloppy decision making in this area reflects this freedom from evaluation.

Nevertheless, as the amounts have gotten larger and the visibility of waste in charitable contributions has increased, corporate officers in some more progressive companies have become interested in evaluating the quality and effectiveness of their charitable gifts as a basis for a more efficient allocation. Possibly some have also sought an escape from tedious and subjective boardroom arguments about the relative merits of everyone's favorite charity. One application of social auditing that has developed in this area is the *charitable gift impact evaluation*. I developed a procedure for making such evaluations for a large corporation which involves major components of social audits. (In addition, it incorporates process evaluations,* since the output and impact evaluation required for a social audit may not be available or feasible in the period between the time when the charitable gift is made and the time when it is evaluated for refunding.) The sample "Corporate Contribution Project Grant Evaluation" form (Figure 4) indicates the kinds of questions involved in social audits of corporate charitable giving.

A social audit of the corporate charitable contributions budget for one of the nation's largest insurance companies concentrated on the relationship between the money and time inputs to various charitable efforts such as slum rehabilitation, education, health services, and support of artistic activities and the outputs and social impact of these activities. A general finding was that the investments in "bricks and mortar" (the building of facilities for charitable purposes) was substantially less cost-effective than were the contributions to various types of human services. Specifically, the money that was poured into urban renewal projects achieved no significant social impact, while absorbing great amounts of money. Financial support to health, education, and artistic activities, on the other hand, had a

---

* A *process evaluation* considers the effectiveness of the internal administrative and operations processes and procedures in achieving program goals. The judgment is made by independent evaluators who observe the program in action and interview both the administrators and participants.

Figure 4. Corporate contribution project grant evaluation (short form).

Indicate Data Source(s): R = Record Review; O = Observation; I = Interview
Write in NA if a particular question is not applicable

Project/Grantee Name: _____ Location: _____

Term of Funding, from: _____ to: _____ Date of Evaluation(s): _____

Evaluator(s): _____ Reviewed by: _____

Overall Evaluation: _____

  (Average of 2.7, 3.11, 4.6, 4.8, 5.3, 5.17, 5.18, 5.21, 5.22, 5.23)

Recommended Action: _____

_____

1. | Project Objectives | (Please quote if possible from project application or plan)
                          (R,I)

1.1 What is to be accomplished? (R,I) (In measurable, quantitative terms if possible)

Major: _____

Secondary: _____

Minor: _____

1.2 Where? (R,I) _____1.3 Over what time period? (R,I) _____

1.4 By *whom*? (R,I) _____1.5 For/with whom? (target population) (R,I) _____

1.6 How is it to be accomplished? (R,I) _____

1.7 Within what cost and other constraints? (R,I) _____

2. | Resource Inputs |

2.1 $ Funding: (R) Initial: $ _____ This past year: $ _____

                Annual: $ _____ Total to date: $ _____

Final Total Expected: $ _____

2.2 Staffing: Name   Salary   Qualifications

Leadership:			
Senior Staff:			
Other Staff:			

2.3 Major changes/turnover in staff: _____

2.4 Facilities & Equipment (if any are to be contributed): (R) _____

64

2.5 Information Resources (special access, unusual skills, etc.): (R,I) _____

2.6 Time available: (R) _____

2.7 Unique Company capabilities for execution: (R,I) _____

3. Process Evaluation Findings	(Essential at early stages when outputs & impacts are not yet present. For each question, indicate "yes" or "no" *and* reasons why (or why not).

3.1 Have the needs of the target population been identified? (R,I) _____
What are they? (R,I) _____

3.2 Are the project objectives relevant to the needs? (R,O,I) _____

3.3 Are the project plans (tasks, staff assignments, budgets, schedules with milestones) relevant to the objectives? (R,O,I) _____

3.4 Are the activities and operations proceeding according to plan? (O,R) _____

3.5 Are planned interim milestones being met? (O,R) _____

3.6 Are costs according to plan? (O,R) _____

3.7 Are the staff optimistic about the project achieving its objectives? (I) _____
Why or why not? (I) _____

3.8 Are a representative sample of the target population optimistic about the project achieving its objectives? (I) _____

3.9 Are representative members of the target population in favor of the project and its activities? (I) _____ If not, why not? _____

3.10 Do members of the target population approve of the project staffing? (I) _____
If not, why not? _____

3.11 How effective and efficient is the operations management? (O,R,I) _____

4. Output Evaluation Findings

4.1 Degree of accomplishment of objectives (%): (O,I) Major: ____% Reason ____
Secondary: ____% Reason _____ Minor: ____% Reason ____

4.2 Objectives achieved as a result of project activities: (O,I) _____

4.3 Additional achievements not planned? (O,I) _____

4.4 Negative side effects as a result of project activities? (O,I) _____

4.5 Net results of the project (positive achievements less negative side effects): (O,I) _____
_____

4.6 Overall effectiveness, in terms of results relevant to objectives: (O,I) _____
_____

4.7 Comparison of project effectiveness with comparable other projects, if any: (R,O,I)

Superior? _____ About the same? _____ Inferior? _____

4.8 *Overall efficiency,* in terms of results per dollar cost: (R,O,I) _____

4.9 Comparative overall efficiency with respect to other similar projects? (R,O,I)

Superior? _____ About the same? _____ Inferior? _____

4.10 Unique information obtained? (I) _____

4.11 Major project strengths: (O,I) _____
_____

4.12 Major project weaknesses: (O,I) _____
_____

4.13 Recommended improvements: (O, I) _____
_____

---

5. Impact Evaluation Findings

5.1 *Number* of people affected by the project? (R,O,I) _____

5.2 % of lifetime the average affected person is affected by the project? (R,O,I) _____ (Degree of effect)

5.3 *Total people years affected* (5.1 times 5.2): _____

5.4 New knowledge created: _____

	Estimated Equivalent Dollar Present Value
5.5 Social impact of new knowledge: _____	_____
5.6 Impact on public health: _____	_____
5.7 Impact on employment: _____	_____
5.8 Impact on income: _____	_____
5.9 Impact on education: _____	_____
5.10 Impact on housing: _____	_____
5.11 Impact on transportation: _____	_____
5.12 Impact on public safety: _____	_____
5.13 Impact on environment: _____	_____
5.14 Impact on quality of life: _____	_____
5.15 Total estimated equivalent dollar present value: $= \Sigma$	_____

5.16 Total project lifetime cost: _____

5.17 *Benefit/Cost Ratio:* (5.15 ÷ 5.16): _____

5.18 *Overall Social Return on Investment* $\dfrac{5.15 - 5.16}{5.16}$ (100): _____ %

5.19 Compared to similar projects (if any), is this project's ROI:

Superior? _____ About the same? _____ Inferior? _____

5.20 Is the project replicable? _____

5.21 *Impact on company image?* (I) _____

5.22 *Impact on company staff involvement?* (I) _____

5.23 *Impact on generating new financial or other resources?* _____

Additional comments: _____

_____

Recommendations: _____

_____

much greater human impact in terms of the number of people helped and the degree to which they were helped. As a result, the company changed most of its charitable contribution of investments from the purchase of facilities to the development and support of human services, with a correspondingly greater social impact and visibility.

Payroll Costs and Employee Benefits

Employee benefits now require budgets of the same order or magnitude as corporate pre-tax profits, assuming that labor costs are about half the amount of company revenues and that one-quarter of labor costs are employee benefits. (For 1976, labor fringe benefit rates averaged slightly over 30 percent for U.S. industry, and even higher in European industry.) That is a large sum to be spent inefficiently, yet it is often so spent without the guidance of social audits of benefit policies and plans. Employee benefits are "worth" to employees what the employees would be willing ot pay for them: their "shadow price," using the economist's term. Yet the portfolio of benefits is hardly ever optimized to provide the maximum shadow price to employees for a particular budget commitment or the minimum funding cost to the company for a fixed "shadow price" worth. The information on employee preferences needed to establish the shadow price can be readily obtained by employee surveys. (See the section on personnel management, later in this chapter.)

Labor cost is another area in which management decisions can be made incorrectly if lacking the input of social audits. On the basis of a purely financial analysis of the labor market, a company may decide to pay minimum wages and benefits in the belief that it is thereby minimizing labor costs. In many such cases a social audit would reveal that the short-term cash savings from low wages and benefits are more than offset by high social costs, and opportunity costs, to employees in wages and benefits not received and, moreover, that, realizing this, employees "turn over" more rapidly, the result being higher recruitment and training costs and lower labor productivity.

Also in the field of personnel policy, a decision might be made to discriminate against a particular class of employees, such as women or old people, on the basis of a perceived financial advantage in terms of labor costs. The group discriminated against might have to be willing to work for lower wages than others doing the same kind of work with no more skill. A purely financial analysis might suggest a wage policy offering lower pay to the group discriminated against. A social audit, on the other hand, would identify the social cost of the inequality in job opportunity, measured by the cost to the employees of the wages they lose as a result of discrimination. Sooner or later this social cost is likely to be translated into a financial cost greater than the financial savings originally hoped for, as the employees who are discriminated against become aware of their exploitation and organize themselves to put matters right. Furthermore, *this* cost is likely to be imposed suddenly and in a concentration more difficult to absorb than fair wage costs. Legal class action suits against employers in the United States are becoming common, and they cost the employers not only the abrupt costs of making up the wages lost from discrimination but also much loss of goodwill among consumers and the general public.

Equal Employment Opportunity policy and procedures involve management decisions that recently cost companies millions of dollars in compensating damages costs when made incorrectly. The AT&T and General Motors settlements are recent cases in point. Social audits cannot eliminate the exposure to EEO actions, but they can forecast what that exposure is so that a farsighted management has sufficient lead time to take the corrective actions required without incurring major disruptions. Social audits attempt to measure the amount of *in*equality of employment opportunity, providing personnel management with estimates of the size, nature, and location of EEO problems. They measure the degree to which the company diverges from EEO regulations and objectives and quantify the divergence in terms of the cost to the individuals who are discriminated against (albeit unintentionally). This indicates to management the areas of injustice that must be corrected, the amount by which they must be corrected, and the costs of that correction. Management then has time to start tackling the problem, rather than being forced to digest a sudden large cost change.

The social audit quantifies the cost of discrimination by measuring the discrepancy between an "equal pay for equal work" policy and "unequal pay for equal work" realities. This is done by testing for systematic salary discrimination against women or members of minority groups who are performing the same jobs as men and majority-group employees. For every type and level of job, a regression equation can be determined that provides the best "fit" to the average salary growth curve and reflects the relative impact on salary of such typical criteria as education, experience, age, seniority, race, and sex. If race or sex turns out to contribute significant components to this descriptive salary regression equation, the amount they contribute indicates the degree of de facto discrimination. Management can then examine individual cases to determine the presence of other, possibly nondiscriminatory factors that may have eluded the analysis and, in cases where no such explanation exists, take corrective action to eliminate the salary discrimination by race or sex. What is more, management will then be able to prove it has taken appropriate action on the basis of the best information available.

It should not be a surprise that widespread discrimination persists, despite the apparent goodwill and absence of prejudice on the part of many executives; factors of prejudice still operate as regards the degree of educational preparation among possible employees, the general nature of the labor market, and so on. The decision required of progressive management is to determine the degree and location of the discrimination which is most probable and to create an explicit policy designed to eliminate it. The social audit provides the information necessary for this action by measuring the cost of discrimination to those who are discriminated against, spotting its location, and determining its trends.

Antipollution Programs

Antipollution investment decisions are an obvious application for social audits. Consider the example of the Ideal Cement Company of San Juan Bautista, California. As reported in *The New York Times* of September 8, 1973, the factory closed its gates on 130 workers on September 7, after 60 years of operation, "because of" stringent air pollution laws. This factory was the principal employer of the entire small community of 1,200 persons located 80 miles south of San Francisco, and many other inhabitants of the town relied on its $2 million annual payroll as it circulated through town commerce. The plant's owner, Ideal Basic Industries of Denver, announced that it would close the plant rather than spend the $2 million needed to reduce emission of dust particles from four 80-foot smokestacks that violated air pollution laws. Here is a management decision that might have been made differently if it had been based on the inputs from a social audit—a decision that might not even have been needed if previous investment decisions had been made with the aid of a social audit.

The social costs to the San Juan Bautista community in unemployment, loss of commerce, corporate taxes, retraining needs, and moving costs of workers were probably much greater than the cost of the capital and the operating costs for the dust-emission-reducing equipment. Unemployment benefits alone come to an average of $125 per month for 130 workers, or $195,000 per year. Assuming that they were unemployed for an average of six months, that amounts to $97,500 just for unemployment. Add to that an estimated $1,000 moving cost for 100 workers who moved to find work elsewhere, and the total comes to $197,500. Assume another $100,000 for tax losses and retail trade losses to the town, and the minimum social cost of shutting down the plant is about $300,000, more than enough to pay the capital costs ($2,000,000 × 8% = $160,000), and probably the operating costs, of the antipollution equipment needed to keep the plant in business.

It might be argued that the $300,000 cost of shutting down the plant is a social cost not chargeable to the company. The private (vs. public) cost to the company is likely to be comparably high, however. Assuming a $5,000,000 annual revenue and a modest 8 percent pretax profit of $400,000, the tax-deductible investment in antipollution equipment, at a cost of $160,000–$200,000 a year, would still have been worth it.

Unfortunately the Ideal Cement Company was not farsighted enough to consider air quality in time to do anything serious about it. Ten to twenty years ago, air quality was not a fashionable issue, and scientists at the University of Southern California were just beginning to investigate smog. If Ideal Cement had done a social audit at that time, it might have been able to forecast the social liabilities it was generating and their ultimate costs in killing its business.

If the management of Ideal Cement Company had had the benefit of regular annual social audits, it would have known years before that it was generating an increasing contingent liability with its air pollution. On the social audit, this would have shown up as a major social cost, the abatement of which would have shown an increase in social assets at least equivalent to the social costs of shutting down the plant. With social and financial statements integrated—social costs translated into financial costs—it could have been seen that an investment in pollution abatement would have paid off. Furthermore, Ideal Cement would have had excellent ammunition for a proposal to the State of California to help it finance the pollution-abating equipment in the interest of minimizing social costs to the state.

Corporate Strategy

What can social audits contribute to decisions concerning general corporate strategy? The basic question for corporate strategy, according to teachers at the Harvard Business School, is "What business are we in?" That is, what combination of markets, products, and factors of production is most desirable for the firm? This question is fundamental for investment decisions concerning diversification, acquisition ("buy"), R&D ("make"), plant location, personnel policy, and the associated financing decisions. Any rational and well-organized business manager would consider the most obvious alternatives: present lines of business, simple extrapolations of these in planning similar products for new clients or new products for established clients, and the exploitation of particular company assets in attempting to reach attractive new markets. He would then select the best mix of the alternatives on the basis of market estimates, the estimated competitive advantages of the firm, return on investment based on market price and the costs of production and distribution, the costs of market entry or product development, and financing requirements and their feasibility. If he did this on the basis of financial data alone and without benefit of social audit inputs, his answers might be wrong.

Why might his choice of business lines be wrong without his having made use of social audit information? Because all the elements in his decision—the markets for new products or services, the production costs, the competitive position estimates, and even the financing requirements and their feasibility—might measure up very differently if the social assets and liabilities of the new lines of business and their associated financial costs and benefits were considered.

For example, consider the differences that might result from a purely financial evaluation and a financial-plus-social evaluation of a *new product line* requiring a chemical plant. Assume that the chemical plant produces both a caustic effluent and a noxious odor (as many chemical plants do); it also employs, like many plants of this kind, processes that are hazardous to health. To operate efficiently it must be run 24 hours per day, 7 days per week. A social audit of the proposed new product line would identify the social costs of pollution, nighttime and holiday work, and safety hazards that the purely financial estimates would neglect, beyond what was currently required by law. We know from experience that what is legally required tends to lag behind what is socially desired, so that the social audit would be a better predictor of future legal and hence financial requirements for the new line.

The social audit of the new line would identify the additional financing requirements to achieve an acceptable social cost and provide a basis for a trade-off, balancing the social benefits of pollution abatement—with the resulting higher production costs and higher prices to consumers—against the social benefits of lower production costs and lower prices to consumers, along with higher social costs from pollution. Similar estimates could be made for the costs of safety devices or automation as compared with the costs of insurance or compensation in both social and financial terms.

Corporate Ethics

Product quality and *advertising* decisions can also be made incorrectly if based on purely financial considerations. Partly unsafe or misleadingly advertised products may maximize profits temporarily, but the social costs of these policies will quickly be converted to financial costs by an angry public when awareness spreads of the consumer risks imposed without informed consent of consumers. Social audits can anticipate such social costs and provide a basis for a sounder social investment decision that will also yield better long-term financial returns. An example is a recently marketed educational kit that included poisonous chemicals. Had the distributor of the kit listened to his more socially minded staff, he would have saved himself a bad reputation and the loss of his inventory because of legal actions.

Plant Location: The Case of Bodega Bay

Another example is the decision on plant location. Suppose an electric power company must meet increased demand for electricity by building additional capacity. A management decision to expand capacity at existing plants or to build another plant at a particular location, if based on purely economic and financial considerations, might be quite different (and disastrously so) from a decision reached with the added input from social audits of the alternatives. A purely financial analysis might indicate a site involving the least expenditure to be one that a social audit would reveal to be extremely expensive in terms of social costs, anticipating the subsequent expenditures for compensating the outraged citizenry or somehow designing the plant in a more socially acceptable way. Power company after power company has made this particular mistake, resulting in long and expensive delays in approval of new construction and power shortages that the power company unsuccessfully blames on public opposition to its plant site choices.

In 1956 the Pacific Gas and Electric Company began to plan a nuclear power plant at Bodega Bay, some 50 miles north of San Francisco. The same site was desired by the State of California for a recreation area, by the University of California for a marine study facility, and by the owners of the land as a private estate. In 1964, after spending over $4 million and seven years in image-damaging controversy with opposed public interest groups, Pacific Gas and Electric Company abandoned the project. In terms of deflated present-value dollars and lost goodwill, the company had certainly wasted over $5 million by its mistake. (See Appendix C.)

What could social audit methods have done to avoid some or all of this expensive mistake? Beginning with the original site decision by PG&E—probably made as early as 1955 but not announced until land purchasing negotiations made it unavoidable in 1958—a social audit of the Bodega Bay site could have immediately identified the social costs * of nuclear power plant use as follows:

Social costs to community: Loss of recreation area;
Loss of local fishermen's income;
Loss of employment of fishermen;
Loss of tourist income as a result of aesthetic (visual) loss.

Social costs to general public: Loss of unique marine biology study area;
Loss of opportunity to use millions of dollars worth of resources for social purposes other than to make the plant earthquake-proof (it was located within a mile of a major fault in the earth's crust!).

Balanced against these social costs would be the social benefits of building the plant at Bodega Bay rather than at an alternative location. This would require detailed consideration of the major alternatives, but one could anticipate that the social benefits of this particular site would include:

Social benefits to community: Taxes paid on land use and income;
Consumer benefit of cheaper electricity.

Social benefit to general public: Consumer benefit of cheaper additional electric power, as compared to power from alternative new sites.

Even before quantification of this primitive qualitative social audit, the analysis could have identified the major potential opposi-

---

* For the sake of making a relatively conservative case for the direct social costs involved, we do not even estimate the controversial risks to life and health from reactor safeguard failures—a possibly small but at least psychologically not insignificant risk.

tion groups and their probable degree of determination and ability to mobilize supporting public opinion and political clout. PG&E would have realized that it was simultaneously scheduling battles with environmentalists, influential university professors, the fishing industry, and the broad spectrum of the public that is concerned about the dangers of atomic radiation. That would have at least made it fairly clear that the policy of minimum communication with the public followed by PG&E was unlikely to be acceptable to the public or ultimately to the federal regulatory agencies, particularly in view of the seriousness of the issues involved.

A quantified social audit could have been accomplished as early as 1960, by which time the decision had probably been made to build a nuclear plant, with its attendant additional costs and benefits. Table 3 gives a crude estimate of what this might have indicated.

Table 3. Social cost of nuclear power plant at Bodega Bay.*

	(In millions of dollars per year)
Social costs to community	
Loss of recreation area	0.5
Loss of fishing income	0.5
Loss of employment	0.5
Loss of tourist income	0.5
Social costs to general public	
Loss of marine study area	0.5
Opportunity cost of resources needed to make reactor earthquake-proof ($5 to $10 million total)	0.5 to 1.0
Estimated total social costs to community and general public	3.0 to 3.5
Social benefits to community	
Taxes paid on land	0.3
Consumer benefit of cheaper power	0.2
Social benefits to general public	
Consumer benefit of cheaper power than from alternative sites	0.5 to 1.0
Estimated total social *benefits* to community and general public	1.0 to 1.5
Estimated total net social *cost* to community and general public	1.5 to 2.5

* As estimated by the author.

Even at this stage in the evaluation of alternatives, PG&E might have noted that with over $1 million per year of net social cost at the proposed site, the economies in production might be insufficient to justify a decision to proceed *at that site*. Furthermore, by investigating in detail the concerns expressed by the opposition groups to arrive at a "shadow price" of the social costs, PG&E probably could have obtained a more realistic estimate of the depth and intensity of the opposition.

Even at this stage a crude dollar analysis would also have shown that by far the largest potential social cost was the "opportunity cost" of earthquake-proofing (or the even greater potential cost of a radiation spill in the event that an earthquake—frequent in the area—ruptured the reactor). This would have suggested immediate additional attention to the question of locating the plant somewhere else rather than within a mile of a major known geological fault.

The costs to PG&E of its lost credibility and reduced community goodwill was not even considered. To the extent that the company needs broad community support for other projects, the public relations costs of obtaining that support in the future have undoubtedly been increased by the company's unfortunate handling of the Bodega Bay controversy.

Financial-Plus-Social Criteria. Figure 5 shows costs for three sites: A, B, and C. The financial cost is lowest for site A, and this simple

Figure 5. Social audits for plant location decision.

SITE	A	B	C
FINANCIAL COST	10	15	20
SOCIAL COST	15	8	10
F + S COST	25	23	30
X BEST CHOICE, FINANCIAL BASIS	①	②	③
√ BEST CHOICE, F + S BASIS	②	①	③

form of accounting would indicate that obviously the best decision is to locate the plant at site A. But it happens that in this example the social cost of locating in site A is the highest.

Let's say the question is whether to locate a nuclear power plant at a seaside resort. This site offers the lowest financial cost because of good access to suppliers and consumers but the highest social cost because of disruption of the environment. The best choice on a financial basis is different from the best choice on a social basis, but the best choice on a financial-plus-social basis is still different. In this example, the investment decision should be made on the basis of the combined financial and social payoff.

Social Audits in Personnel Management

The personnel manager's mission is to satisfy the personnel needs of the organization as efficiently as possible. This usually means recruiting, selecting, placing, orienting, evaluating, training, developing, and *retaining* the most cost-effective personnel and doing all this in a way that maximizes overall company effectiveness within a given personnel budget.

To attract, retain, and develop to their fullest capacity the most effective employees, personnel policy must maximize the attractiveness of employment for the types of employees sought. This must be done within salary, benefit, and other budget constraints.

How can the attractiveness of the company—as perceived by employees and potential employees—be maximized within budgetary constraints? A social audit of the current and potential social benefits and costs generated by the company for its employees can identify the steps that would maximize the company's attractiveness within any fixed level of budget. In social audits, this would be accomplished by the following sequence of actions:

1. Questionnaire survey of employees' perceptions of the relative worth of different current and potential social benefits and the cost of different social disadvantages associated with company employment. (See Figures 6 and 7.)
2. Follow-up interviews to clarify any ambiguities in responses to the sample survey.
3. Formulation of an employee benefits preference inventory, with relative perceived worth associated with each item.
4. Inventory of current social benefits supplied by the company to employees.

Figure 6. Employee questionnaire: company benefits.

We are interested in your opinions of how the company should allocate its employee benefit monies. In the first two columns below, you will find the approximate dollar and percent allocations for the major benefits provided by the company. Please indicate your preferences for how the monies should be allocated in the third column. Spaces have been provided for benefits not currently provided by the company.

BENEFITS	DOLLAR COST PER YEAR	CURRENT % OF TOTAL BENEFIT MONIES	PERCENT YOU WOULD ALLOCATE
Paid vacation	$548,000	37.8%	_____ %
Health & Life insurance	273,000	18.8%	_____ %
Paid sick leave	183,000	12.6%	_____ %
Paid holidays	153,000	10.5%	_____ %
Retirement income	104,000	7.2%	_____ %
Attractive working environment	46,000	3.2%	_____ %
Free parking	45,500	3.1%	_____ %
Luncheon facilities at office	38,000	2.6%	_____ %
Free breakfast & coffee	26,000	1.8%	_____ %
Child care facilities	10,000	.7%	_____ %
Organized recreation (athletics and parties)	10,000	.7%	_____ %
Tuition reimbursement	10,000	.7%	_____ %
Recreation facilities (tennis, swimming)	5,000	.3%	_____ %
Other (please specify)			
_____	0	0	_____ %
_____	0	0	_____ %
_____	0	0	_____ %
_____	0	0	_____ %
_____	0	0	_____ %
TOTALS	$1,451,500	100.0%	100.0%

Besides providing staff with a number of social benefits, there are usually social costs associated with working for certain companies. Previous surveys of Abt Associates employees have indicated that the major social cost to staff members arises from staff commitment to task completion resulting in overtime worked but not paid. On the average, during the last year, how many hours per week have you worked beyond those for which you were paid?

_____ hours per week

Figure 7. Employee questionnaire: on-the-job opportunities.

Listed below are different kinds of opportunities which a job might afford. If you were to seek a job, (A) How much importance would you personally attach to each of these opportunities, and (B) To what extent does your present job actually provide such opportunities?

(Please check one answer for each line in (A) and (B)).

	(A) Importance to You Personally					(B) Extent Provided by Your Present Job				
	Not Important	Moderately Important	Important	Very Important	Extremely Important	Not Provided	Minimally Provided	Adequately Provided	Well Provided	Completely Provided
1. To make full use of my present knowledge and skills	1	2	3	4	5	1	2	3	4	5
2. To grow and learn new knowledge and skills	1	2	3	4	5	1	2	3	4	5
3. To earn a good salary	1	2	3	4	5	1	2	3	4	5
4. To advance in administrative authority and status	1	2	3	4	5	1	2	3	4	5
5. To build my professional reputation	1	2	3	4	5	1	2	3	4	5
6. To work on difficult and challenging problems	1	2	3	4	5	1	2	3	4	5
7. To have freedom to carry out my own ideas	1	2	3	4	5	1	2	3	4	5
8. To contribute to broad technical knowledge in my field	1	2	3	4	5	1	2	3	4	5
9. To reject working on anything that I consider unethical	1	2	3	4	5	1	2	3	4	5
10. To work with colleagues that share my goals and beliefs	1	2	3	4	5	1	2	3	4	5
11. To depend on my work for my preferred rewards	1	2	3	4	5	1	2	3	4	5
12. To expect that I can predict the results of my work	1	2	3	4	5	1	2	3	4	5

Thank you for your cooperation. If you have any comments you feel are relevant to this Questionnaire or the Social Audit, please feel free to note them in the space provided below.

5. Comparison of employee preference inventory with current programs inventory and identification of "low preference, high cost" components to be eliminated and "high preference," "presently unavailable" or "underavailable" components for possible addition.
6. Redesign of company benefits program to respond maximally to employee preferences within some budget and associated reallocation of subbudgets.
7. Review and analysis of additional, highly valued social benefits requiring additional budget to determine if potential return on additional investment is justified.
8. Consistency check, using a survey of employee responses to the new benefits plan and determination whether significant improvement in perceived worth has been achieved without significant budget expansion.
9. Communication of the resulting changes to employees and stockholders, demonstrating the improved benefits gained with no diminution of return on investment.

If such a social audit of employee benefits and costs is executed annually and followed up with the actions indicated, employee recruiting and retention should improve, with attendant reduction in personnel costs from undesired turnover.

Some examples of employee benefits and costs that are widely underestimated by corporations are listed in Table 4.

Corporate social audits directed at measuring company social performance with respect to employees provide an item-to-item, year-to-year, and company-to-company comparison of the social benefits and costs created by the company for its employees. These comparisons can then be used to allocate personnel resources more efficiently and in conformance with employee preferences and perceived valuations, as well as to make them more effective with respect to corporate objectives.

Consider the practical example of designing a plan for employee pay incentives and benefits. If it is assumed that a fixed budget is available, as determined by overall corporate financial constraints, the problem is to maximize the incentive impact and perceived benefits to employees of various combinations of compensation, incentives, and benefits. The social audit approach would permit the maximization of these objectives within the corporate financial constraints on the basis of the following procedure:

Table 4. Typically underestimated employee benefits and costs.

Benefits	Costs
Career development opportunities.	Inequality of advancement.
Education and training opportunities.	Insecurity of employment.
Attentive management recognition of significant achievements (nonmonetary).	Inadequate job satisfaction.
	Overtime worked and not paid (particularly by professionals).
Flexibility of working hours and vacations.	Unaesthetic work environment.
Child care available at work.	Health (including mental health) hazards.
Pleasant lunch facilities available at work.	Insecurity or inadequacy of disability and retirement real (deflated) income.
Payroll savings, investment and loan opportunities.	Losses from theft and other crime at or around the work environment.
Aid in economical transportation and housing.	Unusual transportation expenses of commuting.
College tuition support for parents of college-age youth.	Inaccessibility of various types of staff on the social level.
Opportunities to socialize with diverse levels and functions of staff.	Offensive management styles (excessively authoritarian, cold, formal, bureaucratic, hypocritical, confused, etc.).
Good-humored, strong, competent leadership.	Minor administrative management decisions, made in the alleged interest of efficiency, that seem arbitrary to employees.

First, the social audit team would survey the employees (on a stratified sampling basis minimizing costs) to determine the employee-perceived worth of various social benefits and costs created by the company. Typical benefits would include pay, career advancement, training, health and life insurance benefits, pleasant working conditions, and interesting work. Typical social costs imposed by the company might include risk of layoff, overtime work not paid, perceived inequality of employment opportunity, risk of accident, and tedious work.

Second, the social audit team would estimate the equivalent money worth of the social benefits and costs currently imposed on the employees by the company. This would be done by the method of shadow pricing, which economists use to determine the equivalent monetized worth of so-called free goods not on the commercial market. For example, the market-equivalent cost for an employee to obtain day-care service equivalent to that provided at cost by a company, plus the time-worth of colocation, would determine its social worth to the employee.

Third, the social audit team would analyze the monetized value of social benefits and costs created for the employees by the company, together with the survey results, which would include responses to open-ended questions about additional benefits desired. The objective of the analysis would be to identify the highest perceived benefit and highest perceived cost items on the menu of current or possible practices, to augment or increase the items of high perceived benefit, and to reduce or eliminate the items of high perceived social cost.

Fourth, the social audit team would develop a revised menu of incentives and benefits, review it with management for its consistency with company policies and budgetary constraints, and then review it with a sample of employees for final corrective feedback. Following the corrective feedback from management and employees, the final package would be developed and made ready for implementation.

Fifth, the social audit team would summarize—in quantitative money terms—the increase in social benefits achieved for employees without increasing the budget, and this might be included in company reports to stockholders and staff. Such employee social audit information would presumably be useful in comparing overall company personnel management cost-effectiveness from year to year and from company to company.

Such a social audit of corporate social performance with respect to employees could be used to reduce the risks of equal employment opportunity violations and corresponding legal actions, job dissatisfaction, high labor turnover and retraining costs, and declining morale and unit productivity, as well as increasing the efficiency of personnel management. Included in the personnel social audit are regression analyses of compensation as a function of all major determining factors for all levels and types of employees, to identify any job/pay inequities. Also included are responses to projective questions that tend to identify major organizational and structural sources of employee dissatisfaction. Thus the personnel social audit can serve to provide early warning to management of significant areas in which it is failing to meet its personnel goals, and offer quantitative data for efficient allocation of resources to correct such discrepancies. The personnel social audit can provide these services for about the same cost as a conventional financial audit, and without any more disruption than would be occasioned by routine employee surveys. Furthermore, experience has shown that a positive morale effect is often created merely by asking employees what their concerns are, so that even the data-gathering phase of the personnel social audit is likely to have some social benefits for the corporation.

In our own company, the internal social audit benefits and costs created for the employees as a result of corporate actions in a recent year identified the two major costs as being professional overtime worked but not paid for and inequality of opportunity for women employees. As a result, management made specific efforts to reduce the average amount of professional overtime and to correct the inequality of opportunity among women. As a result of these efforts, the average professional work week was reduced in the next year from about 55 to about 50 hours per week, and the opportunity cost of wages forgone by women employees was reduced by over 50 percent from the previous year's estimate of $26,000, with an improvement in morale and productivity.

In the course of the second year's social audit of Abt Associates Inc., the survey of employee performance and satisfaction identified three major deficiencies. These deficiencies, as perceived by employees, were the inadequacies of retirement income, opportunity for career advancement, and in-company training. As a result, management accelerated the development and implementation of a retirement plan that had been pending, initiated a company information program on the past and current opportunities for career advancement (which were better than most recent employees were aware of), and resumed in-company schooling (an activity that had been dropped two years previously because of an apparent lack of interest). It is anticipated that these management decisions will have significant positive impact on the productivity of this labor-intensive professional services firm.

Social Audit as an Information System

The social audit should be considered as a particular type of management information system, which is designed to help managers make decisions about operating policies. Although the social audit is also a rating system for comparing corporate social performance among different companies and assisting government in enforcing the requirements of social legislation, its area of greatest impact is likely to be in aiding management decisions. Questions might be raised as to whether the financial statement is the most effective format for a management information system. A good management information system is parsimonious in presenting only that information which is directly relevant to management decision making. The financial statement supplies both more and less information than is immediately relevant. Nevertheless, we believe in the usefulness of the financial performance statement even in its present form, because it is widely understood and has the authority of tradition. The different effects for different types of companies for which different social benefit and cost line items would have to be constructed can be integrated into the accounting format, just as different financial data have been integrated into the financial format by using different line items.

For the social audit to be most useful in management decision making, the line items will probably differ somewhat from company to company, just as they do for financial items. They may also change from year to year as different aspects of social investment and social activities are emphasized. The main rule in deciding whether an item is included is the same test of "consequentiality" that is applied to conventional financial statements; this will determine whether a particular item deserves to be included as a line item, or is already encompassed by other line items.

To sum up: Social costs and benefits presently forecast may often predict financial costs and benefits which will occur in future. By forecasting social costs and benefits, the social audit can provide early warning of future financial requirements—and future opportunities.

In some cases, businessmen may decide that future social costs and benefits are *not* the best predictors of private costs and benefits; they may regard other predictors as being better. For example, a businessman may engage in activities of high social cost in the belief that it is his most profitable long-term course because he assumes there will be enough advance legal warning of government or consumer reaction for him to reform these activities in time to minimize their financial backlash. Even in such cases, however, the businessman would do well to execute his own social audit to make sure he has enough lead time to change course, particularly if a change in his operations will require more time than legal warnings permit.

From some corporation executives' point of view, social audits—or corporate social performance reviews—may in fact seem unnecessary and even risky. The anxiety of some executives is that the information developed will not be reassuring, and may even be threatening. All the better! Better an early warning of future threats in time for corrective action than damaging action without notice, such as costly community opposition to new facilities, disruptive employee opposition to new working arrangements, damaging consumer protests against unsatisfactory products and services, interference and fines from government regulatory agencies, unfavorable local tax actions in response to negative public opinion.

It cost AT&T at least $15 million to pay damages for back pay to women employees who were discriminated against. A social audit of company social performance with respect to employees might have warned of the magnitude of the problem and led to earlier and more economical corrective actions.

There are also many positive reasons for doing social audits, with potential gains in productivity and improved financial performance either by continuing to supply the same level of net social benefits more efficiently at reduced financial cost, or by increasing the social and financial productivity of social investments at the same financial cost.

Conflicts of Interest

Corporate management is responsible to several constituencies: the public, owners or stockholders, consumers, employees, and the residents of the communities in which it operates. These constituencies are not always in agreement, but no one constituency can be neglected.

Social science offers several techniques for resolving conflicts among different interests to achieve something close to a social optimum for all the competing groups. By a social optimum (also known as a Pareto optimum, after the 19th-century Italian economist who developed the concept) we mean a maximization of the benefits to some or to all groups without cost to any group. That is, the competitive "game" played among these groups is not of the kind called a "zero-sum game" (in which the sums of wins and losses are zero, and the wins of one group are always at the expense of the losses of another) but rather a game in which the wins of one group increase the wins of another group—or at least do not decrease them.

The scientific techniques for resolving conflicting interests include econometric ones in which the interests of the different groups are expressed in common terms, and the optimum "mix" of them all is achieved by equalizing the marginal benefits of each group. Operations research has provided techniques to optimize the mix of responses to conflicting goals as well. Finally, there are many qualitative negotiating techniques that generally work toward mutual satisfaction of conflicting interests. It is thus no longer possible for a competent manager to claim that because he has conflicting constituencies it is impossible for him to formulate a policy responsive to all interests.

=5=

Implementing the Audit: Intracompany Considerations

THE technical feasibility and social desirability of social audits does not assure their implementation. There are many obstacles to implementation in the corporation that have little to do with technical feasibility (although that is often raised as an excuse for nonimplementation).

The questions often asked by executives are: "Why do it? What are the risks? What are the probable consequences? Are the possible useful results worth the risks and costs?"

Straightforward explanations of why a social audit should be done leave many executives grudgingly acquiescent but basically unenthusiastic. Improved efficiency of social investments is rarely their first priority; they are often almost entirely occupied with improving the efficiency of financial investments. There already appear to be so many legal, union, public relations, operational, and financial constraints on social investment decisions that many executives feel they have little to decide about social issues and therefore do not need a complex decision aid.

The demands on executives are many and the perceived costs of failure are high. Thus *any* new managerial activity is reviewed immediately for its necessity. Managers will ask, "Do I really have to do this additional thing, too? What if I don't? Will it matter?" If they think that not doing it won't matter, they are unlikely to do it. And why should they be convinced that it matters, when so many colleagues don't do social auditing and it doesn't seem to make any difference?

Meanwhile, the pressures on executives to attend to things that do matter—palpably, immediately, and unavoidably—encourage a certain coolness toward novel activities that seem only indirectly related to their central concerns—production, growth, profits, promotion. The indirectness of the impact of social audits on classical management problems is a major obstacle to their implementation. However, legislation and consumer actions are now beginning to relate social concerns more directly to the classic business concerns, as in instances in which pollution fines affect profits or worker protests affect production.

The risks of implementing social audits are sometimes seen as outweighing the risks of not implementing them, mainly because the former are more proximate in time. Businessmen, like politicians, use a high discount rate; they are conditioned to do so by annual reviews and reports. Social audits may seem to them to impose assured one-year risks for possible ten-year benefits. Among the immediate risks are poor publicity from the exposure of damaging social actions, immediate outlay of additional cash, and an apparent legitimization of social demands that may increase the difficulties of labor-management negotiations.

How to Motivate Managers

In the course of studying the implementation of social responsibility activities at middle-management levels, Robert Ackerman, formerly of the Harvard Business School, found that middle-level executives operating under purely financial incentives are unlikely to respond to requests for social responsibility activities unless these are also tied in with the corporation's incentive system.* Mere exhortations by top management to respond to social needs, coupled with an incentive structure that emphasizes rewards only for purely financial performance, tend to result in increasing disdain for social actions which go unrewarded. A widespread example of this has been the failure of middle managers to respond to requirements for Equal Employment Opportunity outreach activities to recruit minority and women employees in rough proportion to their presence in the surrounding population. For the many years during which such recruitment was merely a matter of exhortation by top management, little actually changed. However, when the enforcement of federal EEO regulations put pressure on top managements to make something actually happen, the more effective top managements decided to put their salary money where their mouths were and to make middle-management rewards at least partly contingent on EEO performance. With incentive rewards tied to the new social objectives of companies, most middle managers took the social objectives more seriously and began to turn in more effective EEO performance.

Implementation of social action at lower middle-management levels is likely to operate in much the same way: no effective implementation until the program is tied into the conventional reward system. However, if middle managers perceive social measurements as a way of helping them to get their ordinary nonsocial jobs done more effectively, then they may adopt these methods independently of the incentive system. Social research methods have helped to improve conventional unit performance by such programs as cost-effectiveness and benefit/cost analysis, sensitivity training, transactional analysis, organizational development, and programs to increase interpersonal skills—all of these originally developed by social scientists to analyze and improve productivity. For a pragmatic incentive to implementation to be present, there usually has to be something of a crisis of confidence in the old way of accomplishing ordinary work objectives, so that middle-level managements are willing to take the risks of trying something new because they perceive the risks of continuing what they are doing to be even greater (because it obviously doesn't work any more).

Gradually, even the lowest-level employees have begun to hear about the social purposes of the business enterprise, quality of life is-

* Robert Ackerman, "How Companies Respond to Social Demands," *Harvard Business Review*, July/August 1973, pp. 88–89.

sues, honesty of reporting and advertising, and trade-offs between benefits to the stockholders and benefits to the public, and have begun to develop their own moral ideas on what is just and proper in these areas. For many years now, company policy has not been regarded as having the legitimacy of the Ten Commandments, and the policy of most contemporary corporations is open to critical review at all times by anyone inside and outside the company. This critical review is becoming more and more informed by a more sophisticated awareness of the social impacts of an organization's decisions and the perceived legitimacy of claims by minorities and other previously disenfranchised and disadvantaged groups. It is not only the students, blacks, and women who have become politicized in the past decade, but also majority group employees in general. This politicization is not particularly related to unionization; on the contrary, the old authoritarian, top-down dictation of organizational ethics and procedure has been reluctantly relinquished (in some places) by union leaders as well as by large corporation managers, who once shared with them a style of nonparticipatory management.

The risks of implementing social audits are perceived somewhat differently by middle managers than by those at the top of an organization. Top management perceives possible dangers of unfavorable publicity since the social balance sheet is likely to contain some unfavorable items. They also envisage that the documentation of the social costs created by the company may result in exposing the corporation to damage suits, class actions, and consumer protests. Further, they fear the loss of their independence and freedom in making decisions—as might happen, say, to a supervisor if he or she were required to write out in detail and to publish all the reasons why he or she decides to promote one individual and lay off another. Public disclosure of the human mixture of fact, emotional bias, superficial judgment, plain fancy, and irascible whim, which is usual in decision making, is not likely to be reassuring to outsiders. Outside criticism may inhibit executive action or lead to even greater secrecy.

At middle-management levels, the limits to implementing social measurements are less political and more economic, that is, more pragmatically concerned with possible waste of time and less concerned with the fear of political and legal costs. To middle managers, social measurement seems like an additional chore that will take both time and energy without any corresponding return in increased productivity—just one more hassle that they would rather avoid and one more risk of being distracted from their financial and production targets.

Companies Now Using Social Measurements

Despite this kind of business resistance to social audits, strong interest in such audits continues, and may be growing. The survey of efforts to measure the social performance of business which was conducted by John J. Corson and George A. Steiner * (see Chapter 1) reveals some interesting possible reasons. The survey questionnaire was sent to 750 corporations, and 284 of them returned it in completed form. Most of the companies responding were large, with over 45 percent having annual sales of over $1 billion. Almost half were engaged in manufacturing, 28 percent were in finance, insurance, and real estate, 12 percent were in communications, transportation, and utilities, and the remainder were in extraction, wholesale and resale, and services. Of the 284 responses, 52 were returned by senior officers of corporations, while the remainder were generally returned by public affairs officers having responsibility for corporate social performance.

In response to the question as to whether the company since the start of 1972 had attempted to inventory or assess any social performance activities, 76 percent responded affirmatively. Attempts to measure social performance were not uniform for different types of industry, although the mining and oil refining and primary metals and scientific instruments industries all had an over 80 percent participation. (This is not a significant variance in a sample of this size, the average for all the industries being 76 percent.)

The results of the social performance inventory or assessment were made available to executives only in 38 percent of the cases and to executives and directors in 14 percent of the cases; in only 22 percent were they made available to executive directors, stockholders, the public, and anyone else who was interested. The main method by which the results were made public (45 percent) was in the corporate annual report, with 24 percent reporting "through all media" and 17 percent "by special report." (It is important to bear in mind

* *Measuring Business's Social Performance: The Corporate Social Audit* (New York: Committee for Economic Development, 1974).

here that the questionnaire used the term "social audit" interchangeably with the terms "inventory" or "assessment" (of corporate social activities) and in fact defined social audit by the use of these terms.

The motivations for such assessments as given by the respondent companies were very diverse and included at least a dozen different reasons. Here are some of them:

To examine what the company is actually doing in selected areas	17%
To appraise or evaluate performance in selected areas	14
To identify those social programs which the company feels it ought to be pursuing	14
To inject into the general thinking of managers a social point of view	11
To determine where the company may be vulnerable to attack	9
To ensure that specific decision-making processes incorporate a social point of view	8
To meet public demands for corporate accountability in the social area	7
To inform the public of what the company is doing	6
To identify those social programs which the company feels pressured to undertake	5
To offset irresponsible audits made by outside self-appointed groups	4
To increase profits	3
All others	2

It should be noted that 196 companies of the 284 responding, or about two-thirds, checked more than one of these purposes for making their social audit. It is also interesting to note that the dominant reasons appear to be, at least according to the respondents, to identify and clarify the view of what the company is doing in managing itself. Only secondarily is the company concerned about being responsive to external social needs or to improving its decision making in the social area.

Another question asked was: "What do you see as the most important obstacle to the development of social audits?" Six different replies were allowed, and here they are ranked in order of importance:

1. Inability to develop measures of performance which everyone will accept (98 companies gave this the first order of importance).
2. Inability to make credible cost/benefit analyses to guide company actions (58 companies reported this as the first order of importance).
3. Inability to develop consensus as to what activities shall be covered (38 companies listed this as the first order of importance).
4. Inability to develop consensus on ways to organize information (15 companies gave this the first order of importance).
5. Danger to the company in publishing the results of social audits (only 8 companies gave this the first order of importance; 18 gave it the second order of importance).
6. General decline in pressures on business to undertake social programs (only 9 gave this the first order of importance and even fewer gave it the second order).

Note that the major problems most companies have had with the development of social audits are technical ones: "inability to develop measures," "inability to make credible cost/benefit analyses," "inability to develop consensus as to what activities shall be covered," "inability to develop consensus on ways to organize information." The first four of the six different reasons are all problems of method. Only 8 of the 284 companies assign first importance to the danger to the company in disclosure of its social performance, and only 9 assign first importance to a lack of external pressures to undertake social programs. Clearly it may be concluded, at least from this survey, that the most important obstacles to the development of social audits, as perceived or claimed by large corporations, are methodological ones.

This point requires some discussion. Methodological problems may be a "screen issue," if there is no great impetus to solve them. For example, before Equal Employment Opportunity legislation and its fairly vigorous enforcement, many companies which discriminated against minorities and women claimed rigidities of job pattern and technical and institutional problems ("Can't find anyone qualified!") as reasons for not being able to respond to demands for equality of employment opportunity. As the pressure became greater for EEO affirmative action, most companies found ways to overcome these technical difficulties. Similarly, one reason why

methodological obstacles to social audits appear decisive in the view
of the majority of the large corporations, may be that the impetus
for overcoming these methodological obstacles is not perceived to be
very great. This hypothesis can only be checked by comparing companies that are under great pressures to develop social performance
measurement with those that are not, and comparing the vigor with
which the two types of companies overcome the methodological obstacles. Neil C. Churchill's in-depth survey * of 11 large corporations
(see Chapter 11) suggests quite strongly that where there are great
pressures for overcoming methodological difficulties corporations
find some way to do so.

Another question was: "In general, do you think that business
firms will be required to make social audits in the future?" The
response was almost evenly divided, with 46 percent answering yes
and 54 percent answering no. Again, a larger percentage of the
firms over $10 billion (59 percent) answered yes. There was no par-
ticularly significant pattern by type of industry.

The question was then addressed to those firms that thought
businesses would be required to make social audits in the future,
asking whether in their opinion this prospect was acceptable to them
as businessmen. Here 52 percent answered yes, and another 44 percent answered yes with some reservations, with only 4 percent finding the prospect unacceptable.

The next question asked was: "Has your company given any
person, organizational unit, or group the responsibility for surveying
more or less continuously the evolving demands on your company
for social action programs?" Here again, the largest firms of those
over $10 billion answered affirmatively (86 percent), with 82 percent
of those between $1 and $10 billion answering affirmatively, and 68
percent of those between $0.5 and $1 billion answering affirmatively. Again there was no particularly significant breakdown by type
of industry.

The titles of the persons and staff groups to whom responsibility for social programs was assigned were predominantly in the
public and community affairs department (42 percent), with a substantial number (14 percent) under a senior vice president, and a
significant number (11 percent) under the environmental and urban
affairs officer. A surprisingly small percentage came under cor-

* "Toward a Theory for Social Accounting," *Sloan Management Review*, Spring
1974.

porate relations (6 percent), personnel (6 percent), board of directors (3 percent), and corporate contributions (2 percent).

The next question asked was: "Would you please check, as requested, which of the listed activities your company is engaged in?" Table 5 gives the types of activities mentioned in order of rank.

Asked which activities were noted most frequently to involve significant commitments of money or personnel time, the respondents gave similar replies but did not rank the items in exactly the same order. For example, although minority employment and advancement ranked first both in importance and in commitments of money and time, the second most important activity was listed as increasing productivity, while the second-ranked activity, in terms of money and time devoted to it, was financial aid to educational institutions.

The question was also asked in a negative way to arrive at a rank

Table 5. Response of leading corporations when asked to list their social action programs.*

Rank	Activity	Number of "Highly Important" Responses (of a total of 284)
1	Ensuring employment and advancement opportunities for minorities	232
2	Increasing productivity in the private sector of the economy	201
3	Improving the innovativeness and performance of business management	188
4	Improvement of work/career opportunities	180
5	Installation of modern pollution abatement equipment	178
6	Facilitating equality of results by continued training and other special programs (civil rights and equal opportunity)	174
7	Supporting fiscal and monetary policies for steady economic growth	169
8	Direct financial aid to schools, including scholarships, grants, and tuition refunds	167
9	Engineering and new facilities to minimize environmental effects	167
10	Active recruitment of the disadvantaged	157

* According to John J. Corson and George A. Steiner, *op. cit.*

order of those activities which responding companies believed to be relatively *unimportant*. The most unimportant activity was deemed to be the establishment of schools, with the second and third most unimportant activities being aesthetic restoration of depleted properties and provision of day-care centers for children of working mothers. The fourth least important was given as building plants and sales offices in ghettoes.

The question was also asked which social activity *least frequently* involved significant commitments of money and time. Curiously enough, the provision of day-care centers for children of working mothers ranked second here, indicating considerable ignorance of what is involved in establishing and operating such centers.

The spectrum of current corporate social activities included items under economic growth and efficiency, education, employment and training, civil rights and equal opportunity, urban renewal and development, pollution abatement, conservation and recreation, culture and the arts, medical care, and government. The number of responses to these questions, of the sample of 284 companies responding, is given in Table 6.

In summary, one can conclude that there is an apparent wide degree of large corporation interest in and support for social audits, including qualitative inventories and assessments of social performance, but that the major perceived obstacle to effective implementation of social audits and efforts to measure the social performance of business is, in the corporations' view, the difficulty of overcoming the methodological problems. Professor Steiner's survey unfortunately did not go into sufficient depth to determine whether this perception of methodological difficulty is indeed controlling and whether, if the necessary methodology were developed, corporations would adopt annual social audits more aggressively. There are data from other investigators, however, that suggest that while this is a sincere objection on the part of a substantial number of corporations, another large percentage of corporations might find other reasons to object to carrying out a corporate social audit if the methodological obstacles were removed.

Social Audits and Business Competition

A common criticism of attempts to improve corporate social performance unilaterally is that this damages the company's compet-

itive position, adding to its costs without yielding corresponding increases in revenues. This applies to such social factors as added
product quality, increased employee benefits, and pollution abatement equipment. Even an unusually high degree of corporate charitable contributions is cited as cutting into stockholders' dividends
and ultimately making the company less competitive by raising its
cost of capital. Thus the company's social performance is said to be
impeded by financial disincentives.

Until such criticisms are effectively answered, businessmen in
highly competitive industries are not likely to innovate improvements in corporate social performance to any great degree. They
may perceive that to do so brings them significant penalties in their
financial performance, which is still seen by them as their first responsibility—even though it is not their only responsibility.

There is frequently an error in such criticisms: the assumption
(noted elsewhere in this book) that all or most social performance
improvements require the sacrifice of profitability. The contrary is
more often the case. If major polluters had invested in antipollution
facilities early rather than waiting till now, their current profits
would be higher and they would have increased their average cumulative earnings per share by not having to sell as much equity now
(which brings less capital now than it used to) to pay for the antipollution equipment (which costs more now than it used to). If the
most backward employers in terms of labor relations had been more
farsighted in their concerns for their employees' health and security,
they might have saved themselves the later costs of the most aggres-
sive unionization.

Most social performance improvements generate benefits that
are economic and financial as well as social, provided that they are
applied and operated efficiently. This is strongly the case when social programs are applied to intracompany operations involving employees and production. Corporate charitable contributions may also
yield more indirect economic benefits, if made wisely and with the
objective of improving the labor market, the consumer market, and
the overall environment for efficient company operations.

On the other hand, failure to make social improvements results
in costs that are not only social but also financial. In view of this, a
company cannot afford to *not* improve corporate social performance
merely to remain competitive. As this fact is more widely realized,
there will no doubt be competition to improve corporate social per-

Table 6. Spectrum of current corporate activities and frequency of response.*

Activity	Please check those activities which involve significant commitments of money and/or personnel time	Please check one of the following columns as appropriate		
		Highly important to our company	Moderately important to our company	Of minor importance to our company
Economic Growth and Efficiency				
Increasing productivity in the private sector of the economy	180	201	13	11
Improving the innovativeness and performance of business management	174	188	32	4
Enhancing competition	69	87	39	34
Cooperating with the government in developing more effective measures to control inflation and achieve high levels of employment	121	148	59	10
Supporting fiscal and monetary policies for steady economic growth	109	169	37	7
Helping with the post-Vietnam conversion of the economy	37	54	59	49
Education				
Direct financial aid to schools, including scholarships, grants, and tuition refunds	238	167	90	10
Support for increases in school budgets	38	34	55	62
Donation of equipment and skilled personnel	139	59	114	43
Assistance in curriculum development	83	45	84	59
Aid in counseling and remedial education	67	34	64	73
Establishment of new schools, running schools and school systems	38	19	40	95
Assistance in the management and financing of colleges	120	70	80	48
Employment and Training				
Active recruitment of the disadvantaged	199	157	66	26

* From *Social Responsibilities of Business Corporations*, Committee for Economic Development, A Statement by the Research and Policy Committee, New York, June 1971, pp. 37–40.

Table 6. (Continued)

Activity	Please check those activities which involve significant commitments of money and/or personnel time	Please check one of the following columns as appropriate		
		Highly important to our company	Moderately important to our company	Of minor importance to our company
Special functional training, remedial education, and counseling	134	97	73	38
Provision of day-care centers for children of working mothers	26	18	40	80
Improvement of work/career opportunities	191	180	47	12
Retraining of workers affected by automation or other causes of joblessness	80	67	52	64
Establishment of company programs to remove the hazards of old age and sickness	139	130	55	25
Supporting where needed and appropriate the extension of government accident, unemployment, health, and retirement systems	93	93	48	51

Civil Rights and Equal Opportunity

Activity		Highly important to our company	Moderately important to our company	Of minor importance to our company
Ensuring employment and advancement opportunities for minorities	244	232	30	2
Facilitating equality of results by continued training and other special programs	176	174	47	5
Supporting and aiding the improvement of black educational facilities, and special programs for blacks and other minorities in integrated institutions	159	128	78	25
Encouraging adoption of open-housing ordinances	31	28	55	66
Building plants and sales offices in the ghettos	39	31	36	86
Providing financing and managerial assistance to minority enterprises, and participating with minorities in joint ventures	134	84	75	54

Table 6. (Continued)

Activity	Please check those activities which involve significant commitments of money and/or personnel time	Please check one of the following columns as appropriate		
		Highly important to our company	Moderately important to our company	Of minor impor- tance to our company
Urban Renewal and Development				
Leadership and financial support for city and regional planning and development	135	110	67	40
Building or improving low-income housing	75	58	53	67
Building shopping centers, new communities, new cities	78	66	36	67
Improving transportation systems	88	85	56	35
Pollution Abatement				
Installation of modern equipment	189	178	32	19
Engineering new facilities for minimum environmental effects	169	167	28	22
Research and technological development	145	142	27	26
Cooperating with municipalities in joint treatment facilities	84	79	58	36
Cooperating with local, state, regional, and federal agencies in developing improved systems of environmental management	126	127	57	23
Developing more effective programs for recycling and reusing disposable materials	97	90	52	42
Conservation and Recreation				
Augmenting the supply of replenishable resources, such as trees, with more productive species	42	40	34	74
Preserving animal life and the ecology of forests and comparable areas	41	35	45	72
Providing recreational and aesthetic facilities for public use	80	57	55	65

Table 6. (Continued)

Activity	Please check those activities which involve significant commitments of money and/or personnel time	Please check one of the following columns as appropriate		
		Highly important to our company	Moderately important to our company	Of minor importance to our company
Restoring aesthetically depleted properties such as strip mines	38	36	26	81
Improving the yield of scarce materials recycling to conserve the supply	61	64	49	45
Culture and the Arts				
Direct financial support to art institutions and the performing arts	177	74	104	65
Development of indirect support as a business expense through gifts in kind, sponsoring artistic talent, and advertising	96	45	67	80
Participation on boards to give advice on legal, labor, and financial management problems	138	73	96	53
Helping secure government financial support for local or state arts councils and the National Endowment for the Arts	49	31	48	76
Medical Care				
Helping plan community health activities	111	93	52	45
Designing and operating low-cost medical-care programs	42	47	39	62
Designing and running new hospitals, clinics, and extended-care facilities	42	37	40	69
Improving the administration and effectiveness of medical care	89	82	52	43
Developing better systems for medical education, nurses' training	52	44	51	64
Developing and supporting a better national system of health care	40	50	45	51
Government				
Helping improve management performance at all levels of government	100	113	49	28

Table 6. (Continued)

Activity	Please check those activities which involve significant commitments of money and/or personnel time	Please check one of the following columns as appropriate		
		Highly important to our company	Moderately important to our company	Of minor importance to our company
Supporting adequate compensation and development programs for government executives and employees	31	37	55	55
Working for the modernization of the nation's governmental structure	51	65	52	44
Facilitating the reorganization of government to improve its responsiveness and performance	69	89	50	36
Advocating and supporting reforms in the election system and the legislative process	39	59	54	49
Designing programs to enhance the effectiveness of the civil services	22	32	41	64
Promoting reforms in the public welfare system, law enforcement, and other major governmental operations	62	68	58	31

formance. This is already evidenced by the many corporate social performance reports being published annually by banks, insurance companies, manufacturers, and service companies. It is also reflected increasingly in the institutional advertising of the larger corporations (although such advertising will eventually backfire unless the claims are substantiated with real and measurable improvements in social performance).

It cannot be denied, however, that since competitive social performance requires innovative leadership in needs identification, measurement, and design of implementation programs, there are some risks involved. It follows from the above discussion that *in*effective social programs are doubly noncompetitive because they incur both social and financial costs. Given such criticality concerning the effectiveness of social programs, it is all the more essential to

exert the available scientific performance measurement and evaluation techniques that are currently available. Thus the more competitive the business environment, the greater the rewards for scientific
management of social investments.

Effective Management of Corporate Social Programs

Social performance and social responsibility must be related to
financial performance and financial responsibility if the traditional
and continuing primary concerns of management and owners are to
be addressed. The attention and active agreement of operating executives to social responsibility efforts must be motivated by demonstrating the relevance of those to the achievement of financial performance objectives since the first responsibility of executives is still
the meeting of investment objectives for the owners. Since it is our
belief that the achievement of social objectives enhances achievement
of financial objectives as well over a long-range period of time, the
relevance of social performance to financial performance can only
be demonstrated by stretching the corporate time horizon beyond
next year's financial statement.

While many current social actions will not affect this year's bot-
tom line, all of them will affect it from five to ten years hence.
Boards of directors and chief executives are much more likely to
take the longer-range viewpoint required in order to see the relevance of social performance to financial performance than are their
line operations managers. This is understandable since boards and
chief executives have to plan further ahead than the operators of
line divisions. In order to stretch the time horizon of the line managers forward to make social performance relevant to financial performance, it may be advantageous to ask line operations to develop
five-year and ten-year financial and social performance plans as well
as annual plans. In this way the financial impact of social performance will tend to be more clearly demonstrated.

Leverage

For effectiveness in their social programs, corporations need to
identify *high leverage* areas of social action. They need to focus on
feasible propositions rather than waste their scarce resources in fu-
tile battles against the inevitable. This seems obvious, yet many large

corporations continue to pour human and financial resources into such low-return activities as urban redevelopment, "consulting" to minority firms, and contributions to high-overhead charities. At the same time they may miss opportunities to have major social impact by improving their own employment practices, the quality and honesty of their own production and product marketing, and other activities of high social impact over which they have much greater leverage.

"Leverage" may be defined as a high degree of control over an action, a high degree of productivity resulting from it, and a "multiplier" effect (the action achieves positive impact far beyond its initial application). High leverage areas of social action include those over which the company has a high degree of control (its own employment practices, environmental practices, production and marketing practices, and procurement practices), those which hold high promise of being socially productive (equal employment opportunity, upward mobility, employment security, environmental improvement, economic development, health, education and training, and all the things that augment human assets), and those activities that have a high degree of potential for replication (including innovations that have broad appeal and can be implemented widely).

From a line operating point of view, social actions of the highest leverage are likely to be those that can be implemented directly by line operations management. Furthermore, these are the actions most likely to be identified by line operating managers because they are closer than top management usually is to the needs of the employees, community, and markets in which they interact. To motivate the initiation of positive social actions by line managers, it is necessary to provide incentive rewards for such actions. These should be related to the real financial returns of the line operations' performance over an extended period of time.

Measures of Performance

To distinguish between high and low leverage areas of social action, and to determine whether progress is actually being made toward socially responsible objectives, it is necessary to *measure* social performance. Social performance measurement must be regarded as a decision-making tool for social investment. Unless the relative returns on social investment have been measured, there is no rational basis for allocating investment among competing social actions. Unfortunately, thus far various approaches to measuring social performance, such as the social audit, have been used as a management toy rather than a management tool.

It has been argued by Ray Bauer, Robert Ackerman, Neil Churchill, and others that social performance is difficult to measure. While it is true that social performance may be difficult to measure with extreme precision and in a manner with which everyone agrees, it is intrinsically no more difficult to measure than financial performance. Measures of financial performance, such as net return on investment, are notoriously manipulable by differences in the classification of component elements and differences in measurement practices and procedures. We are well aware of the differences in depreciation rates, discount rates, capitalization, estimates of market worth, and so on that can change a company's profit into a loss, or vice versa, despite the spurious exactitude of the dollars and cents of the financial statement.*

The same is true of social performance estimates and measurements, and the limitations of measurement must be understood if the audience is not to be misled by numbers. However, this is not an argument against measurement itself but only an argument against the misleading use of measurement and against unsophisticated interpretations of results.

To be useful and operable at the line management level, measures of social performance should be expressed in units and categories directly meaningful to the line operations level. For example, in the employment practices area such measures might include percentage of employees advanced by ethnic and sex category and shifts in the composition of the middle-management population. Impacts on the environment might be measured by a "public overhead" cost imposed on operations from environmental cleanup costs, not dissimilar to the overhead costs of physical facility maintenance to which line managers are accustomed.

Scientific Methods

Whatever the limitations of the measurement of social and financial performance, both should take maximum advantage of the

---

* For an amusing set of examples, see Charles Raw, Bruce Page, and Godfrey Hodgson, *Do You Sincerely Want to Be Rich?* (New York: Viking Press, 1969), Adam Smith [pseud.], *The Money Game* (New York: Random House, 1968), and Abraham J. Briloff, *Unaccountable Accounting* (New York: Harper & Row, 1972).

most effective and current methods of *social and economic science* and research findings. Just as professionally competent measurements of financial results use the latest accounting methods, microeconomics, and statistical sampling, professionally competent measures of social performance should also make use of relevant methods and findings from the social sciences, such as survey research, group psychology, and evaluations of educational and health programs impact. Unfortunately this is still rarely the case.

The modest number of businesses that have seriously attempted to measure their social performance have in most cases either limited themselves to the crudest, most incommensurable qualitative measures of performance, or they have attempted to "reinvent the wheel" in developing measurements of social performance without regard to what others have already done and published.

Effective application of social science methods and findings to the measurement of social performance is more difficult at the line operations level than at the corporate level because the intellectual staff resources available to the president are not likely to be immediately available to line operations as well. Except in those businesses that make extensive use of social science for market and opinion research or for detailed behavioral and econometric studies, operating division managers are unlikely to have staffs who are well trained in both the methods and the findings of contemporary social science.

This problem can be solved by brief training programs for managers to acquaint them with the basic tools of social research—research design, survey methods, statistical sampling, impact evaluation, and the like—and the major substantive findings of the over one billion dollars' worth of social research (primarily government-sponsored) concerning the relative effectiveness of different types of social programs carried out annually. (For example, findings that increased literacy does *not* increase the standard of living of migrant farm workers, that housing rehabilitation in ghetto areas costs more and produces less satisfactory results to the residents of the area than do comparable expenditures on housing allowances and health and education, and that effective equal employment opportunity programs require active outreach.) For larger businesses, it may be efficient to provide a small team of social scientists to move from division to division providing training and technical assistance in social measurements and their application to the measurement of social performance through social audits.

Development of Standards

A major issue in the multidivisional firm is *development of widely agreed-on standards*. Contrary to the opinion of some negative critics of social auditing, there is already almost unanimous agreement on the qualitative content of corporate performance. These generally agreed-on areas of social performance include employment, environment, product quality, working conditions and safety, and truthfulness in advertising (see Chapter 1). There are many quantitative measures of social performance for all these areas, which are well known to social scientists but not generally known to or accepted by business. Although there are currently no social performance procedures directly analogous to the "Generally Accepted Accounting Procedures," the application of "GAAP" to social performance measures that are already available in the social sciences can produce measurements for most areas of social concern that will meet standards of precision and confidence for both accounting and social science.

The principal problem, therefore, is one of education—training plus dissemination of what is already known about standard methods of social measurement and about standard ways of combining components in a meaningful business formula.

Standardization of measures of social performance is presently a more important problem between divisions within a company than between companies. If one division's performance in social responsibility areas is to be fairly compared with that of other divisions and with its own previous performance, common standards must apply, just as they do in comparisons of financial performance. Otherwise, inconsistent interdivisional standards will destroy incentives to good performance. Corporate management has both the information and the administrative authority to provide a standard set of measurements for its line operating divisions. To maximize the acceptance by line operating managers of social performance measurement, they should be involved as a group in formulating the measurements and then be held accountable for meeting the standards. This has already been done to some extent for many years in companies which have policies concerning fair employment practices, work standards, safety standards, and the like. Thus there is a good precedent of standard divisional performance measures to build on.

Effective Government Relations

Another major issue in implementing social responsibility at the operating levels of corporations is that of *the division of responsibility and authority between company managers and government officials.* This is a particularly salient problem where line operations of multinational or national firms dominate one or more aspects of a political unit, such as a town or region. It might be asked if it is business's responsibility to anticipate government action by absorbing social costs which have previously been "external" to the business, or merely to respond to such action.

It might be said facetiously that ITT had a strong sense of social responsibility in Chile, that United Fruit had a strong sense of social responsibility in Costa Rica in the early years of the century, and that the California farmers have a strong sense of social responsibility to migrant laborers. Obviously the way one defines social responsibility will be a matter of some controversy among the various publics. Mere involvement in social issues is not the same as *responsible* involvement. Some of the specific issues in "company towns" are: Who decides what social services should be available to the local population? Who pays for them? If the company denies responsibility for anyone but its own employees, despite the fact that it dominates a local community, it can be accused of callous irresponsibility. If it takes another tack and assumes responsibility for organizing and maintaining local social services, it may be accused of paternalism, controlling the lives of the individuals in its vicinity and generally engaging in sociopolitical behavior that is commonly thought to be more appropriate for government than for industry. Certainly this has been one of the criticisms of affirmative corporate social responsibility activities made by Milton Friedman and by Henry Manne of the University of Miami Law School.

There are various ways of dividing responsibility and authority between governments and companies in local situations where a company plays a dominant role. The company can define its own social responsibility very narrowly—limiting it to the company's own employees during their working hours only—or very broadly, covering all the individuals in the community whether employed by the company or not, and involving all major aspects of their lives. Besides its degree of community involvement, the company can also exercise various degrees of benevolence and self-restraint in refraining from economic exploitation. Note that I use the term "economic exploitation" rather than "economic utilization." The latter term describes a legitimate mobilization of local economic resources for the common benefit of the community and the corporation.

The characteristic life cycle of a large company as regards its degree of community involvement and of benevolence (or "enlightened self-interest" or "unselfishness") goes something like this: In the first phase, which might be called the "imperialist exploitation" phase (and is so called by many people in developing nations), the company limits itself to purely economic functions in its locality, administering them with ruthless self-interest.

The second phase, which might be termed "ambiguous paternalism," involves the corporation in providing community services beyond its own immediate economic activity, and we get such allegedly benign but actually often exploitive phenomena as the company store and the company housing area.

The third phase more often than not involves pressure from liberalizing factors and includes attempts by the corporation to impose sincerely benevolent but still paternalistic policies on line operations in the company towns. This is the phase in which schools, hospitals, day-care centers—even parks—are developed by corporations to improve the local communities in which they operate and are proudly displayed as evidence of the benevolent intent and superior capability of the company. Often this also fails. At this level of control, which is not responsive to local political counterforces, the company acts in a sense as a dictatorship—benevolent but nevertheless a dictatorship. Feeling hurt by increasingly violent displays of adverse feelings, the company management often tends at this stage to back off from its entire social services program and go back to phase one, the purely economic phase, though with somewhat more respect for the feelings of the local community.

Counting the Costs of Change

Another major issue is the sense of responsibility on the part of the social innovators regarding the *costs of change*—from boards and presidents to radical leaders. There are social costs to forcing social changes in an organization as well as social benefits. They include the generation of conservative reactions, the human costs of interpersonal conflicts, the time and morale costs of changes in policy, and the possible disruption of delicate working relationships.

The entire corporate social responsibility movement has never been too concerned with measuring the *costs* of change; it has been intent on motivating change by measuring the positive *benefits* of it. However, to mitigate some of the realistic anxieties of hard-nosed managers and convince them that their basic business operations will not be disrupted or damaged by social changes, comprehensive social analyses of actual and potential social policies in an organization must include the costs of the changes as well as the benefits. The costs of organizational change are usually greatly underrated by the innovators and greatly overrated by the defenders of the status quo. In order to make those two opposed viewpoints converge, analysis and estimation of both the benefits and the costs of change are needed. Social audits can help provide this.

This problem is particularly pertinent at the line operations level, where division managers may feel that their authority is being questioned when they are asked to initiate new socially responsible actions. If they are provided with checklists, social audit guides, and other measurement instruments for estimating the costs of change, they will be more secure about the cost-effective changes and better able to prevent changes that are excessively disruptive. Corporate incentive and reward structures should also include compensation for risks and costs incurred in the service of social responsibility as well as recognition for achievement.

6

Organizing the Audit: Costs and Time Required

THE cost to a company of setting up social accounts is generally comparable to that of setting up financial accounts. Correspondingly, the costs of auditing the social accounts is comparable to the costs of a financial audit.

Considering that a typical middle-size corporation has major social impacts on five constituencies—stockholders, employees, consumers, neighboring communities, and the general public—the first task is to determine the general priorities and areas of concern for each of these constituencies. This can be accomplished by economical sample surveys within a month or two; an archival search of already collected survey data can be done in a few weeks. The estimation of the market worth of the various social benefits and social costs generated by the company for its several constituencies can be determined in a month or two on the basis of local economic data related to behavioral changes resulting from corporate social actions.

Where no market prices can be found for social benefits or costs created by company actions, as for example the creation of a park used by local residents without an entry fee, shadow prices can be determined by analyzing the cost of achieving equivalent benefits. This shadow pricing analysis would probably take a few weeks, covering a fairly substantial number of individual line items.

An interdisciplinary team—social scientists, survey researchers, data specialists, economists, and accountants—can accomplish a social audit in a period of three or four months for a particular major location or operation. The work is organized as follows.

Working directly under the team leader, there is a management adviser (both of these assigned by the company) and an outside social audit expert. There are three subordinate technical teams: an audit design team, a data collection team, and a data analysis team. The design task (Figure 8) takes one to two months. Data gathering takes two to three months. Analysis and evaluation take about two months. Reporting takes about a month. In terms of staff time needed to cover a medium-size to large-size company, the design effort requires about twelve person months. The data gathering would take about eighteen person months, analysis and evaluation about twelve person months, and reporting about three person months, for a total of roughly forty-five person months.

Figure 8. Schedule and budget for large-company social audit.

Tasks	Months			
	1	2	3	4
Design	12 person months			
Data gathering		18 person months		
Analysis and evaluation			12 person months	
Reports				3 person months
Person months per month (Total: 45)	6	15	15	9

Figure 9. Organization of a social audit.

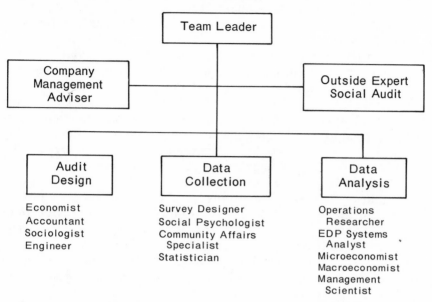

In the United States in 1977 that much professional effort costs between $200,000 and $300,000, including direct costs and the usual 100 percent or more of overhead costs. (Salaries are generally a quarter to a third of the total costs.)

The audit design team for a fairly large company (Figure 9) should include an accountant, an economist, a sociologist, and (in a technologically intensive industry) an engineer. The data collection group should have a statistician, a survey designer, a social psychologist, and a community affairs specialist. The data analysis group should have an operations researcher, an electronic data processing systems analyst, a microeconomist and a macroeconomist, and a management scientist.

If a large corporation has many diverse locations and operations, additional parallel social auditing teams might have to be deployed. Thus, for example, a concentrated industry producing a limited number of products might be socially audited in three or four months by an interdisciplinary team of about five professionals devoting a total of one and a half to two person years of effort. The cost might be $75,000 to $125,000 for both establishing the social ac-

counts and auditing them the first time. Perhaps 20 percent of this
might be spent each subsequent year for periodic auditing of the
social accounts. A large corporation having about ten divisions in
different locations might require something like five times the cost—
although no more elapsed time. The reason the cost would be only
five times as much instead of ten is that company functions and
socially relevant activities would no doubt be duplicated at different
locations, so that not all the work would have to be repeated for each
location. The reason there would not be a significant increase in
elapsed time for the larger company is that the social audits of different locations can be accomplished simultaneously, although ideally
they would be staggered slightly to maximize learning.

Elapsed time for establishing social accounts might increase in
the event of "behavioral problems" on the part of company middle
management. Specific changes of attitude toward the social audit
and toward the company's social responsibilities can of course occur
during the course of the activity. The very act of attempting to
measure social performance obviously focuses the attention of middle and upper management on the functions of individual managers
and on units of social performance. This will probably result in some
changes in these areas and also some bureaucratically defensive behavior. Some of the defensive behavior may take the form of un-
cooperative attitudes about supplying data, rapid attempts to improve performance, or explaining decisions of various types and
their social impacts as perceived at the management level. Such behavioral and attitudinal problems are typical in the implementation
of any new management information system; while helping some
managers to achieve their objectives more efficiently, any new system
is often perceived by other managers as threatening some of their
objectives or their hidden agenda. This problem is no different in
the implementing of social accounting than it is in implementing any
form of performance measurement in any organization. The new
measure is always regarded by some individuals as a little threatening and by others as an exciting opportunity to demonstrate better
performance.

Probably the most effective way of dealing with the attitudinal
and behavioral problems on the part of middle management is to
include all levels of management in the initial process of deciding
whether and how to establish the social accounts. Companywide participation in the decision to measure social performance, and in the

definition of objectives and gains to be achieved, should facilitate the process greatly. It is essential that not only top management, but middle and lower levels of management as well, be involved in the decisions concerning the selection of line items to be measured in the social audit and the procedures for collecting and evaluating data.

The social audit should not become an avenue to attack any particular function of management, and fears that this might happen should be anticipated and allayed by making it clear what the social audit is: a management information system designed to improve the efficiency of investment decisions at all levels. It should not be used to criticize or constrain any particular level or function of management.

The first effort should concentrate on using the social audit as a decision-making aid to management. If the results are satisfactory it may later be published in both the public interest and the corporate interest.

The team leader should be selected from inside the company and he should have a high status. Ideally he should be an officer. Most managements regard a social audit as a little threatening, so it is important that the team leader be highly respected inside the company and be considered very loyal. He should try to do his honest best for the company, and not look for ways to discredit it. This is particularly important, so that if the social audit shows negative results they will be believed by management to be objective, and not merely a political attempt to discredit the company.

The chief financial officer or a senior vice president can be the social audit team leader; in companies of medium to large size, that is generally the ideal choice. It is *not* advisable to select the head of public relations as team leader. If you buy public relations you will get public relations. Social accounting and auditing are not public relations.

To compare the results of your audit with those of other companies, the format of your study can be prepared in suitable form so that it can be sent to your respected competitors in the industry with an explanation of what you are doing and a promise that you will send them your results if they will send you theirs for comparison, in privacy. If this is done, industry standards can be established in a way that will be to everybody's benefit and nobody will be hurt. In due course social audits can also be promoted through trade or industry asociations and then be disseminated by them. In the United States, competitors often circulate questionnaires asking what companies in their field are doing and then send the results to all the participants in the survey.

Another approach is to publish your own social audit and to invite other companies in the industry to follow suit. The social audits of most companies will show a net social equity—and one can assume that the companies that publish the results of their audits contribute more to the public than competitors who do not communicate their social performance.

7

The Government as a Social Auditor

GOVERNMENT auditors have a long and honorable history of reviewing the financial and other management performance of government contractors to ensure compliance with government regulations and good practice. In the past few years, government review has begun to include aspects of the social performance of government contractors as well as their financial and technical performance in equal employment opportunity for minorities and women, environmental impact, product safety, employee health and safety, truthfulness of reporting, and overall technical quality and management efficiency.

The Government as a Monitor

The role of the federal auditor can also be expanded to provide formative evaluation—a kind of "technical assistance" to the project evaluated to help it perform better. This can be done in ways which do not contaminate the objectivity of the audit process itself. The best example is the current practice of public accountants to provide the firms that they audit with what is commonly known as a "management letter." After they have completed their objective audit, they often also supply advice and technical assistance on what it would be well to change so that next year's audit may reveal better results.

It has been the general obligation of government auditors to provide warning to the government of serious management problems on the part of major government contractors, even if such contractors operate within the formal regulations; this seems prudent audit practice. When the social performance of a government contractor is so poor that there is a risk the company will not continue to perform with adequate technical quality within budget and schedule constraints, it would also seem within the area of responsibility of government auditors to give appropriate warnings. On the other hand, when a government contractor performs his or her social responsibilities unusually well, this is worth being noted by government auditors, and possibly called to the attention of other contractors by formal or informal means. The informal means include the "management letter" assistance just mentioned.

What are the aspects of corporate social performance that might be audited by government? Besides meeting such statutory or regulatory requirements as those of the Equal Employment Opportunity Commission or the Environmental Protection Agency, it is my feeling that all actions of a government contractor that have significant social impact on any one of the five major constituencies of the corporation—the employees, the customers, the stockholders, the neighboring communities, and the general public—should be reviewed by the government, and when the impact is materially negative, the actions should be corrected by the government. By "corrected" I do not mean to imply that the government should exercise direct management control of any government contractor. That's not desirable or necessary. It is quite adequate to provide recommendations and technical assistance where needed and requested, possibly with some long-term incentives and enforcement.

For the government to do otherwise than to provide this correction is to risk the failure of the contractor on a major long-term contract as a result of possible work stoppages, employee protests, significantly reduced productivity as a result of loss of employee morale, organizational conflict, or unusual legal or other expenses incurred as a result of damage actions by individual groups or government agencies. When AT&T has to pay $15 million of back pay to women workers that are discriminated against, and Detroit Edison has to settle for $4 or $5 million damages for racial discrimination, and when some chemical companies are forced to shut down (as in the recent shutting down of a steel mill on one of the Great Lakes because of environmental pollution), this incurs major costs to the stockholders and to the clients of those companies—costs which are usually passed on to the consumer in some form. This is very much of concern to any auditor acting to protect the consumers of a company's products or services—in this case a government auditor protecting the government itself as a consumer.

How can government auditors measure corporate social performance to a degree sufficiently accurate to give warning of possible material changes in contract performance? This problem has been greatly neglected until the last few years, and it is greatly neglected because there is an easy excuse available both for corporations and for the people who measure the performance of corporations: the assertion "Well, these things are insubstantial; social values are a matter of individual preference and opinion; they can't be measured; it's all very mushy, so let's keep out of it." The fact is that "these things" can be and indeed are measured—quantitatively, mathematically—with as much precision as cash flows are measured. We measure opinions, we measure preferences, we measure the market worth of different services and commodities just as accurately as we establish the market worth of an inventory, not to the last penny, of course, but with sufficient accuracy on which to base meaningful judgments and decisions. If an audit reveals that the net social income or the net social equity of a corporation is declining rapidly, or is already negative and not improving fast, it is a clear indication of trouble for the overall organizational health and longer-term financial and productive viability of the organization as well.

Consider a few examples. Imagine a large government contractor producing machinery under a multiyear contract, with the machinery including a high component of advanced technology. The contractor employs many skilled technicians and professionals. Their productivity is dependent upon good morale, cooperation among employees, and a "can do" attitude toward solving the technical problems continually arising in fulfilling the contract. Now imagine that this contractor begins to develop morale problems with its employees as a result of either failing to take some widely demanded action involving employee benefits, or behaving in an offensively discriminatory way toward some large class of employees. Internal conflict resulting in reduced morale, personnel turnover, and losses in productivity could seriously threaten the contractor's ability to meet its obligations to the government. Since an audit can measure the costs of various social actions by the corporation, it can provide a warning to government auditors that corrective actions are required.

Human Resources Development

Another quite different and even more complex new area for government auditing of government contractors is the human resources development area. Here government auditors have traditionally played a generally defensive role, attempting to hold down the contractor's overhead costs by questioning proposals for benefits to company staff. In some cases this questioning has been sensible and has led to economies in production. In other cases, it has led to false economies, with expensive long-term costs because of the depletion of human capital. Government tax regulations currently provide tax depletion allowances for certain mineral resources such as oil, and investment tax credit for such material goods as machinery, yet government policy has not yet caught up to the realization that our most important assets in most contracting organizations are the human assets and that these too can be depleted and need reinvestment to avoid further depletion. The human resources of an organization—the network of communications, relationships, mutual trust and understanding, the skills and abilities of the people involved— are a major organizational asset that takes years of time and investment to build up. This fact is almost totally unrecognized in current forms of accounting, with the exception of the human resource accounting used in the social audit.

Government auditors probably should use the new social accounting tools to make their own trade-offs between the financial savings achieved by reductions in staff training, morale building efforts, and support of mental and physical health and the longer-term benefits to both contractor and government from significant overhead investment in improved human capital in the organization. Gary Becker and others have shown that the return on investment of higher education is higher than that of most profitable large

businesses. (Becker estimates it at between 13 and 15 percent.*)
Since the pressure of annual reports to stockholders forces on corporate managements a relatively short-range point of view, it is possible that only the government's expression of the public's long-term
interest will motivate the long-term investment needed for the development of human resources. It is long-term because the payoff takes
a few years to bear fruit but, when it does, it pays for itself more
handsomely than any other investment.

The trade-offs between short-term measures and long-term investments in human resources can be made only through some form
of social accounting, with some quantification. If present-value analysis is used, there have to be values to discount. The investment and
returns must all be expressed in commensurate present dollars in
order to use the same units. Otherwise, one is always comparing
today's program costs with a benefit which is realized in the distant
future. From a purely short-term point of view, this always means a
loss on the income statement and a disincentive to investment.

Government auditors may find excellent career opportunities in
broadening their horizons to cover the larger social accountability of
contracting organizations. In a few months of study they can master
the basics of social performance measurements, social accounting,
and social auditing, learning the basic methods of shadow pricing
from economics, demand surveys from sociology and political
science, and present-value expressions of human and other resources from financial analysis methods.

The fundamental mission of government contract auditing is to
ensure that the government gets good value for its public money.
"Good value" should include corporate responsiveness to national
social policies and the social concerns of the public.

Encouragement to Corporate Growth

A major issue in public policy for both private enterprise and
government regulatory agencies is the optimal distribution, rate, and
type of corporate growth. Government cannot effectively formulate
a policy in this area without knowing the social costs and benefits of
alternative rates, types, and distributions of growth in different in-

*Human Capital (New York: National Bureau of Economic Research, distributed
by Columbia University Press, 1964), p. 120.

dustries. Historically, the issue that has received the greatest attention is that of monopoly regulation, or the growth of one competitor to a point of dominance over the others in a particular industry. More recently, the issue of growth has been put in terms of a rather simplistic opposition to conservation of the environment, on the assumption that environmental conservation and growth have to be traded off against each other. Still largely neglected, and addressed only in individual organizations, is the issue of the social costs of growth * which are attributable to reduced interpersonal communication and impersonality of the work situation, versus the economic and social benefits of growth through economies of scale, as well as the increase in employment security which results for the large-scale business because it is better able to survive fluctuations in the market.

Measurements are needed both by government planners and officials and by individual scholars and social scientists that will enable them to identify the most socially productive patterns of corporate growth. On a microeconomic level, we need to estimate the social costs to employees, surrounding communities, and stockholders which result from large fluctuations in employment levels as a result of rapid growth (and its frequent concomitant, rapid temporary decline). On a slightly larger microeconomic level, the impact of the growth of one dominant competitor on the overall social efficiency of an entire industry needs to be estimated on a more comprehensive basis than that provided by classical economics. Finally, on the macroeconomic scale involving national and international economic activity, the relative growth of different types of industry and the distribution of growth rates nationally and internationally both have important social cost/benefit implications, affecting such matters as unemployment rates, inflation, availability of goods and services, and efficiency in using world resources to minimize the dangers of starvation or economic instability.

The optimum trade-off in social productivity between production itself and the reducing of the negative side effects of production, such as pollution, raises the important question of how to regulate industry to produce the optimum kinds and degrees of output. If the question is what level of production we should aim for to balance the economic benefits of production against the social cost of its

* See, for example, the discussions in E. F. Schumacher, *Small Is Beautiful* (New York: Harper & Row, 1973).

polluting side effects for the maximum social benefit—and if this can be calculated—the question remains as to how to make sure that industry will choose to concentrate on output of the correct types and levels. Such ends can be achieved either voluntarily or by government regulation or by some sort of market mechanism involving taxes or prices. Government needs to determine which mechanisms are most effective in different types of industry and for different types of social issues.

Protecting the Public Equity in Private Enterprise

If government is to accomplish its role of securing the maximum of social welfare for all the people, it must recognize that its powers are not total, particularly in a democracy, and that much of the social welfare of the population of the country is determined more by the actions of industry and business than by the actions of government. Certainly government can and should do what is necessary to aid those elements of the population not directly engaged in business or industry, but it should also ensure that the employees of business and industry are well served socially.

Employment is probably the single largest source of social benefits to most of the people in the society. Since the exact form and nature of employment is more directly under the control of business enterprises than of government (despite the many government regulations on such activity), the actions of business toward its employees will probably have the major impact on their social welfare.

Government has accepted the responsibility for moderating the antisocial excesses of business and industry for many years. From the Clayton Antitrust Act of 1890 through the child labor laws and fair employment practices legislation to current regulations providing for equal employment opportunity, occupational health and safety, environmental protection, and health, accident, and old age security, government has traditionally assumed major responsibilities in requiring business enterprises to exercise social responsibilities toward employees, consumers, investors, and residents of adjacent environments. The issue now is what further directions the federal, state, and local governments will follow in providing not only controls but positive incentives to business for exercising their social responsibilities more effectively.

Since the Securities and Exchange Commission has for many years required public corporations annually to disclose information about their financial status, economic productivity, and overall financial viability for the sake of the financial safety of the investing public, it would seem only reasonable to provide similar information to the public concerning other investments that it makes in private corporations. The opportunity to use various uncosted environmental resources is not an intrinsic right but a privilege granted to corporations by the public. This grant of the use of unpriced public goods such as air and water, and of labor (in the sense of opportunity costs to other employers of labor), is actually an investment by the public in the business enterprise. The public deserves to have information concerning the productivity of that investment relative to other investments and the uses to which the investment is put, just as a stockholder (I believe) deserves to have financial information about the uses to which his or her investment is put and the productivity of those uses. Thus the public investment in private corporations, in the form of various national resources, needs to be accounted for on an annual basis to determine whether a particular reporting company is really making the best use, or at least a socially adequate use, of those resources from the public investor's point of view.

P. Walker offers five major roles for government in the context of social responsibility.* These are: the assessment of national opportunity in the context of the world as a whole; laws requiring that commercial activities be "fair, open, and just," avoiding practices which give unfair advantage to a few to the detriment of the many, and assuring that decisions will be made on the basis of adequate and open information; assuming responsibility for the quality of life itself; efforts to reduce regional and international imbalances and inequities; and encouragement of the fullest application of the talents and abilities of each individual, including interpersonal equity, self-realization, and upward mobility for all employees. To carry out these and other responsibilities, government needs to provide incentives as well as controls for industry to work toward these objectives. For example, in the area of individual self-realization and work satisfaction through such strategies as participative management and job enlargement, government needs to provide encouragement, assistance, and incentives to industry to achieve these objectives. One

* *Productivity and Amenity—Achieving Social Balance,* The Stockton Lectures (New York: Crane, Russak, 1973).

means of doing this is to require industry to report regularly on the achievements and the costs as well as the benefits of its actions toward any of its constituencies having social implications—that is to say, all those actions that it takes that affect people.

As the late Eli Goldston stated in a 1971 lecture at the London Business School,* it is important to try to quantify social concern because it tends to focus choices, requires thinking in practical terms, and provides yardsticks for estimating progress toward social goals, thus providing stimuli for further efforts. Government can do much to provide incentives to industry to quantify its social performance if it requires such quantification as part of tax or SEC reporting. Government can also provide positive incentives for unusually substantial net social contributions (or negative sanctions for non-reporting) in the form of possible tax or cash flow savings.

Another argument for government's requiring quantification of corporate social performance is that it is impossible for government officials to make rational trade-offs among public policy choices without examples of the impact of subchoices about which corporations probably have the most amount of information. For example, it would seem obvious that the federal government could make better decisions about unemployment insurance if it had company data about the incidence, frequency, causes, and estimated social impacts of employee turnover and layoffs. As another example, environmental protection legislation and regulatory actions could be much more efficiently formulated if industry were required to provide government with more detailed environmental impact data on its operations. This policy is in fact already being pursued actively in the United States by the Environmental Protection Agency.

Social Audits at the National Level

Broadly speaking, there are two kinds of measurements of social benefits and costs: aggregate measurements to estimate overall national social performance and more detailed measurements applied within individual units such as communities or corporations or particular sectors of the economy.

The national measures have recently been published by the U.S.

* Published as *The Quantification of Concern* (New York: Columbia University Press, 1972).

Office of Management and Budget,* covering the national performance in health, public safety, education, employment, income, housing, leisure and recreation, and population. These annual indicators of national social performance could be used by both governments and voters at general elections to determine the overall performance of a particular administration. They could also be used to compare American performance with that of other nations, identifying areas of particular social weakness where we have failed to exploit our opportunities as other nations have done; or areas in which we are more socially advanced, in which case we might have reason to export our ideas to other nations. Our national social cost/benefit measures give us information which can be used in national-level planning to improve our overall social welfare and in stimulating political pressure to improve our overall social policy through the regular political machinery.

Measurements of the more detailed type, applied in local communities, particular sectors of the economy, or corporations are most useful in deciding policies for the socioeconomic unit concerned or for a group of such units, including the social benefits and costs to all the relevant constituencies.

One of the major theoretical issues of social policy and welfare economics is the correspondence between the national level of social performance measurement and the local institutional or sectorial level. In the absence of a set of socioeconomic categories by means of which all the local social performances can be aggregated into a national performance level, there is no likely correspondence between the two scales of measurement. Nevertheless, the two need not conflict, and as theory and data develop to cover the gaps between local and national social policy and economic analysis, the two should gradually be woven together in a consistent web of logical and quantitative relationships.

Measurements of the performance of local institutions are analogous to those of the financial performance of companies. They provide a means to compare the organization's performance over periods of time and to evaluate techniques for optimizing the internal allocation of resources.

On the national scale, we already measure our national income accounts and gross national product (GNP). Important corrections

---

* *Social Indicators for 1973* (Washington: U.S. Printing Office, 1973).

might be made in these accounts, including a measure of national socioeconomic welfare as proposed by Eli Goldston: "a measurement of economic welfare" (MEW).* Here the idea is to correct the figures for GNP or total economic performance by deducting "regrettables"—items that the public would prefer to do without if it knew how—such as expenditures for pollution, police, and weapons. Further corrections might involve the addition of such unpriced items as leisure time, unmonetized services contributed by housewives and others, and productive hobby activities. The total is Goldston's "MEW."

The relationship between the microeconomics of the company and the local community and the macroeconomics of the nation with respect to social performance measurement will probably have to await the development of a mezzo-economics relating individual economic units such as firms and communities to economic regions and sectors and then in turn relating these to the overall national economy.

Social Audits at the Community Level

On the level of local government, corporate social accounts include many line items directly affecting community improvement. The direct social benefits and costs to the community, measured in money terms, include taxes paid and tax-supported public services consumed, environmental improvements (such as beautification) and degradations (such as pollution), the tax worth of jobs created and tax-base losses when jobs are eliminated, and social services (such as child care provided or absorbed). Indirect social benefits and costs to the community created by the corporation include the social benefits and costs to employees (such as career advancement benefits and costs in inequality of opportunity) and social benefits and costs to consumers (such as the "consumer surplus" benefit from supplying economical, safe, and useful products, and the cost of physical, environmental, and human resources consumed).

The corporate social audit can thus measure the absolute and relative amount of social contribution of a corporation to a community, in equivalent dollar terms. This suggests opportunities for city

* *Op. cit.*

governments and community action groups (as well as corporation managements) that have not been previously available.

City governments, using social audits of corporations to assay their social contributions to the community (or their withdrawals), can identify the most desirable corporations to suit their aims in urban development. They can then attract the desired corporations with tax and other incentives, and encourage the social improvement of undesirable corporations (or hasten their departure) by added taxes and user charges. They can also influence corporate operating policy and investment decisions in directions responsive to urban development needs by offering tax and municipal services incentives or by threatening additional taxes and fees, in proportion to the corporation's responsiveness to urban needs.

Community groups, particularly minority groups suffering from inequality in employment opportunities, can use social audits to measure the social costs to them of different types and degrees of discrimination and the social benefits of various corporate affirmative action programs. Using such data, they can more effectively bring legal and consumer pressures to bear on socially backward corporations, thereby also indirectly rewarding the socially more effective corporations with the competitive advantage of freedom from the costs of such legal and consumer pressures.

Corporate managements sometimes use social audits to anticipate the social needs of their neighboring communities and to determine the best balance of social investments with financial ones. All corporate financial decisions have social consequences and all corporate decisions have financial consequences. Using social accounting systems, managers can make the best trade-offs among essential social and financial requirements.

Community leaders cannot know what to reasonably ask of corporations, and corporate managements cannot know what actions to take without some measurement of the social impacts on the community on the part of its major private and public organizations.

"External Audits" by Public Interest Groups

Social audits may be executed internally with the cooperation of the management of the organization being audited, or externally and involuntarily. There have been some examples of each, offering some insights into their relative advantages and disadvantages.

The major examples of external audits are those conducted by Ralph Nader and his associates, the publication *Business and Society Review/Transition,* and the Council on Economic Priorities, in the United States, and the journal *Social Audit* in England. *Social Audit,* partially subsidized by the Joseph Rowntree Social Service Trusts, Ltd., has as one of its purposes the compilation of "external" social audits of major industries; it has completed social audits on Tube Investments, Ltd., a diversified manufacturing company, and the Alkali Inspectorate, as well as the Lowson Group of Companies.

These external audits, usually involuntary on the part of the audited, almost invariably concentrate on social liabilities and costs, since it is assumed (incorrectly, I believe) that organizations already have publicized all the information that is favorable. Thus there tends to be a somewhat negative bias in external audits to date, perhaps motivated in part by the unwillingness of the audited organization to share its social performance information openly. Conversely, internal, voluntary audits tend to be optimistic. The speed, efficiency, comprehensiveness, and reliability of internal audits should exceed that of external ones, since the information for them is more accessible internally than to outsiders. However, the reliability of internal audits can also be questioned on the basis of self-serving bias.

Thus the most comprehensive and precise social audit requires both internal and external auditing—internal for comprehensiveness and external for reduction of bias. Much the same double approach has been found effective in financial auditing and cost-effectiveness evaluations. It is probably in a company's interest to do its own social audit rather than vacate the field to its adversaries. In any case this will help to keep outside critics honest while providing early information to management for corrective actions.

8

Case Histories

THE following case histories present examples of social audits in various states of development and implementation. None are ideal, but they demonstrate the diversity and feasibility of the concept.*

R. G. Barry Corporation

The R. G. Barry Corporation of Columbus, Ohio, was 25 years old in 1971. At that time it had revenues of over $34 million and after-tax income of over $0.25 million. Its major business is the manufacture and marketing of leisure-time footwear for men, women, and children. In 1969, it instituted for the first time a full year of human resource accounting.

In the R. G. Barry Corporation's "total concept," human resource accounting is used as part of the information system to provide "data on the investments and write-offs related to the internal human resources of the business and changes that occur in these resources over time." According to the company, "We continue to feel that human resource accounting is an important information element in the achievement of our long-term objectives."

The R. G. Barry concept involves a human resources balance

* I am indebted to my colleague Peter Merrill for several of the critical observations in these case histories.

sheet of human assets and human liabilities as well as a human resources statement of income, both of which are independent of the financial statements and not directly related to them. In fact, there is a very specific warning printed on the page containing the human resources balance sheet and income statement stating that "the information presented on this page is provided only to illustrate the informational value of human resource accounting for more effective internal management of the business. The figures included regarding investments and amortization of human resources are unaudited and you are cautioned for the purposes of evaluating the performance of this company to refer to the conventional certified accounting data further on in this report." The public auditors, Peat Marwick, Mitchell and Company, in their opinion of the financial accounts, say nothing about the human resources accounting.

In the R. G. Barry Corporation total concept, the balance sheet combines the current financial assets with net investments in human resources to yield a total net investment. An explicit comparison is made of conventional accounting and conventional-plus-human-resource accounting. The difference between the two is the net investment of human resources, which is defined as "the total outlays for human resources for recruiting, acquisition, familiarization, training, and development minus write-offs and amortization."

The difference between the conventional liabilities and stockholders' equity on the conventional balance sheet and the combination of conventional and human resource accounting in the "total concept" balance sheet is that in the human resource accounting version the deferred federal income tax is based upon full tax deductions for human resource costs counted as a liability, while they are not so listed in the conventional accounting. The retained earnings of human resources are also counted as a form of equity, while they are not so counted in the conventional accounting.

In the comparison of the conventional and the "total concept" accounting on the income statement of the R. G. Barry Corporation, all is the same except for the addition of "net increase in human resource investment" in the total concept, increasing overall net income by that amount.

The applications suggested for human resource accounting by the corporation in its 1971 annual report include "a monetary employment replacement turnover index" to "reflect the nature and character of turnover by comparing investment write-offs incurred by people leaving and the investment required to replace these people."

Another application that the company suggests which may be significant is the comparing of alternative investment opportunities because the decisions might change when return on investment is determined on an investment base that includes human resources as well as physical and financial resources. Other than these statements, the actual application of R. G. Barry Corporation human resource accounting to its management decision making is not stated, and we have not yet obtained any further information on how this has been applied to management decision making.

A major limitation of the R. G. Barry approach is that its own version of the "social audit" is limited entirely to human resource accounting and gives no quantitative information on the impact of the corporation on its employees, consumers, and communities concerning the net impact of social benefits and social costs generated. On the other hand, the R. G. Barry Corporation is to be commended in making an advance in dealing explicitly with the creation of a social asset (its human resource investment) and in integrating this social investment with its financial investment. It is the first company that has accomplished both of these advances and published them in its annual report.

Bank of America

The Bank of America publishes a report called "The Community and the Bank" dealing with its social policy and activities on an annual basis. The contents include a description of its public policy, its social policy committees and social policy department, and the cost/benefit analyses used for evaluation; and also sections on consumer issues, urban programs, agricultural area activities, environmental concerns, employee issues, employee volunteer programs, education, and contributions.

The report is quite detailed in providing cost input data to the various social responsibility programs and in providing quantitative information on the degree to which various goals (such as equal employment opportunity) have been achieved, in absolute numbers and in percentage terms.

However, the evaluation of the *effectiveness* or the actual benefits of these programs seems completely innocent of any social impact research measures. Basically, benefits are analyzed in terms of the number of people benefited and the inputs by the bank to give them benefits in terms of costs or of nonmonetized efforts. There is no attempt to evaluate the impacts or outputs of the bank's social responsibility activities, so there is no way of determining whether the bank got its money's worth in terms of social productivity per dollar invested. Furthermore, since many of these social responsibility activities are measured in terms of either the percentage level or the absolute level of some goal achievement, there is no commensurability among rates of achievement of different goals, and the bank really has no basis for allocating resources efficiently among its different social policy activities, except the basis of personal judgment. This does not seem a very businesslike and scientific optimization of the "social portfolio."

Steag A.G. (Germany)

The first known example of a German application of the corporate social audit is described below. The information is from a translation of an article in *Manager Magazin* (Germany) for November 1973: "To Build on Figures Rather than Dialectics," by Karl-heinz Bund.

The article claims that Steag A.G. is the first German firm to present a social audit. Dr. Bund, then president of the firm—an Essen energy producer—and now head of the Ruhrkohle A.G., describes the Steag approach, which was patterned on U.S. examples, evaluating entrepreneurial performance on the basis of social benefits.

Steag A.G. first published a social audit in 1971–72, in the form of a cost-effectiveness analysis. Costs were described verbally and expressed in deutsche marks. Benefits were described mainly in verbal form. The cost-effectiveness format was selected to illustrate concretely an analysis of relationships to the environment.

The social groups for which the company presented a cost-effectiveness analysis included employees; the community (those affected by pollution and by the product, various consumer groups, the science community, education, mass media, labor unions, political parties, and churches); the government and tax agencies (federal, state, and local); consumers and suppliers; and also that part of the community that provides the capital: lenders (particularly savers) and stockholders. Social groups were seen as confronting the firm with various demands.

The social audit was broken down into an internal and an external portion. Company activities were included regardless of whether they were intended to increase profits, or were undertaken to comply with legal requirements.

The company recognized that cost data are not always easily available and that benefits to society are hard to quantify. Descriptions were mainly in verbal form. The audit was regarded as a progressive step because:

Social efforts of the firm were identified.
Its social efforts were analyzed in context with profits and their uses.
Comparisons were made of the firm's efforts over time; the efforts were also compared with those of other firms.
Items identified could be monitored on a continuing basis.
Weaknesses in social performance were identified.

The author stated that the form and content of social audits, and whether they can be published, depend on the business and its motives.

Some of the "side benefits" of the audit were an assessment of the performance of public administration in comparison with the performance of business administration, and an evaluation of inflationary impacts on employees and on capital suppliers.

Kansai Electric Power Company (Japan)

In the fall of 1973, I was asked to undertake a five-day educational workshop on social audits for Kansai Electric Power Company in Osaka, Japan, and to conduct a preliminary design for a social audit for the company with the senior executives. (See Appendix D.)

Some of the major social action issues facing the power company at that time were the problems of locating and obtaining public and government approval for additional nuclear-fueled electric power plants, and determining appropriate electric power rates that would satisfy both the internal financial constraints of the company and government and consumer requirements to limit inflation.

A third and somewhat less pressing issue was the question of placing power transmission cables underground as an aesthetic benefit to the communities involved, and the problem of determining whether this social benefit was worth the cost.

In all these management issues concerning socially significant questions, the company was seeking a quantitative planning and decision-making technique for improving the rationality and defensibility of management decisions with respect to these socially significant actions. In the course of the five-day workshop the social audit approach was explained and demonstrated in the course of an actual preliminary design of the company's own system of social accounts and social audits.

The major problem of social impact measurement for the company was the question of how to estimate the social worth of additional electric power since the creation of additional electric power incurred some very definite social costs—principally to the environments of the communities in which additional nuclear power plants would be installed. Table 7 shows the content of the workshop, where five methods for estimating the social worth of additional electric power—along with the advantages and disadvantages of each—were discussed.

Eastern Gas and Fuel Associates

In an insert to its 1972 annual report, Eastern Gas and Fuel Associates' late president, Eli Goldston, introduced an example of social accounting for "self-auditing" purposes. The report, titled *Toward Social Accounting,* presents statistical information on the company's social performance in industrial safety (accident rate reduction), minority employment (increase), charitable giving (increase in contributions and change in distribution), employee benefits (pension impovement).

A particularly useful innovation included is a questionnaire (Figure 10) soliciting stockholder comments and recommendations. The questions contain specific alternatives for stockholder consideration in the area of minority hiring and charitable contributions.

Table 7. Five methods of estimating the social worth of more electric power.

Method	Advantages	Disadvantages
Accounting approach: Electric power's social worth = what is paid for it, or *revenues*	Good clear data available Simple	Fails to internalize the external social costs of added power production Understates value in use
	Easy but weak	
Welfare economics approach: Electric power's social worth = *consumer surplus* produced, *net of external costs and benefits*	Relates well to net consumer benefits	Difficulty of obtaining demand functions data Possible inelasticities and discontinuity in monopoly situation defeating theoretical basis
	Difficult but strong	
Development economics approach: Electric power's social worth = *GNP growth contribution*	Relates well to available input-output data Rationale for relating plant location to regional development	Assumes all of GNP growth is socially beneficial GNP change assumes average market values but change in power should change marginal value Neglects domestic consumption in input/output
	Moderately easy but a little weak	
Environmental economics approach: Electric power's social worth = *net social internalized externalities* (aggregation of total social benefits less total social costs)	Theoretical consistency and simplicity	Data problems of aggregation
	Difficult and strong	
Socioeconomic approach: Electric power's social worth = *social worth of only the socially useful additional applications* of electric power	Clarity of idea to laymen	Data problems of aggregation Value controversy among different consumers over what constitutes "useful" applications of power
	Difficult and weak	

Figure 10. Questionnaire soliciting stockholder comments and recommendations.

1. Should this sort of social accounting report be:
   □ enlarged
   □ continued in about same manner
   □ condensed
   □ omitted

2. Should such reports cover:
   □ Industrial Safety
   □ Minority Employment
   □ Charitable Giving
   □ Pensions
   □ Environment
   □ Female Employment
   □ Consumer Rights
   □ Other (please list)

3. How does our record on industrial accidents seem to you?
   □ Good, taking problems into account
   □ Fair
   □ Mediocre
   □ Poor

4. Should the company continue to move ahead of legal enforcement pressures in the following areas:
   Employment and promotion of minorities
   □ Yes   □ Moderately   □ No

   Preferential hiring of minorities
   □ Yes   □ Moderately   □ No

   Special counseling, training for minorities
   □ Yes   □ Moderately   □ No

   Environment?

5. In charitable contributions, should the company give:
   □ Present level of about 1% as is common practice
   □ Up to permitted tax-deductible level of 5% of taxable income
   □ Above 5% even though not deductible
   □ Nothing, letting individuals choose their own charities

6. Should company charitable contributions be:
   Limited to programs likely to serve our own employees and families
   □ Yes   □ No

   Limited to social welfare programs such as hospitals or United Funds
   □ Yes   □ No

   Include urban or minority programs
   □ Yes   □ No

7. Should the company continue its "Matching Gifts" program as a way of bringing employees into charitable giving decisions
   □ Yes   □ No

8. Should the company move in direction of the following current proposals for pensions
   More complete funding   □ Yes   □ No

   Improved vesting and portability   □ Yes   □ No

   Inflationary adjustments for retired employees   □ Yes   □ No

Information about respondents

Male □   Female □   Institution □
                              (Fund, Bank,
                              Trustee, etc.)

Age _____

Shareholdings
□ UNDER 100   □ 100–500   □ 500–1000
        □ 1000–5000   □ 5000–over

Location
□ New England   □ Midwest
□ Far West   □ Middle Atlantic
□ South   □ Foreign

In its original form, this questionnaire included space for additional comments by respondents and provided for return by mail.

The questionnaire lists additional options for the company's social accounting, notably environmental impacts and consumer rights, which are absent from the present report, even though they would make the report a very useful document.

Scovill Manufacturing Company

The Scovill Manufacturing Company of Waterbury, Connecticut, produces housing products, sewing notions, apparel fasteners, housewares, industrial products, and automotive and fluid power devices. It is a diversified manufacturing company with net sales of over $500 million in 1972 and with over 20,000 employees. In its 1972 annual report, Scovill for the first time presented a "Social Action Report" on the basis that "we thought our stockholders would be interested in a report on our activities in this area."

The Scovill "Social Action Report" (Figure 11) presents a list of social assets and liabilities in four categories: employment opportunities, environmental controls, community involvement, and consumerism. There is a rather widely varying degree of quantification among the different items, and no monetized measures are given of the outputs and impacts of the socially relevant actions and activities.

Examples of partly quantified items include the percentage gain in one significant variable ("Minority employment has grown from 6 percent in 1963 to 19 percent in 1972"), cost inputs to a particular social improvement program ("$3 million air filtering system for Waterbury Mills 80 percent completed"), qualitative statements of nonmonetized numerical results ("Scovill partnership with minority businessman is rebuilding 12 vacant apartments and 4 storefronts"), and straight qualitative statements having no numerical or quantified aspect whatsoever ("Hamilton Beach made its product tags more informative and simplified and clarified its warranties").

Some general comments first. The essence of a balance sheet is that it is comprehensive, yet the Scovill Social Action Report does not make clear the *net* of social assets less social liabilities. Without all line items quantified in commensurate dollar terms (real or shadow prices), there is no way for management or owners to determine if they are positive or negative producers socially, or to compare their performance with that of previous years and that of other companies. The layout shows a longer list of social assets than liabilities, but

Figure 11. Scovill Manufacturing Company Social Action Report.

Since there is much discussion today about corporate social responsibility, we thought our stockholders would be interested in a report on our activities in this area.

A Social Action Report: This is an admittedly imperfect attempt to report on our corporate social action. We have used the balance sheet method of reporting—not because it is possible to attach monetary values to all of the things we are doing or should be doing, but aren't—but because it allows for brevity in highlighting strengths and weaknesses in this area. We will welcome comments on the contents and on whether to continue this report.

Assets	Liabilities

Employment Opportunities

Assets	Liabilities
Company expansion has provided approximately 10,000 new jobs since 1963.	Fluctuating employment levels still a problem at some plant locations.
One of first members of Plans for Progress (3/17/64), a voluntary program to provide more job opportunities for minorities.	Need more upgrading of minority employees into higher labor grade jobs.
Minority employment has grown from 6% in 1963 to 19% in 1972.	Need more upgrading of women employees into higher labor grade jobs.
Women now constitute about 40% of total employment.	Closing of Waterbury work training center after Scovill investment of $33,000. State & Federal grants to support it were terminated.
Established National Alliance of Businessmen training program which resulted in hiring of 280 disadvantaged and 170 veterans in last 18 months in Waterbury area.	
Began first major pre-retirement counseling program for employees with U.A.W. in 1964.	
Established one of first effective alcoholism control programs for employees in 1954. (now includes drug control program)	

Environmental Controls

Assets	Liabilities
$3,500,000 Waterbury water treatment plant completed Nov. 1972.	Problem of disposing of semi-solid sludge from new Waterbury water treatment plant still being researched for a solution.
$3,000,000 air filtering systems for Waterbury mills 80% completed.	
$55,000 water treatment facility for Canadian plant completed March 1972.	Intermittent nitrogen dioxide emissions from Waterbury plant a problem requiring further research.

Figure 11. (Continued)

Assets	Liabilities

Environmental Controls (continued)

$1,100,000 water treatment facility 70% completed at Clarkesville, Ga. plant.

All 10 new plants added since 1959 were built with all necessary pollution control equipment.

New brass chip dryer ($700,000) installed one year ago to reduce air pollution in Waterbury must be modified to comply with new state standards.

New OSHA (Occupational Safety and Health Act) standards may require additional expenditures.

Community Involvement

Scovill charitable contributions averaged 1.2% of company pre-tax net income over past 5 years (1972 contributions were 8% of common stock dividends).

Local non-profit group to which Scovill contributed $163,000 has sponsored 174 units of subsidized housing.

Scovill partnership with minority businessman is rebuilding 12 vacant apartments and 4 storefronts to demonstrate benefits of rehabilitating deteriorating neighborhoods.

Support other such community projects as alcohol and drug control centers, inner city parks, recreational programs, public safety committees. . . .

Employee participation in such community activities as selectmen, state representatives, school board members. . . .

Scovill loaned executives to federal, state and local governments in 1972.

Programs to provide more low-income housing have not been productive enough for time and money expended.

Not enough rehabilitation of inner city neighborhoods.

Still much to be accomplished in revitalizing core cities, controlling drug addiction, extending educational opportunities to the disadvantaged, etc. . . .

Failure of programs to help youth groups establish minority owned businesses after Scovill investment of $20,000

Consumerism

Corporate programs utilizing more effective quality control procedures throughout the company have upgraded product performance.

New and improved procedures to upgrade quality and service to insure customer satisfaction not foolproof —problems still occur and are corrected as soon as possible.

Figure 11. (Continued)

Assets	Liabilities
Consumerism (continued)	
"Dial NuTone" established—a nation-wide telephone network to speed up service and customer communications.	Improper use of products despite more informative product tags and installation instructions.
NuTone added over 100 authorized service stations to its national network in the past year—and expanded its Parts & Service Dept.	Pending or future legislation which may impose more stringent standards for quality and performance.
NuTone simplified its product installation books and added a new Consumer Assurance Laboratory.	
Hamilton Beach made its product tags more informative and simplified and clarified its warranties.	
Hamilton Beach established new nationwide service organization—trained factory personnel contact independent service stations weekly to insure warranties are enforced.	

that doesn't mean they add up to a larger total asset than the total liabilities.

Without quantification of assets and liabilities, there is also no information for management on the relative return on investment in alternative social actions. Without such "ROI" information, rational investment and prioritizing decisions are impossible. Further, each line item has both social and financial assets and a larger component. For example, Scovill lists the environmental asset of pollution control equipment, but does not subtract the financial cost of the equipment from the monetized social benefit to yield the net benefit (or cost). Instead Scovill either states the benefit as if it had no cost, or states the cost of the benefit as if that's all it were worth.

Another general point is the inconsistent time base. Some numbers apply "since 1963," others to the "last 18 months," others since 1945, others to 1972, others to the future. The standard financial method to make values from different times commensurate is to reduce them all to discounted (or appreciated, if from the past) present values.

Without some comparative information, at least with last year's performance, if not with that of the industry, it is impossible to determine if Scovill is improving, doing worse, or staying about the same in its social performance.

There is such a diversity of types of data and so many qualitative rather than quantitative statements ("effective," "the first," "more," "participation," "not enough") along with partial quantifications and varying time periods that the balance sheet is perhaps really more of a working list than a comprehensive statement. Many items are also misclassified (research for sludge disposal is given as a liability but should be an asset), so that it would perhaps be more appropriate to list estimated social benefits and costs generated by company actions rather than assets and liabilities.

Some comments on specific line items follow, in the order shown in the report.

Employment Opportunities: Assets

Ten thousand new jobs . . .

What are they worth? (Low-paying jobs are worth less than high-paying ones)

. . . since 1963

But how distributed in time? Job worth some time ago was not the same as it is now.

One of the first members of Plans for Progress . . . [a] program to provide more job opportunities for minorities.

But how many have actually been provided? At what average level, with what average lonevity? Being "one of the first" is admirable but not of clear social worth. What were the jobs worth?

Minority employment has grown from 6% in 1963 to 19% in 1972.

At what levels? How is this related to minority representation in the community—to what is legally required and to what is common practice? Does it indicate discrimination or not, and what is the monetized cost or benefit of such discrimination to those concerned?

Women now constitute about 40% of total employment.

Why is this an asset? Women constituted most of the employment of sweatshops, too. The issue is the degree to which they share equal opportunity with men at all levels, and equal pay for equal work.

Established National Alliance of Businessmen training program which resulted in hiring of 280 disadvantaged. . . .

At what cost? With what net benefit?

Pre-retirement counseling . . .

What net benefit? (Difficult to measure. Perhaps assume benefit equals cost or market, whichever is less, as in accounting practice.)

Established one of the first effective alcoholism control programs.

What is "effective"?

What was the dollar worth of working man-days saved to the program, less the cost of the program? Same for drugs.

Employment Opportunities: Liabilities

Fluctuating employment levels.

How much? What is the social cost in lost income?

Need more upgrading of minority employees . . . of women.

Upgrading *need* is not a liability, and if equal opportunity is worthwhile (and I think it is), then the *need* is an asset; the failure to meet it may be a liability. This can be measured by the monetized cost of less-than-equal pay for equal work or equal work capabilities.

Closing of Waterbury work training center after Scovill investment of $33,000.

How much was accomplished in terms of trainees placed, and income worth of these placements, net of costs incurred? What benefits did Scovill obtain net of its costs?

What is the total employment income lost as a result of the center closing, controlled for non-center-related employment variations?

Environmental Controls: Assets

$3,500,000 Waterbury water treatment plant completed Nov. 1972. (Also "$55,000 water treatment facility" and "$1,100,000 water treatment facility.")

Has it produced $3,500,000 worth of social assets? What has it produced? What is the social worth of the amount of treated water produced versus untreated water?

$3,000,000 air filtering systems . . . 80% completed.

Presumably this is a 0.8 times $3 million financial cost at this time, but not yet a social asset, except perhaps in the employment it has generated. What is the discounted present value of the future budget?

All 10 new plants added since 1959 were built with all necessary pollution control equipment.

What is meant by "necessary"? Legally required? That wouldn't be enough for large social assets. Socially necessary? As defined how? By whom?

What difference has all this pollution control equipment made? What is the dollar worth of the environmental improvement (if any) or reduction in environmental pollution? This can all be monetized by shadow pricing of air quality, or at its crudest by assuming that it was worth the opportunity cost. If the latter measure is used, it overlaps and is redundant with line items listed under 1 and 2 above.

Environmental Controls: Liabilities

Problem of disposing of semi-solid sludge . . . still being researched.

Research is not a liability, but an asset.

The *problem* is not necessarily a liability.

"Still being researched" implies a discrepancy between aspiration and achievement that is a social liability only to the extent that it costs someone something.

It is the "disposing of semi-solid sludge from new Waterbury water treatment plant" that is the social liability. This is what should be measured. It might be estimated by the actual dollar cost of disposal plus the annual cost of declined real estate values around where it is disposed, compared with what they would have been without such disposal.

New brass chip dryer . . . must be modified to comply with new state standards.

The fact that it must be modified is a *financial* liability, but probably (if the state standards are effective) a *social* asset. The current social liability is not the modification, but the degree to which the environment is degraded sans modification, and the dollar cost of that degradation. This may be estimated by shadow pricing or changes in market opportunity cost.

New OSHA . . . standards may require additional expenditures.

This is a contingent ("*may* require") *financial* liability; again, its fulfillment may be a social asset. Meanwhile, the actual social liability is the cost of occupational hazards to employees, company, and community. This can be computed from lost labor input and the resulting lost revenues and profits to company, income to employees, and taxes to community.

Intermittent nitrogen dioxide emissions . . . requiring further research.
Again, research is an asset.
The *requirement* for research may be a contingent liability and/or an asset.
The NO_2 emission clearly represents some social liability. The amount, while difficult to quantify, can be roughly monetized by the market value of the impact of the emission on the real estate affected.
Which constituency pays the added cost of reducing pollution—the stockholders in reduced earnings, the employees in reduced pay (increases), the consumers in increased prices, or the community in decreased company expenditures on other social amenities?

Community Involvement: Assets

Scovill charitable contributions averaged 1.2% of pre-tax net income over past 5 years.
What were they in cash, and is the trend up or down, and how does it compare with industry standards?
What social good did it do? Some charities are notoriously ineffective, others excellent. The charitable investment portfolio optimization problem is not addressed.
How does this involve the community? Were all the contributions to community charities? Were these the best choices? On what basis?
Local non-profit group to which Scovill contributed $163,000 has sponsored 174 units of subsidized housing.
What is the social worth of the housing—for example, the consumer benefit, or incremental saving to consumers from standard market prices?
How much of the benefit generated is attributable to Scovill's $163,000 contribution? If less than $163,000, it wasn't worthwhile.
Scovill partnership with minority businessman is rebuilding . . . to demonstrate benefits of rehabilitating deteriorating neighborhoods.
What is the worth of Scovill's contribution, and its results?

Is the demonstration the benefit, or the housing, or both?

What is the social benefit from the housing, in terms of direct and indirect consumer benefits?

What is the worth of the demonstration in stimulating other productive activities?

Support other such community projects as alcohol and drug control centers.

What is the support worth, both in input (cost) and output (benefit) terms?

What are the *results* of these projects in reducing community social liabilities? What are the relative results—for example, should more or less be invested in drug or alcohol control? No basis for choice!

Employee participation in . . . community activities.

Is this really a company asset, or is it an individual asset?

What did the company contribute, in dollar costs of employees' working time donated?

What social benefits were generated by this participation, and what was it worth in community services at cost?

Scovill loaned executives to . . . governments.

How many for how long at what cost?

What public assets were generated by the loaned executives, and what are they worth?

What was the opportunity cost of their absence, to local social programs?

Community Involvement: Liabilities

Programs to provide low-income housing have not been productive enough.

"Enough" for whom, by what standards or criteria? That a program fails to meet a need is not a direct social liability—the liability is the unmet housing need, but it is not a company liability since it was not caused by the company. The program may be a *financial* liability to the company to the degree moneys are expended, but the amount is not stated.

Not enough rehabilitation of inner city neighborhoods.

An evaluative judgment is not a statement of liability. (See item 1, above.)

Still much to be accomplished.

Not news. (See item 1, above.)

Failure of programs . . . after Scovill investment of $20,000.
The $20,000 investment is a *financial* liability, not a social one.
(Also see item 1, above.)

Consumerism: Assets

Corporate programs utilizing more effective quality control.
What has been the consumer benefit generated? Its worth?
What is the degree of "more effective"-ness—more effective
than what?
What is the *net* social asset created (benefit less cost)?
Dial NuTone established.
Is a marketing and sales improvement a social benefit? Most
would not agree.

Consumer assets in general seem very weak. Were there really
no new products developed that met major social needs in new
ways? Or generated consumer surplus?

Consumerism: Liabilities

New and improved procedures . . . not foolproof—problems still occur.
What are the social costs of the "problems"? If safety prob-
lems, what costs in insurance, accidents, lost income, etc.?
Improper use of products.
What is the social cost of this?
Is it really the company's liability?
*Pending . . . legislation which may impose more stringent standards for
quality.*
Surely legislation pushing social assets is not a social liability!
It may result in a financial liability, but it should produce a
social asset. This is a misclassification. It also tells nothing
about social actions by the company.

Though it serves a useful purpose, obviously many criticisms
can be made of the Scovill "Social Action Report." It uses such a variety of partially quantitative measures that there is no basis for
measuring a net social effect, or for comparing year-to-year performance, or for comparing the company's performance with that of
other companies. Items are partially quantified in terms of input
costs, but never in terms of outputs or impacts, so that no estimation
of the relative efficiency of different social programs can be made.

Furthermore, the few measures that are applied are in mutually incommensurate units and lack a common time base. In sum, it would seem that the Scovill audit gives only a superficial and very selective accounting of some of the input costs of some of the socially directed programs of the company. It is thus both incomplete and imprecise to the degree that it is of little more use than a purely qualitative list of actions undertaken.

Abt Associates Inc.

At this writing it would be incorrect to state that there have yet been any complete applications of the social audit approach developed by Abt Associates Inc., although partial applications have been made successfully. Our comprehensive approach to social auditing is still in the process of development and improvement.

The major applications of parts of this approach to date have been with an insurance firm, a fruit company, and Abt Associates Inc. itself. The effort for the insurance firm, a corporation with $4 billion in revenue, focused on an audit of its charitable contributions budget. Because of the company's great size and its management's substantial social concern, the contribution budget was in excess of $1 million—sufficient to warrant careful analysis of the social return on the financial investment involved.

A cost/benefit approach was applied to the current and proposed charitable contributions of the company. This involved comparing the monetized social worth of the impacts of the specific programs, determined by the equivalent market worth or shadow prices of such impacts. From this analysis it quickly became apparent that the charitable contributions budget was overinvested in facility development and urban redevelopment building programs, both of which were relatively high-cost items with only marginal social returns. On the other hand, the education, health, and arts programs were found to offer relatively high social returns for the money invested. Partly as a result of this analysis, it is believed, the chairman wrote in the company's "Social Responsibility Report" that charitable contributions by the company would be shifted from building projects into more productive human services projects.

The insurance firm's use of the social audit approach was limited. Only certain parts of the method were used, including the cost/benefit analysis comparing social program outputs and impacts to inputs, estimating a market or shadow price for social impacts, and improving the mix of social investments to achieve greater total social return. The areas of application were limited to corporate charitable contributions, and specifically excluded such other areas of high social impact as employment, environment, and product and service quality.

Another application of the social audit approach was in the case of a fruit company. In 1969, the company was being troubled by various types of consumer protests, many of them expressing strong opposition to what they believed were the company's outdated policies concerning its treatment of people. The president of the company at that time asked Abt Associates Inc. to investigate the company's social impacts and thus provide an independent assessment of the validity or lack of validity of the charges being made against the company. The objective was to apply the social impact evaluation techniques developed in Abt Associates' many federal government evaluation programs to this large private company's social actions. This was Abt Associates' first social audit for private industry and, although it lacked many of the later improvements in quantification, several of the essential concepts of the social audit were developed and applied.

The social audit team proceeded to identify the major constituencies affected by the company's social actions—employees, community residents, and the general public, as well as consumers and stockholders. Interviews and observations were conducted among the first three constituencies to identify the positive and negative social impacts of company operations. A report was prepared describing both the beneficial and detrimental impacts of company actions in the areas of employee and labor relations, health, housing, education, and economic development. While the specific findings of the audit remain confidential at the request of the company, it may be said that some significant negative social impacts were identified and feasible corrective actions were recommended.

The first quantitative and monetized social audit was undertaken for Abt Associates Inc. in 1971 and 1972 and first published in its 1971 Annual Report.* A somewhat unusual social auditing problem arose in the attempt to estimate the social worth of Abt As-

---

* See Appendix E for the 1975 social audit of Abt Associates Inc.

sociates' services to its consumers because, in addition to its social services delivery operations, many of the services were research and evaluation, and knowledge of specific kinds, for which it is very difficult to determine market or shadow prices. In the initial effort in 1971, the multiplier effect of work done by the company was used to compute the social worth of that work in excess of what was paid for it. For example, the net social contribution to clients from an employment training program was estimated by determining the total increased annual income of the estimated number of additional job placements resulting from the company's training and technical assistance activities for the U.S. Department of Labor, less the total contract funds spent by the company in producing that social impact.

Most of the company's other projects, however, were found to have much less direct and more long-term social consequences, not yet accessible to computation. Thus in the company's 1972 social audit, it was decided to assume that the net result of social benefits and costs to clients (consumers) was "a wash," which is what the accountants call an equality of benefits and costs, canceling each other out. This decision was made not because it was believed there was no net social worth to the research and knowledge produced by the company but because of the adoption of the conservative accounting concept that a service or product is worth the lesser of two quantities: market value or cost. Since market values were not available to generate a consumer surplus differential between market value and cost, the cost of the work was assumed to be its worth—and this, of course, exactly balanced the opportunity cost to the clients of the money they paid for it. The firm continues to wrestle with the problem of determining the social worth of its knowledge products, and in doing so has identified several methods of doing this although none of them can be regarded as conclusive at this writing.

9

The Good Company, Profits, and Technology

AS we look at corporate social responsibilities and goals, it seems worthwhile to consider the idea of a "good" company. My own idea of the good company overlaps somewhat with the idea of a just society and the idea of a social experiment.

Fundamental to the idea of a good company is that it is a good place to work. That means that the individual's aspirations have a better chance of being realized in this particular work environment than in others that might be available and that opportunities for the individuals in this organization are enhanced and are congruent with their image of themselves as persons doing something useful, important, interesting, and attractive. This concept sees the company as a small society and a microculture, an oasis in the chaos and decay of much of industrial society.

The company can represent itself as an oasis physically, using landscaping, trees, playgrounds, and art. It can also express the idea of the oasis operationally (despite competitive pressures) by permitting informality and flexibility in work routines and by encouraging individual employees to seek the kind of work which interests them most.

The social ideology of a company largely defines the kind of employees it can attract and the markets it can address. Social ideology often includes not only a devotion to pragmatic social problem solving—applying scientific knowledge and methods to reach large-scale societal objectives—but also the egalitarian principle that the feelings and opinions of individuals count even more than efficiency.

As has been pointed out by Daniel Bell in *The Coming of Post-Industrial Society,** the two doctrines of scientific reform and participative egalitarianism often conflict because scientific suggestions of what people should do are sometimes very different from what they want to do. Also, speed and economy of decision making can't be maximized simultaneously with egalitarian participation in these decisions. We must always sacrifice some of one for more of the other.

The Company as a Social Experiment

Now that corporate managements are becoming more sensitive to the ways lives are affected by what happens to the organization, the concept of the company as a social experiment may get more explicit exploration. There are often several social experiments going on at once in a company, each with its own central question. Some of them are listed here.

- □ How large can business organizations grow before they lose their amiably informal qualities?
- □ How large and successful can a business organization grow when serving markets that often have motivations other than to maximize the quality of life?
- □ Can the quality of the products and services supplied by the company be increased to the highest standards, within the budgetary constraints imposed by the market and the economic requirements of employees and stockholders?
- □ Can social impact research of high quality be accomplished— particularly the sort which requires the services of top quality social scientists—in a corporate funding environment which is continuously unstable?

* New York: Basic Books, 1973.

- Can the ethical and scientific values of high quality and high efficiency production be successfully integrated with the economic requirements of employees and stockholders to create a growing and viable industry with long-term constituencies of consumers, producers, and investors?
- Can intellectual, scientific, ethical, and economic values be successfully integrated in a company, while maintaining a first-rate image in the intellectual, scientific, human resource communities?
- Can industry meet its commitments to social reform, scientific quality, and economic return and still offer the kind of secure learning environment essential in a human development institution?
- Can industry attract, by art or science or sheer effort, the kind of minds and characters that can solve its problems?
- How can industry maintain the drive for quality in the work of its staff, and yet avoid elitist arrogance and the loss of sympathetic feeling for the populations it is trying to serve?
- Can we define and standardize top behavior for scientists and our managers so that sustained quality can be maintained without dependence on key individuals?
- Can we simultaneously maintain the high standards of individual performance and fair dealing among persons which is characteristic of a meritocracy, and at the same time achieve representative participation of minorities, sexes, and generations at all levels of the organization?
- As a social experiment in institutional innovation, are companies confounding too many goals and methods to yield any meaningful indications of what works and what doesn't?

These are some of the issues related to the concept of the company as a social experiment. The process by which these issues are resolved and the results for all the major company constituencies of employees, clients, owners, and surrounding communities will affect the idea of the company as a just society and as a "school of life."

A rather minimal resolution of these issues in the next decade will result in a better than average commercial enterprise. Such an outcome, while not reflecting our ambitions fully, is not to be disdained; a lot of smart people try unsuccessfully to do no more than that.

The ideal resolution of these issues might result in the innovation of a new type of social institution effectively combining most of the best elements—and only a minimum of the worst—of successful industrial enterprises, first rate universities, and effective government organizations. It would be a social invention satisfying both the public and private interests of all the company's major constituencies in a way effective enough to stimulate widespread imitation and thus the rapid development of a more socially constructive industrial form.

The history of corporate social experiments is fairly substantial, ranging from the reforms by Robert Owen in his early 19th-century mills in England and Cadbury's experiments in housing in the later 19th century (which became a model for town planners in the 1950s) to experiments with job development, job enrichment, and advanced social benefits such as the Kaiser Permanente–Kaiser Community Health Plan in the mid-20th century.

Social responsibility has been defined as caring for others actively, by supplying to others what is available in abundance. It would seem that in order to carry out its social responsibilities, a corporation should be encouraged to innovate social experiments and that government should take measures to increase the company's willingness to take part in such social experiments, possibly by tax incentives or incentives of other forms.

Profit or Good Works—or Both?

Milton Friedman and Peter Drucker have argued that it is the first responsibility of business, including its first social responsibility, to achieve profitability and growth—the conventional business objectives.* We have no quarrel with this position as far as it goes. However, such assertions have often been used as arguments against the exercise of business social responsibility, and with this position we disagree.

Both Friedman and Drucker suggest that business cannot exer-

---

* See, for example, Milton Friedman and Eli Goldston, "The 'Responsible' Corporation: Benefactor or Monopolist?" *Fortune,* November 1973; Milton Friedman, "Milton Friedman Responds," *Business and Society Review,* Spring 1972 (an interview); and Peter Drucker, *Management: Tasks, Responsibilities, Practices.* New York: Harper & Row, 1974.

cise social responsibility without also exercising authority over social policy and that the exercise of such authority represents an unjustified expansion of corporate power.

The second major argument Friedman, Drucker, and others employ against corporate social responsibility is that it is competitive with financial responsibility or, to put it another way, investment in the achievement of social goals requires the sacrifice of profitability. Such an assertion involves the assumption that social actions cannot yield improvements in financial profitability and in fact will have a negative effect on profits. Yet there is substantial evidence that it is precisely those corporations which have been most socially responsible that have also achieved the greatest financial success, and that socially irresponsible corporations sooner or later run into financial difficulty. Although much more empirical research needs to be done in this area, a preliminary review of the most socially responsible and the most financially productive corporations in the United States suggests a strong correlation.

The arguments by both Friedman and Drucker against abuses of corporate power in the name of social responsibility are fair enough as far as they go, but miss the main point: that corporate responsibility can and must be consistent with and mutually supportive of financial productivity. Their arguments of course do not prove that corporations have no responsibility for the society in which they exist.

I have tried to eliminate any misunderstanding with Professor Friedman by writing to him to suggest that he actually subscribes to our view of social responsibility when he says "The appropriate way for corporations to accomplish social goals is by setting up rules so that they have to pay for resources they use."

Professor Friedman has replied, "I do not mean that the corporations should themselves set up those rules. That I regard as a basic government function. I rather mean that we, in our capacity as citizens, should set up rules requiring corporations to pay for resources they use. This would mean that consistent with their seeking to maximize profit they would be led by an invisible hand to serve the social interest."

Perhaps our only difference on this point is what is a government function and what is a corporate function, not the need for the function to be exercised. We certainly agree that the social interest should be consistent with a company's natural interest in maximizing its profit (although it may be simplistic to assume that corporations are always profit maximizers; often they are profit satisficers and status maximizers).

However, our assertion that social actions do not require the sacrifice of profitability seems to Professor Friedman (as he puts it) a ". . . strict cop-out. If two criteria give the same answer, they are not separate criteria. It seems to me utterly meaningless to say that social responsibility is a separate criterion, to be regarded as parallel with profitability as an objective for a corporation, unless the two can and do conflict. If they do not, no problem arises. The fundamental justification for a free enterprise system is that, given the proper framework, the pursuit of profit by individual enterprises will, in fact, serve social objectives. But this Invisible Hand Doctrine of Adam Smith is a very different view than the view that corporations should explicitly and directly pursue what they regard as social responsibilities."

We really do disagree here with Professor Friedman: The fact that two criteria sometimes guide us to the same answer does not mean that the same question was asked or that the criteria are identical.

The basic issue is the compatibility of profit and positive virtue. Critics of the concept seem to suggest that company actions must be painful—that is, unprofitable—to be really virtuous and that profit must be gained without virtue. Such puritan masochism cannot allow profitability and other socially benevolent actions to be compatible within the same organization.

Why cannot profitability and other socially responsible behaviors coexist? Perhaps intolerance of the concept is based on too narrow a conception of profitability or socially responsible behavior, or both. If profitability is defined as *maximizing* profitability within very short periods of time and constrained only by the law, then *any* additional operational or financial cost conflicts with that maximization. The short-term costs of *both* social and financial investments then *do* conflict with short-term profit maximization. Most businessmen would reject profit maximization by elimination of investment in future capacity as shortsighted and doomed to mid-term failure, as resources become exhausted without replacements becoming available from previous investments. If they decide to maximize profits by eliminating social investments, it is because they either do not know the relationship between social investments and financial returns or believe that some other agency such as the government will make the necessary social investments.

If socially responsible actions are defined as only those taken for altruistic purposes, then by definition they cannot be profitable (except by accident). I spent an hour trying to convince the board of directors of the Aetna Life & Casualty Insurance Co. that socially responsible actions would be likely to be even more cost-effective if profitable. Their counterargument was that profitable social actions would be interpreted as self-serving and lacking in real goodwill and altruism and perhaps result in unfavorable publicity to the effect that commercial motives were being disguised as charity. That might be a practical risk, but it isn't logical and an educated public would not necessarily view the matter thus.

After all, most so-called altruistic actions—and certainly most government social programs—are motivated by "enlightened self-interest." "Enlightened" implies a self-interest that takes a broad, long-range view. Examples abound: good labor relations, community activities, employee training and health services—all social actions motivated not by altruism but by enlightened self-interest. Otherwise, these social programs simply would not exist, since there are very few saints in the world. Whatever socially benevolent programs we have exist as a result of organized, enlightened self-interest, and not altruism. To insist on supporting social action programs for altruistic motives is to insist that they be hardly supported at all.

If profitability and social responsibility are not mutually exclusive and not always opposed, what relation *do* they have to each other? This depends on the kind of profitability and the kind of social responsibility involved. As pointed out above, short-term maximization of profit is indeed incompatible with both social and financial investments that do not provide immediate payoffs. Inordinate pursuit of unlimited social goals is also incompatible with profitability. Both are extremes. The far more common and likely cases are companies with reasonable requirements as to profitability and limited social goals.

The Myth of Profit Maximization

The ultimate test of the effective exercise of a corporation's social responsibility will be its cumulative social impact on all the people affected by it—owners, employees, neighbors, customers, and the general public. Trade-offs may be made among the conflicting interests of these constituencies, but ultimately they must all be satisfied to some minimum level of what they consider to be just. At least some of them must be unusually well served for a company to have exercised its social responsibilities well. Whether the unusual social benefits generated are primarily for owners or employees or consumers or communities should depend on what a company can do best with respect to what is needed most in its field of action.

Thus a company in the "knowledge" industry, such as a publisher, may elect to emphasize product quality to the benefit of consumers in the social responsibility it exercises. A capital-intensive manufacturing company selling a standard undifferentiated product (chemicals, glass, steel) may elect to exercise its social responsibility in making an asset of its physical environment. A labor-intensive retail business may choose to emphasize an attitude of social responsibility toward its employees. Society as a whole is likely to be served best if all organizational units do what they can do best for their immediate human audiences.

This allocation of social responsibilities is not best served if all corporations are striving to maximize profits. Profit-seeking corporate behavior eventually reaches a point of diminishing returns compared to efforts of other kinds. If the costs of production and market competition do not permit significantly improved profit margins, it is better for a business to invest its surplus resources in efforts other than those seeking immediate increases in profit. It may be better to diversify or to create values that increase the company's likelihood of survival.

In fact, most companies are not really "profit-maximizing"; they are "profit-satisficing" (explained below), because of imperfections in the market and the multiplicity of corporate goals. Even in the theoretical "perfect competition," profit-maximizing behavior does not necessarily maximize *both* economic and social values—it merely achieves an economic equilibrium.

It is a *myth* of American enterprise that profit-maximizing behavior is not only necessary, but sufficient for overall economic and social success! Although profit has always been necessary to provide incentive for the capital that is required to develop enterprises, it was always seen by the great entrepreneurs as an instrumental rather than an ultimate value. Undoubtedly, Vanderbilt, Rockefeller, Ford, Sloan, Carnegie, Watson, Morgan, and the others wanted to be rich, but I believe their principal interest was in building great enterprises. If one studies their behavior in detail, more often than not their profits were used to build their enterprises rather than the enterprise being used to maximize profits.

Even more in the past 50 years (as taxes on income and capital gains have shifted the corporate payoff from direct personal income to appreciation of assets) the personal interests of the leaders of our major enterprises seem better served by growth—with enough profit to support it—rather than by the maximizing of profit. We should once and for all face the deceptive quality of this profit-maximizing myth. Profit-maximizing behavior to the exclusion of all other considerations is both practically stupid and socially destructive and, for just those reasons, practically extinct except in the imaginations of quixotic critics of 19th-century capitalism.

An indirect social cost of the continued widespread belief in the profit maximization myth is the argument against social investments by private industry. This argument is based on two assumptions which we have discussed above: first, that profit maximization by business is in the best interest of our society and, second, that social investments must be made at the expense of profits. Both assumptions are incorrect. It is not in the interest of the general society for everyone to maximize profits. By doing this we tend to minimize important social goals, and slighting these social goals will eventually generate even higher economic costs, more than offsetting the temporary extra "profit." The second assumption is incorrect because many social investments (and often the best of them) need *not* be made at the expense of profit; in fact they may contribute to profit, either currently or on a discounted present-value basis.

It would be constructive to replace the myth of profit maximization with a more realistic doctrine of "profit-satisficing." "Satisficing" is a term used in operations research and systems analysis to describe the satisfaction of a given requirement only to the level of the requirement and not further, as contrasted with maximization or optimization. Business must "satisfy" certain profit requirements: to provide incentives to capital investment, to generate surplus for repayment of investment and the opportunity cost of capital, to generate surplus for reinvestment in its own future qualitative and quantitative development, and to generate tax revenues for government to reinvest in overall social programs.

There is no question that business must generate a profit to survive and flourish. The point is that if some profit is good, more profit is not necessarily always better.

How much profit then? Profit requirements are not an ever-ascending monotonic function but an inverted U-shaped curve: profits grow and decline as a function of the overall satisfaction of all of the participants in an enterprise. This inverted U-shaped curve is obviously a result of politically weighted trade-offs among a variety of satisfaction-versus-profit relationships, differing somewhat for each of the corporate constituencies. For the purely financial investor, the satisfaction-versus-profit curve may appear to be a straight line going upward. Yet even here the wiser investors realize that the steeper the line bends upward beyond some high performance point, the greater the risk of its being chopped down by market competition or government regulatory action. Consider the windfall profits of the large oil companies as a result of the Arab embargo. The sophisticated financial investors in such companies were probably praying that the companies would reinvest the short-term profits in long-term technical and social growth programs to avoid the strongly negative public opinion calling for regulatory penalties for such high profits.

For employees of an enterprise and for consumers of its products, the satisfaction-versus-profit curve is probably an inverted U, with the peak "profit" (maximum satisfaction) at that point where employment security, opportunities for employees to move up, work and product safety, and product quality and economy are maximized. To do all these things will certainly require profits, but it is impossible to do them all well and *maximize* profits. In the long run, however, the maximum total satisfaction of all involved in the organization tends to maximize overall "profit" simply by ensuring the greatest long-term survival and growth.

All the above is not really a radical new concept but simply a practical intermediate position between the theoreticians of profit maximization and the financially naive technological visionaries who always call for the sacrifice of present profits for more investment in research and development or other long-term future payoffs. Business must pay as it goes, but if it insists on trying to pay the maximum as it goes, it will not go very far. I do not believe that I have discovered any new truth here but merely restated an attitude that I believe has been part of the philosophy of the most successful builders of enterprises.

Social Impact of Technology

There is today a deepening pessimism concerning the social role of technology, on which so much of our corporate enterprise is based. The number of students seeking engineering degrees has dropped. Reform politicians accuse governments of neglecting the poor while spending heavily on technology. Weapons of war and the defenses against them—always heavily technological—make some people think of technology as murderous. In the United States today, thousands of unemployed aerospace engineers are being re-trained for careers in public service, health care, and commerce.

The transportation, power, and extraction industries are viewed by the public as principal polluters. Computers are seen as dehumanizing. Mass media are feared as purveyors of cheap commercialism, incentives to violence, and subliminal political propaganda. Drugs, legal and illegal, ruin the lives of many—including housewives as well as alienated youth.

Are these concerns justified by the facts? At least in part, they seem to be. As Table 8 summarizes, technology is still too unit-oriented, rather than systems-oriented, despite the ironic fact that the technologists are our most competent analysts and designers of systems. Partly out of historical momentum, partly from economic and political pressures, technological advances are often advances at the unit level, made at the expense of the system—and this applies in political and economic systems as well as engineering. The negative side effects still have not overwhelmed the positive achievements—most people would still prefer to drive cars and have air pollution and traffic jams and accidents.

Nevertheless, the negative side effects are growing faster than the positive results of technology, and with more mutual support, and this is widely sensed and feared.

In the last 25 years, the United States alone has spent over $200 billion on research and development, with over 80 percent of this devoted to military, atomic energy, and space efforts not directly responsive to major social needs. This may have been history's greatest socially irresponsible investment in technology since the pyra-

Table 8. Effects of technological change.

Sector	Major Technological Change	Unit Payoff	Unanticipated System Cost	Impact on Qualities of Life
Health	Antibiotics	Greater survival from infections	Increasing development of resistant strains	+ Reduced disease mortality – Risk of suddenly increased mortality
Education	Cheap textbooks	Wider access to printed literature	Fragmentation of culture	+ Diversity of choices, self-development
	Programmed instruction	Economies of self-teaching	Decline in quality of teachers	– Less opportunity to learn under great teachers
Entertainment: films, TV, books, music/records	Cheap home audio-visual entertainment	Widened access to A-V material	Superficial entertainment crowds out high quality	+ Democratization of culture (wider access) + Home education opportunities – Violence and trivia on TV may reduce mental health of public – Vulnerability to propaganda, loss of freedom

162

			+ / −
Housing	Cheap high-rise building construction	Lower unit physical production cost	"Vertical slums," crowding, social pathology	+ Higher physical quality of buildings − Lower social quality − Less privacy, quiet
Trailer		Low-cost family enjoyment of nature	Ugly trailer parks	+ Cheap enjoyment of nature for a few − Quantitative pollution of trailer parks
Transport	Cheap cars	Individual mobility	Traffic jams, air pollution, land use waste	+ Mobility, freedom − Less quiet, clean air, safety
Agriculture	Cheap chemical fertilizers	Higher yield per acre, better crops	Pollution of ground water	+ Reduced cost of food, short-run − Pollution of bays and rivers − Tax costs of cleanups and substitute methods
Manufacturing	Automated production line	Higher unit productivity and worker income	Boring jobs, exclusive "worker elite," resisting redistribution	+ Decreased working hours − Job dissatisfaction

163

mids. If most of that $160 billion had been spent on medical re-
search, education, housing, transportation, and the environment, I
wonder if the United States wouldn't be a much better country
today, and more secure, because so much better loved, even though
less well armed.

In this gathering crisis of the perceived social role of technology, there are three major alternatives in the immediate future:

  A. *Continued and increasing public disenchantment with technology,*
     followed by reduced public support and self-fulfilling
     prophecies of technological inefficiency.
  B. *Polarization of opinion* into technological and anti-
     technological factions with great loss of potential useful ap-
     plications.
  C. *Redirection of technology* from military and nonmilitary nation-
     alistic glorification to urgent social roles in health, nutrition,
     housing, environment, education, law enforcement, and the
     like.

I believe we are observing a race between the trend toward the
successful social application of technology and the trend of public
alienation with technology. I fear that if there is widespread disillu-
sion with technology, scientific thought itself will not long be free
and supported, and some dark ages may be upon us.

The Future for Technologists

What does this threat mean to scientists, technologists, and technology planners and managers? First, technologists need to develop
rapport with social scientists and learn from them what the major social needs are and perhaps become at least amateur social scientists
themselves. Second, technologists must not give up being technologists because technology cannot be applied to social problems if technology is not continually being developed. Third, technologists need
to become sensitive to the impacts of major technological changes on
the quality of life and to determine if such impacts are consistent
with a publicly acceptable social role for technology.

To learn what the major social needs are, as perceived by the
public, one needs only to examine the copious literature of contemporary social research. In the United States today, the federal government spends about $1 billion per year, regardless of politics, on
such research. Various federal departments, and corresponding departments in the 50 states, continually research social and economic

Table 9. Some problem-solving technologies.

Application or Activity	Technological Advance	Unit Impact	Quality of Life Impact
Systems analysis and systems synthesis (design) (operations research and systems engineering)	Applied mathematics + physics + systems engineering + computer simulation = system optimizations	More efficient component and sub-system designs, new systems capabilities	+ Efficiency, resulting in reduced consumption of material and human resources − Pressures for centralized controls to avoid suboptimizations
Economic and industry planning and forecasting (economics)	Macroeconomic theory + national income accounts data + computer simulations = econometric modeling	Reduced industrial and national economic instability	+ Job security, econometric stability − Economic controls reduce freedom and diversity of choice for some.
Government policy and program development (political science and sociology)	Survey research + sampling theory + behavioral sciences + phone and mail data gathering + computer processing = opinion, user needs, and decision modeling	Social and economic problem-responsive programs development	+ Responsiveness of governments' policies and programs to people's needs (security with diversity) − Manipulation of public opinion to maintain political power (loss of freedom)
Organizational development (social psychology)	Industrial psychology + small group and individual psychology + sensitivity training = group behavior modification	Changed organizational behaviors	+ Job improvement + Self-development + Mental health − Risk of job insecurity − Loss of privacy
Individual social, emotional, and cognitive development (psychology and psychiatry)	Developmental psychology + psychometrics + psychoanalysis + chemotherapies = individual growth and therapeutic strategies	Changed individual behaviors	+ Mental health + Physical security (reduced violent conflict and self-destructive behavior) + Sociability (reduced hostility and inhibition) + Self-development − Privacy

needs of the population, develop and plan alternative action programs, and evaluate program processes, outputs, and impacts. Most of the problem-solving technologies developed in the course of hardware technology research and development were applied. Some of these are systems analysis and design, econometrics, decision modeling, sampling and statistics, industrial psychology, and organizational development. (See Table 9.)

But the interest must be there for the technologists to assume an active and benign social role. Technology today is too interrelated with politics, economics, and social change for the technologists to assume that all will continue as before if they simply do their assigned job. To be socially responsible, they must take some responsibility for the social applications and quality-of-life impacts of their technology. They cannot take the attitude of the scientific attaché of a major European nation who said to me, "In my country, there *are* no social problems!"

Yet the technologists must retain their expertise. If it is true, as claimed by many scientific and engineering educators, managers, and planners, that only with technology can we solve our social and economic problems, then it is essential to retain technologists. Even if it is *not* true or only partly true, we must still have technological expertise simply to control and minimize the negative impacts of the technology we already have—and cannot help continuing to produce because it is an inseparable part of modern civilization.

If the socially productive technologist of the future is to remain an expert technologist while also becoming at least an amateur social scientist, how can that person find the time to do both? I believe the time is available and needs to be spent. Medical technology gives us increases up to 50 percent in our working lifetimes (from 40 to 60 years) and it is desirable for health reasons alone to spend this time productively. Working lives increased from 40 to 50 years—25 percent—and retirement at 75 rather than 65 are already commonplace. The time will be also clearly available in the aggregate from technologists as a group, if a sane world arms control policy, international scientific cooperation, and efficient division of labor release millions of technologists from unproductive or redundant work.

How can technologists become sensitive to the positive and negative impacts on quality of life that determine the overall effectiveness of technology and its potential survival and growth? First it is necessary to understand the quality-of-life concept—just what quality of life consists of, and some ways it can be scientifically detected and measured. If "QOL" can be measured, then differential technological impacts on it can be experimentally determined, and we will be able to plan the application of technology in the most socially constructive way.

Table 10 lists some of the obvious and less obvious qualities of life, with associated possible indices.

Table 10. Quality-of-life indices.

Qualities of Life	Indices
Obvious Measures	
Aesthetic satisfaction: perceived beauty in the look, sound, smell, feel, and taste of things	Opinion poll
Quiet	Reduction in db above mean library ambient
Privacy	Percentage of time desired visual and audio privacy is achieved
Freedom and diversity of choices	Number of free choices / Number of different choices
Sociability, "gemütlichkeit"	Opinion poll and projective tests
Health	Reduction of mean morbidity (days away from work)
Entertainment	Audience surveys of reactions
Physical safety and security	Reduction of accident and crime rate
Employment security	Reduction of unemployment
Interesting and rewarding work	Job advancements / Job changes
Opportunities for lifelong education and self-development	Voluntary career changes / Number of available careers, adult education enrollment
Subtle Measures	
A certain minimum predictability of things	Reduction in rates of change of key planning variables
Only a limited amount of frustration and difficulty in making arrangements	Inverse of telephone, travel, and hotel error rates
Basic confidence in the goodwill and decency—or at least neutrality—of most strangers	Reduction in crime rates of nonfamily crimes

Quality of Life (QOL): What Is It?

Quality of life is the characteristic that makes life desirable. It is a concept related to happiness by the implicit assumption that the one goes with the other. It suggests there are objective, widely shared criteria for life quality, and indeed we will approach the concept in that way.

Quality of life consists of the aspects of life that are valued. "Standard of living" no longer suffices as a measure because many persons in nations affording a relatively high and improving standard of living, in terms of per capita national income or GNP, nevertheless believe that the overall quality of their lives has deteriorated. One such person would be the middle-class professional who earns more income than ever before, yet breathes worse air, wastes more time in traffic jams, is robbed and threatened more often, is woken up at night by noise more frequently, finds his or her work more repetitive than before, the children offered less thorough education, the neighborhood made ugly by commercial signs, and his or her favorite entertainments crowded out by cheap and superficial trash on TV.

From an economist's point of view, the components of quality of life are those aspects that are scarce, costly, and in demand: freedom amid diverse choices (liquidity of financial and human resources), monopsony in consumption, and high preference returns on investments of effort.

From a sociologist's perspective, quality of life might be expressed in terms of preferred social relations: privacy when wanted, congeniality of proximate peers, role and class mobility in harmony with one's own preferences and security and those of others.

From a psychologist's viewpoint, quality of life might consist of opportunities for satisfying self-development: rich in emotion and fantasy, yet able to deal with reality in ways effective in yielding further satisfactions, unafraid of obsolete threats, uninhibited by anxieties, unimpelled to waste energies on self-destructive or hostile behaviors.

An ecologist might view quality of life in terms of the balanced maintenance of diverse life forms, with no obliteration of natural forms or species.

Quality-of-life indicators from the disciplinary points of view might include disposable income (as opposed to absolute income) for the economist, available rates of social mobility for the sociologist, low rates of interpersonal conflict or depression for the psychologist, and slow rates of ecological change for the ecologist.

Technology in the Solution of Social Problems

Given an awareness of social needs, continued technological expertise, and a sensitive comprehension of the QOL impacts of technological change, what can the technological planner or decision maker do to maximize the productive and beneficial social role of technology? The best opportunities for action probably lie in the application of problem-solving technologies, themselves mainly the fruit of technologically based industry and government activities. Table 9 shows how five of these problem-solving activities have exploited technological advances with resulting impacts on quality of life which are mostly positive, although in some cases partly negative.

One of the potentially most fruitful applications of several of the problem-solving technologies would be the development of a technological division of labor among nations. Currently the technological competition among nations wastes enormous resources through redundant R&D and piecemeal production that does not fully exploit economies of scale. Why should several different nations have to produce operationally similar aircraft, space exploration vehicles, and medical technology? Only for nationalistic and military security reasons—which could be nullified with effective international agreements.

Classically, the efficient allocation of technological resources to social problems would be accomplished by investing each resource to the point where the marginal return equals that from the other resources. To do this, it is necessary to determine the absolute and relative return in quality of life from alternative mixes of technological applications to social problems. Methods of measuring the social efficiency of technology and specific technological applications are therefore needed.

I would propose, as an initial and still crude measure of the social efficiency of technology, the arithmetic sum of the changes (positive and negative) of the quality-of-life components weighted by their relative popular preference among the populations affected, divided by the sum of the costs of the technology in terms of both the equivalent economic cost (using shadow pricing) of the negative impacts on quality of life and the economic cost of the application.

This measure of the social efficiency of technology requires subordinate quantitative measures of the positive and negative changes in quality-of-life components in commensurable terms. These social impacts can be reduced to commensurable terms by expressing them in present economic value, discounting all future returns to the present. The economic returns may be derived by shadow pricing them, or determining what the impacted population now pays to achieve or to avoid comparable social benefits and costs. It is assumed that all social impacts such as health, security, freedom, and environmental quality can be expressed in terms of the money the people concerned have actually paid for equivalent services or what they have paid to avoid equivalent costs: the basis of the social audit.

Governments and industrial enterprises have always invested in data collection and measurements promising decision-making utility. This had led to a preference for hard or quantitative data, typically to the exclusion of social data and the neglect of the measurement of the social performance of organizations or of technological innovations. The social effects, decisive though they may be, have been expressed qualitatively and thus have not been subject to test. This poses difficulties in allocating resources, resulting in much of the present unhappiness with the social inefficiency of technology.

If social efficiency measures can be applied to proposed technological changes in the social audits of both government and industrial organizations, then decision makers will have a quantitative and rational basis for applying technology in the optimal pursuit of social needs.

Even though the net improvements in overall quality of life as a result of technological change are positive—as many of us still believe—we must admit that there is substance to the widespread and increasing public alarm over the degrading impacts of new technology on quality of life. There is also the very serious question of whether our technological efforts achieve the highest possible net positive impact in response to social needs. Clearly, much could be done that is not yet done.

To do it will involve some reeducation of technological planners and decision makers concerning social needs and what social science research can tell us about their relative priority and their interdependence. It will also involve several other factors: the maintenance of purely technological skills; the development of an awareness of technological impacts on the quality of life, among technological decision makers; the development of measurements of the social efficiency of technology, as expressed in terms of quality-of-life impact; and the application of such measurements in comprehensive audits of the social performance of the government and industrial organizations which employ technology.

10

Social Responsibility in Times of Crisis

A rapidly developing test of the seriousness and effectiveness of corporate social responsibility commitments will be the social behavior of corporations during the current and coming times of economic and financial crisis. When sales and earnings are growing, and when the main problem for corporations is coping with success, devoting management time and money to social responsibility activities is not only a capstone to many successful careers but also a healthy long-term investment in human and other resources. However, in times of economic crisis such as the present—combining inflation, stock market vagaries, and reduced consumer demand, with shortages in energy and raw materials, and the liquidity crisis in the capital market—management attention tends to focus on its first priority: organizational survival. In this concentration on finances, corporate social responsibility actions may revert to such a low priority that they go unattended—or are in effect eliminated.

What can the corporate managements do in times of severe economic and financial crisis to ensure at least the minimum maintenance of their social performance and measurement programs and still (as they must) devote their main energies to the immediate economic crises? First of all, it is at these times of economic crisis that

172

corporations are faced with decisions that tend to have larger-than-usual social impacts on the constituencies served. Hence the evaluation of social impacts is all the more critical at times of economic crisis, even though this fact tends to be submerged by the urgency of the immediate financial problems. Typical decisions made by companies during economic and financial crises that have enormous social consequences are:

- □ Reductions in force, involving layoffs and unemployment.
- □ Reductions in overhead expenditures in order to bring total costs within falling revenues, involving possible cutbacks of employee benefit programs.
- □ Liquidation of subsidiaries, possibly involving elimination of pension benefits, despite ERISA (the Employee Retirement Income Security Act).
- □ Reduction in product and service quality in order to make up for rising costs of labor and materials without increasing prices in the face of falling demand.
- □ Unfair competitive practices and untruthful financial reporting to maintain the necessary revenues and working capital for survival.
- □ Defaulting on financial commitments, loans, and vendor payments, or the excessive stretching out of such payments to conserve cash when sufficient working capital is not available from the equity markets or from banks in a liquidity crisis.
- □ Reduction of antipollution efforts in an attempt to conserve working capital by not spending on antipollution equipment, and to reduce operating costs. Power utilities have already made moves in this direction, claiming that increased fuel costs and labor costs (together with consumer pressure not to raise rates at a time of inflation) force them to make economies somewhere, and these can only be achieved by reducing emission standards.
- □ Sacrifice of other environmental protection standards, such as the restoration of land after strip-mining, to reduce production costs and to maintain sufficiently high profits to finance the purchase of primary materials in times of very high interest rates and scarcity of working capital.

It seems obvious that these and other pressures to cut back on social responsibility activities in times of economic and financial stress create difficulties in maintaining corporate social responsibility. The trade-offs between the corporation's responsibilities to its various constituencies of employees (to maintain employment), stockholders (to maintain earnings), and consumers (to maintain good value at noninflationary prices and still satisfy demand) may shift substantially in times of economic recession and inflation. It is precisely at these times that the recalculation of the best trade-off of these competing forces in the public interest requires the most accurate measurement, social as well as financial.

Furthermore, the feedback from social consequences to economic and financial consequences is shorter and more intense in such times of crisis. For example, excessive layoffs to reduce labor costs will feed back rapidly in dissatisfaction among employees who are retained and will reduce their productivity. Community tax burdens increase and are translated into increased corporate taxes. Decreased consumer buying power reduces corporate sales and revenues. In a depression, the social consequences of short-range economic self-preserving actions rapidly translate into further negative economic forces; these in turn cause more cutbacks, resulting in a downward spiral of reduced productivity for the entire economy. It is this spiraling process that must be prevented in a time of economic crisis, and the measurement of the social impacts of corporate decisions at such times can be a positive force for reducing the rate of the downward spiral.

One approach to ensure the measurement of social impacts is to institutionalize the measurement function and to build it into the decision-making process for all major corporate decisions. This could be accomplished by establishing a permanent social impact measurement function, either in the operations office or in the financial office of top management. All major decisions contemplated would be reviewed by the corporate officer who has responsibility for the social impact estimation, and he or she would provide this estimated impact evaluation to corporate top management for consideration in the decision-making process. This need not be a very expensive operation and really requires little more than a concerned and knowledgeable senior officer of the corporation to take responsibility for this social impact evaluation, plus a middle-level analyst to direct evaluation research activities and a few research assistants to gather data. On the other hand, the costs—short-term and long-term—of *not* institutionalizing a modestly funded corporate social impact evaluation activity might be very great. High social costs imposed on employees, stockholders, or consumers in times of crisis will not be forgotten by those constituencies and will eventually feed back to cause negative impacts on corporations. Furthermore, if corporations do not act responsibly in times of economic crisis, the government is very likely to respond to the pressures of public opinion by intervening with additional regulations to protect the public interest, further limiting the freedom of action of corporate management to respond to crises in the way management considers most effective.

Layoffs and Their Alternatives

One of the major social costs imposed by employers on their employees is that of the layoff. This suspension of the social benefit of employment is a common and frequent practice in industry (and increasingly in government and universities) made necessary by a reduction in operations resulting from a reduction in sales, revenues, or external funding and requiring a reduction or redistribution of internal labor budgets.

The iron law of all enterprises is survival. When costs exceed revenues (or in nonprofit organization terms, when costs exceed income from endowment, external funds, or government budgets), costs must be reduced if the organization is to continue. In most organizations a heavy proportion of the cost of operation is labor cost; therefore most cost reduction decisions involve reductions in the labor force: layoffs.

Layoffs impose severe social, economic, and psychic costs both on the laid-off employees and their families and on the employees who are kept on. We have estimated the immediate social costs to the employee laid off as approximately equivalent to the wages he or she forgoes during the average period of time he or she requires to find comparable employment. In the social research industry we assume this to be approximately 30 days. Actually, this estimate greatly understates the total social costs of layoff, since in periods of national crisis the duration of unemployment may be much longer. Also, when the employee does find work he or she may "pass along" his or her unemployment to the individual being replaced on the job. Furthermore, the emotional anxiety and stress for the laid-off employee, for his or her family, and for other employees who are not laid off but fear they will be (suffering the disruption of their working lives as a result), all add to the cost. Next to being summarily dismissed for some infraction of an organization's rules or for inadequate work performance, being laid off is the worst thing that can happen to an employee.

The corporation or other employing organization therefore has a social responsibility to minimize the social costs of layoffs. This minimization does not necessarily mean to reduce the number of layoffs to the minimum. Most organizations would probably go bankrupt if they had no layoffs whatsoever at some time in their histories; and if an organization goes bankrupt and ceases to exist, in effect all its employees are then laid off.

The social cost of layoffs depends heavily on the way layoffs are executed. For example, employees given adequate warning time prior to an impending layoff, and more generous termination payments, may be able to make the transition to other employment with a minimum of personal anxiety and interruption of income. In addition, alternatives to layoffs should be investigated: an across-the-board reduction in salaries might offer a better trade-off than maintaining full salaries and reducing the number of employees.

The agonizing decision faced by most managers who must reduce labor costs (usually the major cost variable) is which individuals should be laid off and when and how. Also, there is usually a range of choices between a smaller layoff early or a larger layoff later. Giving early warning of a layoff may reduce employee morale and productivity enough so that the total layoff is ultimately increased; in the meantime, the organization may lose some of its most critically needed people, whom it had not planned to lay off.

Facing such dilemmas, how can the manager who must reduce labor cost through layoffs minimize the social cost of such action? The social audit approach to this problem is to estimate the relative social cost of alternative layoff plans and then to trade the best of these off against the social cost of not laying off. For example, a manager might estimate the social costs of laying off half a unit's staff after a certain period of time in order to retain the other half for twice the length of time (assuming the entire staff could not be retained within the budget). The manager might decide that to do this would minimize the total social cost—even counting the costs of reduced group solidarity among the employees retained, plus their reduced morale. This plan would then have to be traded off against the social costs of not laying anybody off but achieving the necessary economies by reducing overhead services, social benefits, and the like. This complex trade-off could only be made conclusively with quantitative measurement of the equivalent social worth of the different benefits to the people involved.

It is a noticeable fact that layoffs decided by managers who directly supervise the individuals who are candidates for layoffs often tend to delay acting, while managers who do not directly supervise or do not know the candidates for layoff tend to make the decision more promptly and decisively. The reason is not hard to understand. The manager faced with laying off individuals he or she knows personally tends to feel some guilt at causing this economic and psychological loss to the individuals concerned and tends to feel this much more intensely than the manager who is laying off individuals that he or she does not know personally.

The question here is whether a warm personal relationship that delays a layoff decision is really more socially productive than the colder, prompter layoff decision made by a manager who does not know the individual concerned. This involves a trade-off between the values of personal communication between managers and the individuals they manage, versus the values of long-term social efficiency for all concerned. It might be naively assumed by some not experienced in management that the most socially productive and humane decision is that which delays the layoffs and that the earliest layoff consistent with economic logic is the cruelest one. This is hardly ever the case. On the contrary, the longer layoffs are delayed once they become economically necessary, the less warning time for readjustment is available to the employees who are laid off and (eventually) the greater the number of employees who have to be laid off, because the opportunity to achieve savings early by prompt layoffs has been lost. Thus the social advantages of personal relationships between managers and employees may be offset operationally by the social costs of inhibiting prompt layoffs when economic conditions demand them. It might be argued by the softhearted that means other than layoffs should be found to solve particular economic problems; we of course assume that all alternatives have been explored and that a reduction in staff is the only means of preserving the enterprise and the job security of the employees remaining.

Here we face again the choice of "amenity" versus productivity, operating with different trade-offs at different levels. The maximum social amenity (and often productivity) in a work situation may require personal contact between manager and employee, yet when a layoff situation occurs this personal relationship may work against what is in the long run most socially productive and humane. Conversely, where the promptest possible layoff maximizes social benefits both to those laid off and to those remaining employed, the management whose style offers the least interpersonal intimacy may be in a position to make the most socially productive decision.

Environmental Protection During Economic Crises

In times of inflationary prices, shortages in resources (particularly fuel), increasing unemployment, decreasing liquidity, and depressed equity markets for new growth capital, companies that ordinarily would assume social responsibilities by investing in environmental protection tend to cut back their capital and operating expenditures in this area, in the obvious interest of their own economic survival. Since the Arab oil embargo and the rapid increase in the price of fuel, the power generating utilities are a dramatic example of this trend, with utility after utility requesting delays in the enforcement of environmental protection regulations, reducing capital outlays for pollution abatement equipment, and reducing operating outlays for low-pollution fuels, such as low-sulphur oils.

The best response to this kind of crisis, from the public point of view, is a complex one and cannot be determined ideologically. The conservationists are mistaken in their belief that the public interest is best served by adhering rigidly to the most stringent environmental standards. The decision makers in utilities and other businesses are equally mistaken if they believe times of national economic crisis and fear of bankruptcy should be exploited to delay pollution abatement and other environmental protection activities indefinitely. What is needed is a careful calculation of what combination of cost reduction measures and environmental protection measures yields the best short-term response to the economic crisis in the public interest, while avoiding extremely high, long-term environmental costs. This involves a complex set of socioeconomic and technological trade-offs, including actions to modify consumer demand that cannot be intuitively or crudely calculated but require the best possible impact measurement in order to determine alternative courses of action.

It should be remembered that drastic reductions in capital expenditures for pollution abatement equipment, and for reductions of expenditures for low-pollution fuels, also have dislocating and depressing effects on the economy. Pollution control equipment manufacturers are part of our economy; when orders for such equipment are canceled, this contributes to unemployment and to economic depression. As demand is shifted from low-pollution to high-pollution fuels, the increase in employment and revenues in the high-pollution-fuel field does not immediately make up for unemployment and business failures in the low-pollution-fuel field. Furthermore, utilities need to explore certain courses of action that will help them overcome the problems of rising fuel prices and shortages of capital.

For example, much may be done to reduce the demand for energy, thus helping to alleviate the energy shortage immediately, or at least within a year. Reduction in demand seems the most logical area for short-term policy measures, since the supply components of the energy shortage cannot be rapidly addressed without negative impacts, economically and environmentally.

Demand might be reduced selectively without relaxing environmental and other social constraints, through more efficient timing by government of its incentives to reduce demand, concentrating on those times and those areas where demand is most excessive. For example, a great deal of the additional power generating capacity of utilities is required not to meet the average load but rather to meet peak loads in certain concentrated urban areas of the country. If these peak loads could be spread out in time, and geographically, enormous savings in added power generating capacity could be realized. Some of this spreading of the load could be achieved by staggering working hours (so that the maximum intensity of use peaks could be flattened out), staggering working days by instituting shorter, overlapping 4-day, 40-hour work weeks, reducing overall transportation demand through those shorter work weeks (saving 20 percent in commuting costs immediately), and similar operational measures—requiring no new technology and no new legislation, but simply cooperative efforts by the major business and government institutions to spread peak power loads.

The social costs of instituting such reductions in peak demand, either for energy or for other commodities, are likely to be much less than the alternative of relaxing environmental standards or of trying to go on meeting increased demand (within environmental constraints) without sufficient working capital. During an economic crisis, all the available alternatives need to be considered.

11

Viewpoints and Controversies

THERE is one and only one social responsibility of business—to use its resources and engage in activities to increase its profits so long as it stays within the rules of the game, which is to say, engages in free and open competition without deception or fraud.
                    —Economist Milton Friedman, University of Chicago.

Milt Friedman is right but of course he doesn't go far enough. Friedman overlooks two things. First, the businessman does not exist solely in a world of cold, grey economics; he also exists in a real world where people's needs go far beyond their economic needs. He is a man before he is a business-man. He feels pressure from within himself to become a part of the whole social pattern and to accomplish more than making a profit. Second, Fried-man overlooks the fact that the rules have been changing and are going to change at an explosive rate in the future. We may yet reach that state where a businessman is judged by the social goals he accomplishes as well as the profits he makes.
                    —Thornton F. Bradshaw, President, Atlantic Richfield Company.

In the future, companies that are the most creative in meeting social prob-lems are going to be the most profitable. Creativity in dealing with social issues is likely to flow from a general management confidence. If I am right . . . then you will be bound to take corporate social behavior into account in your investment decision, not as a matter of philanthropy but as a matter of cold, hard-headed business. In the future, we may see corporations . . . which will suffer lack of investor interest due to future costs that will be incurred because of failure to meet social responsibilities. Companies that already have made the expenditures will be considerably more attractive than those which have huge capital costs ahead.

    —G. Robert Truex, Chairman, National Bank of Commerce, Seattle.

Critics—Right and Left

The social audit approach to measuring social performance seems to have attracted as many critics from the liberal left as from the conservative right. The standard conservative argument against social audits is based primarily on the assumption that socially responsible actions invariably come at the cost of profit and are therefore inconsistent with profit-maximizing behavior. We have argued against this view on the basis of two beliefs: (1) It is not in the best interest of society in general or business in particular to maximize profit; it is better to sacrifice some profit requirements for social survival; and (2) even if profit maximizing were the norm, it is possible to apply social auditing to that end in a way more consistent with achieving other social responsibility objectives. In other words, there are many socially significant actions that can be taken that need not be at the expense of profit, and some of these can even contribute to profit.

The criticism from the liberal left is of a less pragmatic and more theoretical sort than might be expected. The concern expressed by some major critics of contemporary corporations is that social audits can be used to defend the social virtue of organizations that should not be defended. They know that a company's social audit can result in rather significant equity for society and a net social income, besides the purely financial stockholder's equity and net financial income, and may justify a favorable judgment of the company's social performance, but they are concerned that the same method applied to some of the corporate giants will result in positive results that will then be used to justify the social negatives of these organizations.

This is a difficult criticism to refute because it is partly correct. I suspect that social audits of large corporations, including these guilty of imposing significant social costs on employees, consumers, and the general public, would in most cases still have a positive social balance sheet and social income statement.

However, even if we assume this to be the case for the moment (and I will explain below why I think it is likely), I don't think this means that the social audit can or must be used in defense of antisocial corporations. A comprehensive and openly discussed social audit of a large corporation will identify major areas of social contribution and social negatives and presumably, even though the net of the two is positive, there will be pressures for making it even more positive by reducing the social costs. I don't believe that a large corporation's disclosure of a social balance sheet and social income statement *together with the social liabilities and costs created by its operations* will persuade the general public or consumers or regulatory agencies to believe that all is well and that nothing need be done to improve the social performance of that particular corporation.

An analogy to the argument made by the liberal critics would be to say that open discussion of financial balance sheets and income statements would result in less pressure for improved financial performance since most corporations show a positive financial balance sheet and income statement. We know that, quite to the contrary, the more disclosure of financial performance corporations make, the more efforts are engendered to improve it.

Now to the interesting question of why most social audits of corporations are likely to yield net equities to society and net social income. The major social contributions of most corporations are to the consumers in the form of consumer surplus and to the employees in the form of a kind of "employees' surplus." The consumer surplus (the familiar economic term) is the difference between what a consumer is willing to pay for the product or service and the price at which the corporation is willing to sell it. The analog for the employees is the difference between the wages and benefits employees would be willing to work for in a given environment and what they actually get. Since both consumer markets and employment markets (at least for skilled and professional employees) are highly competitive, it is easy to see that most corporations that survive and flourish over any period of years are likely to have done so in this competitive environment by supplying these consumer surpluses and employees' surpluses. If they did not offer consumer surpluses, their products would not be purchased, and if they did not have employees' surpluses, they would not be able to retain the employees necessary to produce those products and services.

Consider a corporation like General Motors. We take the example of General Motors because it is likely one of the largest and best established corporations, and yet few corporate critics would argue that it has an unblemished reputation for social performance. Nevertheless, I suspect that a social audit would result in a strongly positive result overall, with significant social equity and very significant net social income generated each year. Why? Because most of the two million plus cars produced annually could probably be sold for as much as $500 more than their current prices with only a small drop in sales, therefore creating a consumer surplus of $500 times two million or $1 billion. There has to be an awful lot of social cost generated by pollution, safety hazards, employment discrimination, and the like to offset that $1 billion consumer surplus.

The liberal left critics of the social audit are mistaken if they see this kind of social audit leading to an effective defense of the social malfeasance of corporations. On the contrary, the theoretical likelihood that most social audits will, in the net, yield positive results is likely to facilitate their acceptance by corporations as a balanced review of performance, a review that recognizes not only negatives but also positives. One cannot expect corporations to discuss only damaging information about themselves, and I believe that the practical price for this is to give fair and equal treatment to positive information.

The critics that look to corporations to participate in discussions of only their socially negative aspects will not get very far because it would seem to be against human nature to cooperate with such hostile efforts. It should be reemphasized that comprehensive and precise financial disclosure has not resulted in ruining or weakening companies, but on the contrary has provided the information and the incentives to both corporate insiders and outsiders to improve financial performance. We would expect that a similar development would occur with the widespread application of social audits.

Problems in Accounting: Neil C. Churchill's Study *

In a study of business social performance measurement, Neil C. Churchill of the Harvard Business School studied 11 U.S. corporations currently involved in socially relevant activities. The companies were selected on the basis of his perception of their being most ac-

* "Toward a Theory for Social Accounting," *Sloan Management Review*, Spring 1974.

tive in assessing their socially relevant activities. Churchill divided the 11 companies he investigated into two types: Type A, in which external stimuli motivated the social programs (five companies), and Type B, in which the programs were primarily motivated by internal stimuli (six companies).

Why Companies Measure

In the externally stimulated companies (Type A), some catastrophic external pressure such as physical destruction, boycott, or intense public opposition resulted in a socially active policy, which in turn resulted in an action program. In the internally stimulated companies (Type B), usually a senior executive interested in social issues initiated an investigation of the company's social impacts, which then led to attempts to measure the social impacts of the company, finally resulting in a social action program.

It is significant that the major difference in social action policy between the Type A and the Type B corporations was that the internally stimulated ones for the most part did attempt to measure their social impact while most of the externally stimulated ones did not. Professor Churchill fails to give the other characteristics of these corporations, but since he does not give them we must assume that as a competent social scientist he kept other relevent factors essentially constant.

It is interesting to consider exactly why social performance measurement was not initiated by the externally "pressured" socially active companies, while most of the internally stimulated ones did attempt to install social information systems, or at least carried out an inventory of their socially significant actions and attempted to measure benefits and costs.

It is Churchill's hypothesis, with which we agree most strongly, that rational management requires quantification as an essential precursor to efficient allocation of resources. Churchill suggests that the immediate "academic" reaction, to the effect that the corporate managers who were not concerned for the measurement of social costs and benefits of their actions were behaving irrationally, was really an insufficient explanation of the behavior. He then questions whether the "rational model" really satisfies the situation and suggests that perhaps the model itself is vulnerable. The managers may be quite rational in not wishing to measure the costs and benefits of socially relevant actions: This is suggested by some of the organizational tensions (identified by Robert Ackerman) * occurring at middle-management levels when middle managers attempt to implement higher-management social action imperatives. Furthermore, great difficulties may be experienced by managements in measuring the impacts of social actions that appear to them to have little relevance to the decisions themselves.

The relatively modest concern of corporations for measuring the costs to themselves of their social actions is not explained by Churchill. He does comment, however, that measurement of a corporation's socially relevant activities has been both limited and difficult, and he offers some characteristics of socially relevant actions that he believes help to explain this failure to attempt measurement.

Churchill found that there were two views of the social purpose of business. One was the concept that the role of business is to make a profit and that it should act socially only in response to society's wishes as expressed by law. The other proposition is that farsighted response to the changing nature of a corporation's social role maximizes profit in the long run by allowing the firm to anticipate both competition and government controls and thus minimize total costs—for example, by building plants with pollution abatement incorporated rather than having to retrofit later at higher costs. Further, this latter view considers that anticipation of social response can make government regulation less restrictive and less costly. The first view considers all corporate actions economic, while the second view considers social actions initially social and then later becoming economic. Churchill states: "Both views argue for measuring social actions in the same way, for if the business of business is business, then social activities are minor and social costs are very small."

I would disagree with him on this. He also argues that what is now social is a precursor of what will be economic, and then says: "A uniform measurement scheme that deals with the same subject in the same way appears desirable." This seems perfectly reasonable.

Moving Targets
Churchill then goes on to a major aspect of social responsibility that he suggests is an obstacle to corporate measurement of social performance. This is the alleged "moving target" nature of social requirements. It is argued that what is "social" today being "eco-

* Robert Ackerman, "How Companies Respond to Social Demands." *Harvard Business Review*, July–August 1973, pp. 88–98.

nomic" tomorrow, "there is a tendency to account for such activities in economic terms and a tendency not to worry too much about separating socially related actions from purely economic ones, since in all probability they will either go away or blend into the economic mainstream of the firm." The suggestion is that since the social requirements will eventually be "captured" by the conventional economic actions of the firm anyway, no social accounting system is required to augment the regular economic accounting system.

It is true that socially effective social policy and performance require continual adaptation to changing social needs and opportunities for response. However, the "moving target" problem, I think, is more conceptual than practical and can be overcome. Dynamic control theory and feedback control systems oriented to continual error reduction both demonstrate the feasibility of homing in on "moving targets." Furthermore, both theory and practical experience indicate that frequent crude error-correction signals are much more effective in goal-seeking guidance and control systems than are infrequent but precise correction signals. The analogy applies in social evaluation research as a system for guiding social policy: Social action can be better guided by frequent, crude, formative evaluations of social needs and opportunities than by infrequent, precise, and summative evaluations. In practice, this means that decision makers should measure social performance frequently (perhaps quarterly, or at least annually).

How Big Is a Social Contribution?

A second factor that Churchill believes tends to negate social measurement in corporations is the allegedly small and ancillary level of expenditure. He argues that few firms contribute even the 5 percent allowed for tax purposes to social causes; thus controllers and managers do not perceive the value of having detailed information on such expenditures because the potential savings from more rational allocations do not seem to warrant examining them in detail. This view, I believe, makes the fallacious assumption that the corporation's most socially relevant activities are its charitable contributions rather than its mainstream activities. This is a common mistake.

"Corporate social responsibility" certainly includes such critically relevant actions as the enforcement of Equal Employment Opportunity regulations, affirmative action programs, consumer product safety standards, truth in advertising, occupational health and safety standards, health, education, and retirement benefits for employees, and the increase in work satisfaction for employees through job development and job training activities. It seems ironic that the most socially impactful areas of business activity are rarely thought of as such by businessmen; corporations often have enormous positive social impacts which go unrecognized.

Churchill summarizes the reluctance of industry to measure its social performance as originating from the "prevailing view of social costs as those beyond economic necessity and beyond the law, the recency of attempts systematically to manage social activities, and the moving-target characteristics of socially responsible activities." In our view these are insightful explanations. They indicate a lack of understanding by many business executives of the opportunities in social and economic productivity that would be afforded by social measurement.

Accounting Theory in Social Auditing

Churchill then examines accounting theory in relation to the measurement of socially relevant activities and raises a number of interesting problems in the application of accounting theory to social measurement that help to explain some of the difficulty managers have with the concept. He seems to believe that the measurement of different aspects of quality of life is "far from attainable" because he cannot accept a common monetary measure for different social values. He claims that there is no ideal measuring unit to express the effects of an action in terms of net benefits or detriments for every individual.

It is my feeling that the perceived market value of such actions in dollar terms does in fact provide such a measuring unit. The argument that no unit will satisfy the differential utility to different groups of a particular social benefit or cost does not really stand up: The utility of a dollar of dividend is also very different for different investors, but this does not prevent us from using the common measure of dollars as a kind of average utility for return on investment.

The difficulty of measuring the effects of social actions is a very real problem raised by Churchill as an obstacle to corporate social performance measurement. Some of the theoretical problems are the spillover effects, the costs of providing adequate control groups, and the difficulties of measuring social impacts without introducing measurement artifacts.

Churchill then uses ten accounting criteria to examine the problems of measuring social costs in an accounting framework:

Continuity
Cost
Revenue (realization)
Matching
Consistency
Materiality
Conservatism
Freedom from bias
Relevance
Entity

Continuity and *consistency* require (1) that the enterprise be a going concern, continuing indefinitely, and (2) consistent accounting principles to provide year-to-year comparability. Churchill states that the "moving target" or changing nature of social concerns makes continuity and year-to-year consistency of social measurement difficult if not impossible. He gives the example of no one's being interested today in calculating the cost of employing child labor, although this was once of great concern, while other social concerns that are currently salient and would be subject to measurement would probably not be included in future years.

We do not find this argument valid because while the specific line items of social costs and social benefits may change from year to year, the overall net social income (or loss) and total social assets and liabilities can be expressed from year to year. We do not agree that "social measurement differs from economic measurement in the applicability of the concept of consistency and continuity" because the social content of an enterprise can change just as the economic content does, while the accounting categories remain consistent. A corporation can change its mix of products and services and assets and factors of production from year to year without changing the consistency and continuity of its enterprise or its accounting. It can also change its mix of social benefits and costs and assets and liabilities from year to year without having to give up consistency and continuity in accounting for them.

Materiality is given as another reason for not measuring social benefits and costs, on the assumption that they are only that small percentage of the net income of the corporation that is devoted to charitable enterprises. Obviously this is completely mistaken if one considers social costs and benefits to be a major percentage of corporate revenues. We believe this is in fact the case and some simple examples should so demonstrate.

Most corporations in our increasingly service-oriented economy are devoting a substantial percentage of their costs to employee payroll—approximately 50 percent. Since the industry average for employee benefits is currently about 30 percent of payroll, we can assume that roughly 15 percent of current corporate costs (or somewhere between 10 percent and 15 percent of annual revenues) represent employee benefits. These certainly involve major corporate social responsibility decisions. Expenditures to increase or decrease environmental pollution are another major cost factor. Since costs of this kind amount to well over 10 percent of the average company's revenues—and probably more than 100 percent of the average company's net income—they definitely satisfy the accounting criterion of materiality. Any cost that exceeds average net profit is material!

Churchill then describes the very real difficulties involved in applying the criteria of *revenue realization, matching,* and *conservatism* to social actions. He states (correctly, we believe) that social benefits should be recognized in the periods during which the changes in social conditions take place—usually the periods during which the social actions occur—and says: ". . . social costs are matched to the period in which the benefits are recognized. These social costs are measured at the enterprise level by the resources expended in producing the social benefit—in this sense a cash rather than an accrual basis of cost allocation. This reflects the recognition and revenue realization and matching principles of accounting." He then states that this treatment stems from the difference between economic and social gains; economic benefits continue from period to period but social benefits are a "moving target." His statement that the social benefits are a moving target is based on the externally determined criteria for, say, a desirable level of minimum pollution, changing from year to year as goals are reached.

While this requires some complex computation, it does not seem to argue against the feasibility of applying the accounting criteria concerned. There is really no reason why social gains cannot be disaggregated to continue on a year-to-year period, much as economic benefits change because of (for example) changes in pollution abatement requirements. This is really quite analogous to changes in price levels for other assets and liabilities that can be treated by conventional accounting approaches.

Freedom from bias is given as another obstacle, on the basis that the perceived social significance of different social actions varies from group to group and from year to year. The specific example given is that conservation of energy was considered predominantly a social issue prior to the energy crisis of 1972, after which it was considered predominantly economic, and estimates of the social costs of energy-saving efforts were changed as a result.

Churchill states that "the less biased approach would account for all costs of energy-saving activities irrespective of the motivation." What he neglects is that the differences in motivation generate differences in real or shadow prices and that the perceived social utility of an energy-saving program is a direct and unbiased measure of it that can be expressed in terms of economic market values, exactly the way the rapid increase in the price of energy as a result of the energy crisis reflected the change in the financial values involved.

There is an unnecessary confusion here between two concepts: change as a result of a change in *bias,* and change as a result of a change in *utility,* the latter being perfectly and logically expressible in terms of a change in price. Naturally, all changes in price reflect changes in relative supply and demand; demand contains an element of consumer preference which expresses bias, but this does not seem a terribly useful way of looking at changes in demand. We therefore conclude that one can measure changes in social utility as expressed in changes in perceived market value in a way just as free from bias as one can measure changes in economic utility as expressed in changes in economic prices.

The accounting criterion of *relevance* is raised as another possible obstacle to the measurement of social performance. Churchill states that "for decision-making relevance, the enterprise's social and economic costs are one and the same. . . . Social actions, however, produce benefits not primarily to the economic entity but to segments of society affected by the enterprise—its constituencies. Economic revenues accrue to the economic entity; social benefits do not."

This is not completely correct since some of the social benefits, particularly those associated with employees, consumers, and the general public and its consumer response to the corporation, certainly do accrue to the economic entity and thus do produce benefits for it. While it is true that social actions also produce benefits not only to the economic entity but also to segments of society affected by the enterprise (its constituencies), the same may be said of the enterprise's economic actions. Its economic actions in employment yield social benefits to the society, and its economic actions in research and development (producing new knowledge) and in production of goods also yield social benefits to the public constituencies.

Thus, although there may be a difference in the degree to which the internal (economic) and external (societal) constituencies of the enterprise are affected by the economic and social actions of the enterprise, both are affected by both. If this is the case, then the relevance of social costs and benefits created is just as great for management decision making and resource allocation as that of economic costs and benefits.

The most confusing issue is raised by the accounting criterion of *entity*, which is central to accounting theory. Under this concept a business enterprise is treated as a separate accounting unit with its own assets, liabilities, revenues, and costs. In social accounting the costs accrue to the entity just as in economic accounting, but the difference is that some of the benefits or revenues accrue primarily outside the entity to the entity's constituencies—the customers, suppliers, employees, community, stockholders, and general public. In economic accounting all the benefits or revenues accrue to only one constitutency, the owners or stockholders. In social accounting benefits accrue to several constituencies, and the concept of entity is more complex since the corporate constituencies are expanded and diversified.

Churchill correctly asserts that this is a major change in or difference between social and financial accounting, in that the concept of entity constituting the economic accounting in social accounting includes not only the firm but also its effective constituencies. Churchill believes that "the inappropriateness of the concept of the economic entity for social measurement explains, in a large measure, why there is so little social cost measurement within corporations today." Most of the social activities in the firms visited were viewed as economic, or soon to be economic, leaving the social costs of the corporation to be counted only in special areas of social action. The broadened concept of "entity and the modified concept of cost benefit matching presented here can produce social measurements that

accord with actions taken and results produced. This would eliminate the conundrum of the firm cited earlier which found that the
more social actions they undertook in their normal business programs the less the social costs they measured. Counting as costs the
resources committed to programs affecting different social groups
would give the firm a picture that they do not now have of their
resource commitments in the current year, comparatively over time
and comparatively with other firms in their industry."

Churchill correctly concludes that as social considerations increase in importance in business operations, the need for social
cost/benefit analyses also increases. Accounting for social costs in a
manner commensurate with the characteristics of socially relevant
actions can be the beginning of "an arithmetic of quality."

A major question raised by the Churchill critique of social auditing is that of how information that was not deemed relevant to a
social audit during one year would be added to it in the following
year. The principle of *continuity* and *consistency* in accounting practice
should be observed in any social audit of social accounts: adding
items of interest from year to year and removing those not considered of interest any longer, but providing enough data for comparisons as long as they are of interest, and explaining any changes in
reporting. This is consistent with a long tradition in accounting practice of providing year-to-year comparability and of describing any
change in line items in any two-year period.

Dollar Audits versus Process Audits

In the January–February 1973 issue of the *Harvard Business Review,* Raymond A. Bauer and Dan H. Fenn, in an article entitled
"What Is a Corporate Social Audit?" commented on the Abt Associates social audit. After a few friendly words of praise to the effect
that the Abt audit "represents a diligent and ingenious pioneering
work," it is criticized as follows.

The strongest criticism is that "this format is not the one most
likely to be adopted by large, complex companies." The reasons
Bauer and Fenn give for this view are these:

> It does not respond to the currently perceived needs of the exec-
> utives of such organizations, nor to the realities of their situa-
> tions. . . . The Abt audit is organized around the total social

impact of the company rather than around an assessment of its social programs. While the approach has great conceptual attractiveness, it is not particularly well adapted to the needs which are expressed by the executives with whom we are familiar, whose concerns, objectives, and aspirations for an audit are far more limited than Dr. Abt's. . . .

The goal of the Abt audit . . . is to render social performance in dollar terms and balance sheet form. Thus, it does not disclose (it may even hide) the firm's performance and social programs in which its executives are interested. For example, a company could be spending large amounts of money inefficiently on pollution control or hard core training or giving substantial sums to irrelevant charities. And, indeed, in the course of conducting his audit, Abt found some unwelcome facts about his organization and changed policy accordingly. But the actual rendering of his findings in balance sheet form was, in our view, a technical exercise. Our sense is that few companies are interested in supporting this last step of technical virtuosity if the information can be meaningfully presented in other ways. . . .

The Abt audit is designed for external reporting. However, most executives are interested at this time in internal reporting for internal assessment. The prospect of external reporting exacerbates the already considerable anxiety of such executives. . . .

The Abt form of a social audit is so abstract and complicated that we find few, if any, executives (never mind laymen) who claim to understand it as an overall entity—nor do we feel we can explain it as a totality.

Bauer and Fenn admit that they "may well be too sharply critical, and indeed, we have a personal bias to which we must confess." Probably the most significant indication of Bauer and Fenn's point of view is their statement that "we feel that the attempt to reduce social performance to dollar terms is perverse. While monetary measures are a great utility in many contexts, their utility is, finally, limited; we feel there are likely to be fatal errors in employing the dollar measures as exhaustive representations of social phenomena. Mainly we are skeptical of the availability and possibility of rendering the social *consequences*—whether positive or negative—in dollar terms."

The Process Audit

Bauer and Fenn then admit that "we judge it a mistake to specify at this time just what the final form should or would be" and suggest that the way to get started on social auditing is with what they call a "process audit." The sequence of steps in the process audit includes, first, an assessment of the circumstances under which each social program came into being, then an explanation of the goals of the programs and the rationale behind each activity, and finally a description of what is actually being done. The goal of such a process audit is given as the assemblage of information making it possible to "intelligently assess the program." Clearly this is a qualitative and fairly conventional management assessment of corporate social programs, which seems perfectly sensible. However, it provides no quantitative information or analysis on which to base corporate social investment optimization decisions, or on which to base an evaluation of corporate social performance relative to that of previous years or of other companies.

In the following discussion we will take up point by point the criticisms of Bauer and Fenn and our view of these criticisms.

Pros and Cons: Bauer and Fenn

It may be a mistake to assume that the "currently perceived needs of the executives" do not include the total social impact of the company, but only the assessment of its specifically intended social programs. To say this is to suggest that executives are concerned only about the social impact of charitable contributions, but not about the social impact of their corporations' employment practices, the safety and value of their products, the truthfulness of their advertising, the environmental impacts of their production processes, or the overall social impact on communities in which their corporations operate. Clearly this cannot be the case because an essential minimum of corporate social performance in these areas other than voluntary charitable contributions is already *required by law* in the United States and in many other nations. No corporation can effectively survive without responding to these requirements for corporate social responsibility and these legal requirements of at least four kinds in the United States—employment practices, environmental impact, safeguards to health and safety in production processes, and product safety. In at least these four functional aspects the law *requires* executives to be concerned with the social impacts of corporate actions. It is difficult to support Bauer and Fenn when they conclude that a comprehensive social audit including these factors "does not appear to respond to the currently perceived needs of the executives."

The second criticism is that the rendering of social performance in monetized balance sheets fails to disclose, and may hide, corporate performance in social programs in which its executives are interested. It is difficult to respond to this criticism since specific line items in the social audit are intended to be devoted explicitly to major social programs which corporations operate, such as air pollution controls or employee training. The assumption is that the social performance of such programs cannot be meaningfully assessed without comparing their social outputs and impacts in quantitative monetized terms with their money cost inputs. This is precisely what the quantitative type of social audit does, and the process audit does not do.

The third criticism is that the social audit is designed for external reporting, or so it is asserted. This is a misunderstanding since the social audit is designed either for internal or external use or both, but its principal emphasis is as an internal aid to corporate social investment decision making. Whether or not it is published in external reports is purely discretionary and is not in any way an intrinsic feature of the quantitative social audit.

The fourth criticism of Bauer and Fenn is that the form of the social audit "is so abstract and complicated" that it allegedly "cannot be understood by most executives." It is our experience, however, after teaching the method to over 200 middle- and upper-management executives in the United States and Japan in several workshops, that the method can be learned and understood in about two days of study—hardly a matter of incomprehensibility. Furthermore, newspaper and magazine articles on the method in both the United States and Japan have demonstrated that journalists with no more than an hour or two of interview time have been able to grasp the concept and its implications and express it clearly in articles. All these factual events would seem to contradict the assertion that the quantitative social audit is so abstract and complicated that few executives can understand it.

Finally, the fifth and really most fundamental criticism of the quantitative social audit by Bauer and Fenn is that it is impossible to reduce social performance to dollar terms and that the attempt itself is "perverse." We believe that Bauer and Fenn are mistaken here in both a positive and a negative sense. They are mistaken in the positive sense in not appreciating that it is essential that social performance be expressed in money terms for any meaningful cost/benefit analysis and investment decisions to be made rationally. We believe that they are mistaken negatively in feeling such a strong antipathy to expressing social benefits and costs in quantitative money terms.

The optimization of any allocation of resources among competing projects or objectives mathematically requires the equalization of marginal utilities among the alternatives. These marginal utilities can only be determined quantitatively and require quantitative measures of cost input and benefit output. Thus any rational decision about alternative financial or social investments having social impacts needs to make use of a quantitative approach in order to optimize the return on such investments. There is simply no way of optimizing investments without quantifying the returns from individual investments.

Concerning skepticism about "the possibility of rendering the social consequences in dollar terms," this possibility has become a fairly well established practice among economists and social systems analysts in the past decade in the United States. There are many examples of cost/benefit analyses in which the social consequences of particular policy options are rendered in quantitative dollar terms and convincingly enough for such analyses often to have become the basis for decision making in the U.S. Department of Defense (using the variation called "cost-effectiveness analysis") and the U.S. Department of Health, Education, and Welfare. There is a large body of evidence of not only the possibility but also the actuality of rendering the social consequences of various policy options in quantitative dollar terms.

A Market Economy in Social Programs?

Another similar criticism has been stated by Daniel H. Gray in a small booklet published in 1973 by the firm of Arthur D. Little, Inc., called *Inventing the Social Audit*. In this pamphlet, Mr. Gray states that "the notion of rendering human and social phenomena into dollar amounts in the way that Linowes [David F. Linowes—see discussion later in this chapter] and Abt are trying to do, and Likert [Dr. Rensis Likert, Director Emeritus of the University of Michigan's Institute of Social Research] has long tried to do, seems to us basically unsound—though all three have helped greatly to heighten the awareness and sensitivity of businessmen with respect to significant 'externalities.' The reason why the effort to apply traditional business accounting to these externalities seems basically unsound to us is that prevailing accounting is married to, and therefore bounded by, the same limits as the prevailing theory of a market economy. Like that theory, it focuses on the world of transactions. But the very problems we want this accounting to cover have become problems precisely because they lie outside the world of transactions."

We believe this criticism is mistaken in asserting that accounting is bound to the operations of a market economy and implying that the social audit fails to focus on the world of transactions. Accounting is not limited to the market economy. Accounting can be applied either in a pure free-enterprise system or in a socialist or communist or fascist economy, or any kind of economy that lacks the features of the market economy. In any case, our approach to social audits does assume the existence of a market economy, presupposing consumer sovereignty and market worth as the basis of all estimates. We see no reason why conventional accounting in our market economy cannot be expanded to cover the market worth and production costs of activities that have social impacts, as well as those that have financial impacts.

Gray's assertion that "profit and loss accounts derive directly from the theory that expressly calls for the exclusion of what it calls 'external diseconomies' and we call 'unrequited social demands'" seems difficult to support. Why cannot profit-and-loss accounts be expanded to include some or all of the known "external diseconomies" and still remain profit-and-loss accounts, reflecting profit and loss to not only the corporation but to society as well?

Gray's proposal for a process audit to assess corporate social performance would appear to be limited to qualitative analysis. As explained previously, I feel that such an approach cannot provide the information required to optimize return on social investment. However, it seems to be a perfectly reasonable way of approaching a basic management review of socially directed corporate activities.

Audits and the "Outside Audience"

Melvin Anshen of the Columbia University Graduate School of Business has made some very useful critical comments on the social audit technique which deserve to be addressed. In his book, *Managing the Socially Responsible Corporation*,* he raises both conceptual and technical questions about the social audit technique.

Concerning the objectives of the social audit he asks,† "Is the primary purpose to enable a corporation to report its socially responsible activities in meaningful terms to an outside audience—its stockholders or the general public? Or is the purpose to provide data for improved internal management decision making and, possibly, to strengthen management's ability to perform? . . . It can be argued that the two objectives lead to quite different quantitative measuring systems. . . . As corporate controllers have long known, the composition and structure of the two sets of information requirements are far from identical and can be standardized within a single system only with some gross adjustments."

This is an important question for the choice of the best means of communicating the results of a social audit. The choice will affect which audiences will be best able to understand the results of a social audit and hence use it in their decision making. Our answer would be that the objective of the social audit encompasses both the reporting of socially responsible activities to an outside audience of stockholders and consumers and the public in general *and* the providing of data for improved internal management decision making as well.

While it is true in the case of financial information that the "composition and structure of the two sets of information requirements are far from identical and can be standardized within a single system only with some gross adjustments," we have somewhat more flexibility available to us in the case of the social audit in satisfying both internal management decision-making and external reporting objectives. One reason for this is that the decision-making information required by internal users is not so different from that required by external audiences—both being concerned with overall company performance from year to year and with comparisons to other companies as well as the major line items of social benefits, assets, costs, and liabilities. In contrast, financial balance sheets and income statements do not break down in line-item format the different detailed sources of revenue and cost, these being aggregated under the general terms of sales, gross revenues, cost of sales, and overhead. In the social audit of my own company, we have in a sense already en-

* New York: Macmillan, 1974.
† Ibid, p. 124.

compassed the detailed revenue and overhead budget breakdowns that are available to most internal managements; these are much more detailed than the overall financial statements.

It might be argued that to maximize the communication of corporate social performance to outside audiences, statements of individual social program activities, their degree of success or failure, and the net social return of each on social and economic investment might be easier to understand. This is indeed sometimes the case. Since year-to-year and intercompany comparisons are of great concern to outside audiences, it seems essential to aggregate the individual line items and their respective benefits in the social balance sheet and income statement.

Professor Anshen also raises the question of socially responsible policies and programs that have no readily defined associated costs (being merely administrative changes) yet deliver significant benefits to customers and the sponsoring company, such as product safety and truthfulness in advertising and promotion. If accounting doctrine strongly requires some costs to offset the benefit created by such apparently costless social actions, then these actions can always be costed out on the basis of a prorated share of the overhead costs of maintaining staff who seek out such administrative changes and the cost of the management time required to evaluate and implement.

A more difficult question is that raised concerning corporate social inactivity: ". . . those policies and programs a company might sponsor but does not, possibly by specific management decisions, often because of management inadvertence or lack of vision." This is related to the economic concept of opportunity costs. Professor Anshen asks whether these opportunity costs should be brought into the company's social audit accounting on the negative side. This question can be answered practically by comparing the company's supply of social services or socially responsible actions to whatever it is that is demanded by the various corporate constituencies. To the extent that something demanded as a legitimate and needed social action is *not* supplied, the opportunity cost of this lack of social responsiveness on the part of the company should be accounted for as a social cost generated by the company.

The social audit of my own company in fact included such an item in its social balance sheet and income statement, listing as a social "opportunity cost" to employees the *absence* of an employee retirement plan. (A company-paid employee retirement plan has since been instituted.) The monetized value of the absence of the retirement plan was based on an estimation of the average industry retirement plan's per capita worth to the individual, multiplied by the number of employees in the company. The decision to include this opportunity cost in the first place was based on a survey of employees to determine the demand for various socially responsible actions by the company and the deficit resulting from discrepancies between such demands and what was actually offered. The employee retirement plan was the only major benefit demanded that created opportunity cost material significant enough to warrant including it as a line item.

Limits to Social Responsibility

A broader issue raised by Professor Anshen is the question of public expectations of corporate behavior and the impression that "there are no defined boundaries for the concept of social responsibility." This would certainly be a great problem if it really did exist. However, we would respectfully suggest to Professor Anshen that the boundaries of the concept of social responsibility are always being defined by corporate constituencies in terms of those social requirements they believe are important. The major social issues which concern the corporate constituencies can be determined annually by survey research, after which all issues that afford material benefits or costs for any of the constituencies can be computed. Those items that are mentioned by the corporate constituencies but which do not involve social benefits or costs amounting to one percent of the aggregate total can be rejected as being nonmaterial.

John C. Burton's objection (quoted by Anshen) that "the measurement of what ought to have been is limited only by the imagination of the proposer of alternatives" is not correct. The measurement of what ought to have been is in fact limited by the materially significant desires of the corporate constituencies. While in a sense this is the limit of the imagination of the proposers, that limit is generally established quite realistically, in our experience. The survey techniques used to determine the social policy preferences of employees and consumers and stockholders can permit open-ended responses in which individual constituents add whatever they think should be added to the "menu." However, we have found surprisingly few such initiatives, offered by only a small minority of those surveyed, and including so many different idiosyncratic suggestions that in the aggregate they did not amount to any significant expansion of the definition of corporate social responsibility. In view of our experience we believe this problem is chiefly theoretical and not really a practical obstacle.

It may be that Professor Anshen is unnecessarily pessimistic when he states that any company attempting to account for its social performance for the benefit of outsiders or for internal administrative use will find it necessary to invent its own measurement techniques. Perhaps he does not consider the widespread and well-developed techniques of social programs impact evaluation as relevant for measurement because this technology has not been transferred to the measurement of corporate social performance, except in a very few cases. Nevertheless, social programs impact evaluations have become quite common and are fairly well developed. Some large and fairly well-known examples are the Coleman-Mood evaluation of equality of educational opportunity and its impact (or lack thereof) on schoolchildren's achievements. Social program impact evaluation research amounts to well over $100 million a year and several thousand social scientists are engaged in this work, primarily for the federal government, at this time. There is a rather large overlap between the skills required for the work on the government programs and those required to measure the social benefits and costs of corporate socially significant actions. A specific example is the environmental impact research now being carried out by the Environmental Protection Agency, by various state and local governments, and by many private research and industrial organizations that prepare environmental impact assessments under federal regulations.

The "Socio-Economic Audit"

In 1973, David F. Linowes, a certified public accountant and management consultant, published a book, *Strategies for Survival,** in which Chapter 11 describes his concept of the corporate social audit. Mr. Linowes' concept of the corporate social audit is both similar to and different from my own.

Mr. Linowes' corporate social audit consists of what he calls the

* New York: AMACOM.

"socio-economic operating statement." It is designed to "tabulate those expenditures made voluntarily with social improvement in mind. Employee welfare, product safety, and environmental protection are typical items that might be included. Expenditures required by law or union contracts do not apply." Right here, there are important differences between the Linowes social audit and the Abt social audit. First, the Abt social audit includes both a social balance sheet and a social income statement, while the Linowes corporate social audit includes only a social income statement. Second, the Linowes socio-economic operating statement includes only those items affecting social impacts that are made *voluntarily,* and explicitly excludes social actions and impacts that may be required by law or union contract.

We disagree with this exclusion of involuntary beneficial social actions from the social income statement since it seems to us irrelevant whether a social benefit was intended or not, in the same way that an unusual profit or an unusual loss is also often unintended but, nevertheless, just as significant. To make such distinctions would open up an impossible mess of intention-testing on the part of every corporate management to determine which social improvements were intended and which were unintended, which were made with a social improvement in mind and which were made for financial objectives, particularly since it is our belief that most social improvements also yield financial benefits and many financial benefits also yield social benefits. This attempt to disaggregate motivation and results would seem to be both theoretically unsound (because it excludes a great many socially useful but involuntary corporate decisions) and thoroughly impractical (because it is not feasible to convincingly and reliably determine the mixture of motivations involved in corporate social actions).

The purposes of the Linowes and Abt social audits are certainly similar, if we assume the purpose given by Linowes is "to report to management and to hold up to public scrutiny what a corporation has done for society on the one hand and what it has failed to do on the other." A modest difference here is that the Abt social audit is intended primarily as an aid to management decision making and need not be held up to public scrutiny to be useful, while apparently it is Mr. Linowes' objective to maximize public visibility and the probable intended pressures for social reform.

Another major difference between the Linowes and Abt social

audits is the degree of subjectivity, which the Linowes approach is more willing to accept than is the Abt approach. Linowes is willing to accept management judgment about the social worth of a particular corporate social action, while the Abt social audit avoids drawing subjective judgments by measuring the actual or imputed monetized market worth of social impacts on the basis of actual consumer preferences and behaviors.

Another similarity between the two approaches is the attempt to measure social impacts in dollars, or what Linowes calls "socio-economic dollars." The definition of the money unit varies drastically, however. In the Linowes approach, the "socio-economic dollar would be a unit of measurement used to identify all socially beneficial expenditures made *voluntarily* by a corporation." Furthermore, these social benefits or costs would be expressed as the input cost or purchase cost rather than the output or impact cost. In the Abt social audit, not only voluntary but involuntary—and indeed all—social impacts are quantified in dollar terms. Regardless of motivation, the monetized market worth of the social benefits or costs created expresses the social impacts on the population concerned rather than the input variables of cost expenditures.

The Linowes corporate social audit in general uses the accounting doctrine that socially significant corporate actions are worth what they cost the corporation, whereas the Abt Associates Inc. approach estimates social worth on the basis of the monetized market worth of the impact on the populations affected. For example, Linowes wants to count as social benefits created by the corporation such items as the salaries expended on personnel engaged in socially productive activities, the contributions to various charities, the costs of setting up facilities for the general good of employees, the public expenditures for safety devices, community improvements, and the costs of landscaping. All these are cost inputs rather than social outputs or impacts.

The weakness of the Linowes socio-economic operating statements in using cost inputs as the basis of quantification of social benefits in its line items is that frequently the input cost may be an extremely poor indicator of the actual social impact. For example, imagine two social programs that cost exactly the same. (They have the same input costs, and on Linowes' socio-economic operating statement would be expressed as having equal socio-economic dollar worth.) Assume, however, that one program is a complete failure and the other is a thorough success. In the Linowes method, these differences in effectiveness—actual impact on the populations affected—would not be stated, while in the Abt social audit, this is precisely the focus.

The great weakness of the Linowes approach of using cost inputs, rather than the impacts of the outputs on the people who are to be affected by social benefits and costs, is that it completely removes the incentive for efficiency of corporate social actions. Furthermore, it places the emphasis on improving corporate social performance on more and more expenditure of cost inputs, rather than on better efficiency and better social impacts or results. Such an approach is not likely to lead to increased efficiency and effectiveness of corporate social actions and may even deter the use of social audits.

Another major difference between the Linowes and Abt corporate social audits is that Linowes offers only a socio-economic operating statement or income statement, while the Abt corporate social audit also includes a social balance sheet. The reason that Abt uses a social balance sheet is that it provides a cumulative description of the overall balance between social assets and social liabilities created by the corporation to date. This is something a socio-economic operating statement or income statement cannot do by itself because it only provides annual incremental data on the social benefits and social costs generated and fails to express completely the cumulative state of corporate social performance.

The practical consequence of the absence of a corporate social balance sheet in the Linowes approach would be essentially to eliminate the net cumulative social benefits or net cumulative social costs created by the corporation in the years leading up to the immediately previous year. This would enable socially irresponsible corporations to select a particular year in which they expected a great deal of public scrutiny and to generate a high degree of net social benefit for that year alone. This would do little to erase the cumulative result of previous years of creating net social costs.

Without a social balance sheet, major social investment in human assets, environmental improvements, and product improvements cannot be justified because they do not create immediate social income. They may look as if they create only modest social benefits, if any, and these can be enormously offset by high initial costs of investment, if only the income or operating statement is used. In other words, the only way one can show the long-term net benefit of major social investments is to express them on a social balance sheet where the discounted present value of future social benefits can be a major offset to the immediate social opportunity cost involved in the particular social investment.

Another similarity between the Linowes and Abt social income statement is that both have line items under the general categories of social impacts on people, on the environment, and on consumers. Minor differences exist in that Linowes, in his socio-economic operating statement, uses the categories "relations with people," "relations with environment," and "relations with product," while the Abt approach is to estimate social benefits and costs to employees, communities, consumers, and the general public.

The Abt social audit is more comprehensive in that it includes social impacts on the community and the general public, while the Linowes socio-economic operating statement does not. This could be an important difference: Many industries that create new knowledge or products and services have social impacts far beyond those on the immediate consumers of the products and services or on the immediate environment. Examples are major scientific and technological and social innovations and inventions created by corporations that advance a particular technology; these can create social benefits far beyond those which have an impact on a corporation's employees, consumers, and local neighbors.

There are currently no known successful or unsuccessful examples of the Linowes approach to the corporate social audit but the concept has received substantial attention in professional accounting publications.

12

The Social
Research Industry

A new industry generally arises at the time when two essential factors come together: a new technology and a new application for it or, if you will, a new method and new purpose. In the 1960s, the new technology—in this case an intellectual technology rather than hardware—was interdisciplinary systems analysis. This was a collection of different disciplines—operations research, systems engineering, economics, political science—applied on a large scale for the first time in the middle sixties to a major national purpose: the solution of new domestic social problems. The national concern with social technology began a little earlier than that in the late fifties and early 1960s when Sputnik spurred our national concern for catching up with the Russians in technical education. This concern was sustained and expanded by the civil rights movement and the "War on Poverty" in the early and middle sixties. Social research at that time began to demonstrate to the general public the many connections between educational and economic inequality and our national inadequacies in employment, housing, health services, crime control, and so forth.

As these connections became more and more apparent and with

the publication of Michael Harrington's book about poverty * and the publication of the Coleman Report † in 1966 relating lagging educational achievements of poor black children to segregation, there was an across-the-board national campaign launched against poverty and inequality in general. Our primary concern in the early 1960s was with the poor, mainly the black poor.

But then a curious thing began to happen. Toward the end of the last decade and particularly the first part of the current one, the socioeconomic front widened to include the previously solicitous but largely uninvolved middle classes. Drugs, crime, youth movements and movements for the rights of women and the aged, consumer rebellions, increasing shortages of materials and energy—all these began to affect very directly the nonpoor and the nonblack, giving us many new social problems. There was also the welfare crisis, to the point where almost 1 million people in New York City were on welfare and the fiscal survival of large urban governments was being significantly threatened by the fact that expenditures continually exceeded revenues. The threat of a default on its financial obligations by the city of New York was only the first of what are likely to be many such crises. So a much wider concern has now developed.

The scope and the pace of these problems have obviously required more than the conventional responses on the part of our established government institutions and our private charities, which until the past two decades have had almost total responsibility for dealing with such problems. In our general recognition of a national crisis in the 1960s, and our mobilization to meet it, which we named the War on Poverty, new agencies sprang up in the federal government—the Office of Economic Opportunity, the Environmental Protection Agency, the National Institute of Education, and others—to deal with the new problems. The established think tanks such as Rand, Mitre, SRI, IDA, and RAC,‡ previously devoted almost exclusively to military and international conflict problems, began to spin off functional units, both internally and externally, to focus on domestic social problems. Most of them began by focusing

* *The Other America: Poverty in the United States* (New York: Macmillan, 1962).

† *Equality of Educational Opportunity* (Washington, D.C.: U.S. Government Printing Office, 1966).

‡ Rand is the Rand Corporation, Santa Monica, California; Mitre is the MIT Research and Engineering Corporation, Bedford, Massachusetts; SRI is the Stanford Research Institute of Palo Alto, California; IDA is the Institute of Defense Analysis, Washington, D.C.; RAC was the Research Analysis Corporation, McLean, Virginia.

on crime and education since they believed these had the most in common with military technology and organization.

Again, in the middle 1960s, as the War on Poverty and the war in Asia became the two most important national issues, some of the experts and technical staffs of the organizations that had been addressing the military problems began to leave those areas of activity and go to work on social problems, some of them out of idealism, some out of a keen sense of the coming market, some out of boredom with the same old military security problems and the desire to apply their bag of intellectual tricks to meet new challenges. Herman Kahn left Rand to found the Hudson Institute. Olaf Helmer and Ted Gordon left Rand to found the Futures Group. Oskar Morgenstern of Princeton University started Mathematica. I left Raytheon about that time to start Abt Associates. Most of us knew each other at least slightly, and we shared a background of interdisciplinary research applied mainly to military security problems: a combination of operations research, systems engineering, economics, and political science—heavily quantitative and up to now hardware-oriented. We brought some of our own flavors to our work. For example, Kahn had been a physicist, so he turned his attention in part to the peacetime application of nuclear energy. I had worked on computer simulations of international conflict and then applied much of this approach to educational systems analysis and instructional games.

So the societal stage was set and here were some new actors to fill the new roles, educated by dealing with questions of military security and bringing with them the new problem-solving technology that had had its origin in weapon systems enginering and military operations research in World War II and to some extent (even in World War I) in a combination of applied mathematics with systems engineering.

There were also a few other strands in this historical development. One of the most important was educational research, in which the outstanding leader is the Educational Testing Service, a nonprofit organization that is probably the world's largest educational testing group. It produces the annual standard achievement tests and the college board examinations. There are also the American Institutes of Research and some others. The development of large educational research institutions was partly motivated by the same drive for educational superiority that was forcefully articulated by Admiral Rickover following Sputnik. It was also in part a result of there being some new data processing technology available, along with new survey research and statistical methods that had been developed in the thirties, primarily through opinion research, and also the availability of computers to process large amounts of data economically. The educational research labs contributed heavily in learning psychology and provided highly trained behavioral scientists schooled in quantitative methods for this gathering movement of problem solvers.

Another group comprised the social services professionals: social workers, urban planners, city government types. These were usually untrained (or undertrained) in quantitative methods, but they were intimately aware of the social problems of the cities—the actual conditions under which the poor and other populations lived and with which the new analytical methods were trying to cope. These professionals added a sense of realism and motivation and urgency and also some degree of race and sex integration since— unlike the technology elite—they were not predominantly white and male and middle-class.

By now, in the middle 1970s, these groups are working, collectively, with about half a billion dollars of government research funds each year, most of it being distributed through competitive bidding, but a small percentage through sole-source procurements. Most of the money comes from federal sources: the Department of Health, Education, and Welfare, the Department of Housing and Urban Development, the departments of Labor, Transportation, and Interior, and the Office of Management and Budget. (Some of the money comes from state and municipal governments, but most of it is federal, either directly or indirectly.) Social research has gotten to be a significant industry.

What the Industry Does

This industry is essentially one of providing social research services to major clients in the form of planning, evaluation, analysis, technical assistance, training, and lately some degree of operations management. In the first few years of the industry, the output was almost entirely paper, and that was a source of great frustration to many of us who wanted to have a little more impact than the production of reports. Many of the reports weren't read; the few which were read were probably not fully understood, and very, very few of the findings were actually implemented. And so again we were spurred to look for opportunities where we could combine the research we were doing with some opportunity to implement the findings and the results.

The first of these opportunities came in the poverty program in the early and middle 1960s with the Job Corps centers, the community action agencies, and other experimental—usually quasi-educational—programs, which were opened up to industry bidding after the universities had tried and failed rather miserably in their administration. Job Corps initially was all university-managed, and it had almost completely fallen apart when the Office of Economic Opportunity decided to spin it off to industry contractors. Industry did somewhat better.

Since then other major social experiments have been started, and we hope some are more successful. One of the large ones, HUD's Housing Allowance Demand Experiment, provides allowances to poor people and replaces the program of subsidized low-income housing (which was very expensive but not very responsive to poor people's needs) with direct income supplements to poor people to let them pick their own housing. This cuts out the administrative middlemen, saves tax money, and is more responsive to people's needs and preferences. Experiments are also going on with health maintenance organizations and income maintenance.

These social experiments are actually being operated by the social services and social research industry, under contract to the federal government. In other words, this is the beginning of a new service industry that is not only doing research and development for the programs and evaluating them, but also handling their planning, design, and operation. For example, the Housing Allowance Demand Experiment has enrolled 3,600 housing allowance program participants; their applications are being processed; their monthly checks are being mailed; and the contracting firm (Abt Associates Inc.) is essentially operating the program just like a Social Security Agency, under government contract.

The country is resorting to such social experiments as these rather than abstract analyses and evaluations, first of all, because they seem to be more economical, and secondly, because we can't really get very conclusive results from theoretical analyses alone. Probably over $100 million was spent on evaluations of the various Department of Labor manpower and employment training programs through the 1960s and, as far as I know, neither the Department of Labor nor anyone else knows how to solve the problems any better now than before. If the same amount of money had been spent in some experimental demonstration programs to increase job opportunities and employment, we might have learned more and, at a minimum, we would have done some immediate good.

So there's been a gradual shift in the disbursement of federal funds in the past few years to a smaller percentage of middle-class intellectuals and to a larger percentage of working and nonworking poor, who are supposed to be the ultimate object of these funds in any case. And I think that's a healthy development. It will force improved methods of analysis and make the methods more competitive.

The Skills of Social Science

The principal resources or assets of the social services and social research industry are the people in it. It is a labor-intensive industry. You don't need much capital. You don't have to buy anything, not even a facility. You can rent that. All you have to do is get some people to work on the problems and risk some of their time. However, the difficulty of marketing such services and managing them effectively is reflected in part by the still relatively small number of profit-making enterprises in the new industry.

There's been enormous growth in the availability of staff for the new industry, and I think it might be of some surprise that in the 1970 census, we find that the social scientists, economists, political scientists, psychologists, sociologists, urban and regional planners, and so forth, expanded as a professional population at the unprecedented rate of 163 percent in the previous decade, the highest rate of expansion of any major occupational group. This compares very impressively with the 20 percent increase for physical scientists and even the 93 percent increase for the life scientists. It's also about three times the average 55 percent increase over the decade in all professional and technical workers. According to the census data, more social scientists (58 percent) possess graduate degrees than either the life scientists (47 percent) or the physical scientists (43 percent). Another surprise is that with average annual earnings of about

$16,000 per year for all three professional scientific groups—the social, physical, and life scientists, the highest average income level was that of the economists (a major segment of the social scientists), with nearly $18,000 per year (1970 data).

The Outlook for the Industry

What is the outlook for the next decade? Is this social research and services industry a wave of the future or just a ripple? I'm probably biased since I'm deeply immersed in the industry, but I do believe that social research and services are not going to go away in the foreseeable future. We have too many unresolved social problems, too many rising expectations, too strong a feeling that everyone should share the good life (efficiently communicated by our advanced telecommunications media), and too many resource shortages and inequities of distribution to make people satisfied with what they have—at least for quite a while. Social research and social services activities are principally concerned with redressing actual and perceived deficits in the distribution of resources and developing more viable organizational means for sharing the scarce resources that we have; these activities are not likely to diminish in the foreseeable future.

Even though these activities continue to grow, there's still a question whether the social research and services industry of the future will serve mainly the private sector or the government or perhaps function as part of the government. It is still difficult to combine the values and the procedures of conventional business practice with the values and procedures of social research. Conflicts sometimes exist between business and the academic and purist points of view. Some also think there's a discrepancy between profitability and social service within the social research and services industry itself. I don't happen to believe that discrepancy actually exists but I know many of our younger and less experienced staff members think that if a company is making a profit somebody must be getting ripped off. That attitude isn't likely to stimulate or encourage the additional development of private enterprise in the social research and services industry. However, I think that as the potential harmony between profitable operations and socially constructive activities becomes better understood by social scientists working in these areas, some of the opposition—particularly youthful opposition—to profitable operations in social research and services will diminish, and I've noticed that it already has in the past two or three years.

I think that the major future growth in the industry will be not only in the United States, but also in Europe and Japan. In the area of social problems, and social research responding to social problems, they are about a decade behind the United States.

As labor shortages have caused northern European nations to import laborers from the southern European countries, and as the cultural conflicts between the natives and the non-natives have been exacerbated, I think a great many social problems have arisen. As resource shortages have increased the intensity of dealings between labor and management groups, these have been another source of problems. So has the issue of who is responsible for paying for environmental pollution.

In Japan, the major issues have been environmental pollution and resource shortages and their impact on social values, stability of prices, and availability of goods. In both Europe and Japan, social scientists have not been available so far to provide the staff for problem-solving activities. Most of these skills are still imported from the United States. Shortages in social science skills constitute major market opportunities for the social research and services industry. Social research services haven't been in heavy demand before now because there hasn't been a recognized need, but I think that's rapidly changing.

Serving Private Industry

This discussion has mentioned government support of the social research and services industry. One might ask whether industrial corporations come to us for help in looking at societal research problems. And if so, what kinds of examples are they interested in?

Applied social research companies do provide such services to corporations in the form of environmental impact analyses, affirmative action planning, employee benefit analyses, and what we put under the general rubric of social audits or corporate social performance evaluation.

Interestingly enough, most of the social research professionals, particularly economists, are employed by private industry. However, the industry market for social services research companies, at this writing, is not as large as the government market for several reasons.

One reason is the cultural gap. I think the social scientists and social services professionals are still regarded by many hardheaded businessmen as naive, idealistic, and more concerned with achieving social reform in accordance with their allegedly liberal ideologies than in solving problems. I think that's partly a misunderstanding, although a very correct understanding of a limited percentage of the professionals in the field. In Europe—for example, in France—a sociologist is often assumed to be a socialist, and leaders of industry sometimes regard sociology as an attempt to redistribute the wealth. There is something of a similar point of view in Japan.

Another cultural gap is the lack of understanding on the part of managers trained in engineering or law or the physical sciences or business of what social scientists have progressed to. Many assume that the social sciences are strictly judgmental and qualitative and have no scientific validity. They're completely innocent of the statistical and highly quantitative methods that have been developed and are now in common use in social research. That's another cultural lag that has to be made up through practice and communication.

And finally, there's the misperception on the part of many businessmen that social reforms are usually paid for out of profits and somehow will reduce the profitability of the enterprise, although the arguments are compelling that even mid-term—and certainly long-term—profitability of enterprises is highly dependent on effective social arrangements. One of the motivations of our developing corporate social responsibility measurements for the social audit is to demonstrate to business managers that progressive social policies are in fact generally financially profitable as well as socially profitable.

Data Bases for Social Auditing

The data bases available for social auditing are numerous and impressive. Consider some examples. Concerning equality of employment opportunity, there are all the data required by federal regulation in the affirmative action plans required of all government contractors. Concerning environment, there are all the impact analyses of the Environmental Protection Agency and the Corps of Engineers and the data collected by environmental groups such as the

Sierra Club and the Friends of the Earth. Concerning employee benefits, there are all the actuarial and other data collected by insurance companies and unions. Concerning consumer and employee preferences and values, there are all the tools of survey research and the data collected by market researchers.

In addition to all the present resources of theory, practice, information, and data available for social auditing, substantial research is continuing. Some of the government agencies supporting this research are the National Science Foundation, the Office of Technology Assessment, the Environmental Protection Agency in its environmental impact research, and the U.S. Office of Education in its long-term educational impact analyses. The General Accounting Office is also looking into social auditing.

Among private research institutions developing better methods of social auditing and its components are the Public Affairs Council, the University of Michigan Institute for Social Research, the Council on Economic Priorities, the Russell Sage Foundation, Harvard Business School, Yale Law School, Abt Associates Inc., and Arthur D. Little, Inc.

Next Steps

Given this state of the art of social audits, what can be done now? For all organizations, public and private, concerned in some way with social responsibilities, whether self-imposed or mandated by the public, at least the following five actions seem immediately feasible and desirable:

1. Organizations can and should do their own social audits, on a regular annual basis, at the most comprehensive and detailed level afforded by the organization's intellectual and financial resources.

Plenty of help is available if resources internal to the organization do not suffice. Technical assistance is available from university business schools and economics departments and research firms such as Abt Associates Inc. and Arthur D. Little, Inc.

2. The organization's social audit should be directly related to management decision making, aiding in balancing the interests of the stockholders (or voters), employees, customers, community, and general public. Thus not only the corporate charities and employee benefits programs should be included but also personnel, research and development, production, marketing, and finance.

Figure 12. Antecedents of social audits.

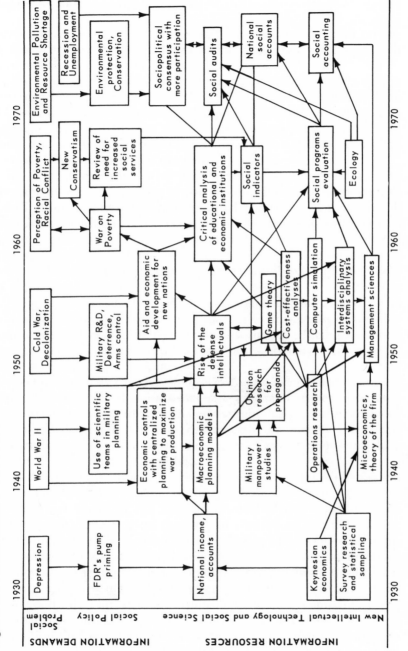

Figure 13. Genealogy of social audits: the four "grandparent" disciplines.

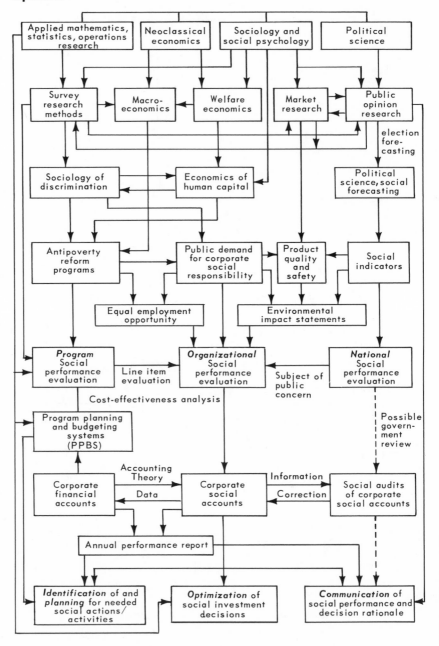

3. The social audit should be conducted as consistently as possible from year to year. As new, more comprehensive, sensitive, and precise measures of social impact are added—and they should be added as they become available—the previously used measures should be continued at least long enough for year-to-year comparisons.

4. Research and development directed toward refining the organization's social audit should be carried out continuously and cooperation should be offered to efforts to standardize the audits.

5. Management should use social audits in seeking a high positive social and economic impact for its organization while keeping a low profile and reporting results modestly. It would generally seem wise to claim a little less social benefit for one's organization than one believes one deserves, to reduce the danger of the social audit being denigrated as merely a more sophisticated public relations device.

Despite the still primitive state of the art of social auditing, we remain confident that it is an art critical to the socially responsible management of both public and private organizations and that it will advance rapidly to meet this need.

Figures 12 and 13 list graphically some of the social and scientific antecedents of social audits.

13

Problems and Prospects

AT this stage of development of the social audit, the major problems have to do with its practical implementation. While controversies continue over some of the theoretical foundations, such controversies also exist in the field of accounting practice but have failed to inhibit the practical application of accounting; therefore these theoretical controversies are not really a limiting factor in application.

The practical problem of implementation is partly one of the unconventionality of the point of view of the social audit. This requires a degree of reorientation and retraining of managers and executives. Similar inhibiting factors apply to any innovation that is regarded as having a high entry cost; managers generally prefer to have someone else break the path first.

Actually, there are two entirely different sets of problems in implementing social audits. The first set pertains to the internal implementation of corporate social audits for management decision-making purposes, and the second set arises from the use of social audits as public expressions of the measurement of corporate social performance in annual reports. The first problem is one of introducing a new type of management information system and training people to use it, while the second problem is an intercompany and publicly perceived validity problem.

There is no risk to managers from bad publicity or unfavorable public comment from the internal application of social audits as an aid to social investment decisions. Nevertheless, there is widespread reluctance to actually apply the method to management decisions. Some of the reasons for this reluctance include a simple cultural lag: Management is reluctant to change its style of decision making regarding social investments from one that is based primarily on personal judgment and tradition to one that is based on social survey data and economics and is open to analysis.

Although the social audit does not require managers to reject traditional values—it merely offers a way of estimating the benefits and costs of such choices—it can be perceived by them as threatening a dehumanizing "mechanization" of their decisions. This is a misunderstanding resulting from a lack of experience with the meaning and applications of social audits. It can be corrected through management education, training, and successful demonstrations of the applications of social audits to improve the quality of work and life.

The second set of problems associated with the social audits is related to the publication of social audits as part of corporate annual reports. Here the difficulty is one of legitimizing social accounts and social audits to match the established legitimacy of financial accounts and the financial audits of such accounts. Annual reports for public corporations are required by law in most nations. Corporations are generally required to publish financial audits of financial accounts, generally in the form of a financial balance sheet, an income statement, and an application of funds statement, plus an auditor's opinion to the effect that these financial data have been presented fairly, accurately, and on a basis consistent with generally accepted accounting principles. In the case of the social balance sheet and income statement, or indeed any other kind of corporate social performance statement, financial auditors have thus far been reluctant to express an opinion concerning the fairness, accuracy, and overall validity of such statements.

This reluctance on the part of the accounting profession to audit and express an opinion on the results of the audit of social performance data, as well as financial performance data, imposes a problem of credibility concerning such social performance statements. In addition, where such social performance statements are integrated with financial performance statements, auditors may be reluctant to express their conventional "clean" opinion on the validity of the financial statements because they are mixed together with social performance statements, which the auditors cannot review with the use of current and generally accepted accounting principles.

A possibly representative situation was experienced by a company which sought to integrate its social and financial audits in its annual report, but was told by the auditors that they could not provide their usual favorable opinion of the fairness, accuracy, and general consistency of the financial statements if these financial statements were mixed together with the social performance statements. This left the company with the dilemma of either not publishing its social performance statement at all, or publishing integrated social and financial statements and forgoing a statement of the auditor's good opinion, or of publishing the financial and social performance statement separately at some additional printing cost. The penalty for eliminating the social statement is of course the cost of not presenting social performance measurement data that have already been invested in, that is, a waste of resources. The cost of publishing the integrated social and financial statements and losing the good opinion of the financial auditors might be a major loss of investor confidence in the accuracy and validity of the financial statements, with such possible consequences as increased cost of capital and protests by stockholders. The cost of presenting the financial and social statements separately is that the two are not integrated in a way that is understandable; there would also, of course, be the additional printing cost involved in printing two performance statements rather than one. None of these solutions is ideal.

Some Solutions

The prospective solutions to the first major problem of implementation, internal management support, is probably related to the second problem, external acceptability. When corporate social performance statements are required either by law or by public opinion, or at least by investor opinion, it seems probable that they will, in fact, be implemented. There is likely to be a back-and-forth process: pioneering companies instituting social audits, and business philosophers, reformers, and critics demanding corporate social performance reports. Gradually the few companies that do publish social audits will be imitated by other companies, and the critics who demand such reports expanding in numbers as the public becomes informed about the feasibility and practical utility of corporate social performance reports.

The solution to the inhibitions on the part of operating management is, first, *top-management support* for the measurement of corporate social performance and the more efficient investment of social resources and, second, substantial *upper- and middle-management training* in the use of social audits to achieve these top-management objectives. A substantial part of the social audit training, if successful, will have to be devoted just to changing uninformed attitudes on the part of middle management about the feasibility of measuring the social impacts of the corporation in quantitative dollar terms, thus providing a rational basis for investment and other social policy decisions. At the same time, top management will have to make social performance a component of its overall rating of company units and their managers and back this up with the usual systems of incentives and controls to convince middle management that it is really serious about achieving improved social performance and will use quantitative methods for measuring such performance and improving it.

Concerning the external validity problem, we will have to wait until either the financial accounting firms learn enough about social accounting to develop some general procedures for auditing corporate social performance or until a sufficient number of social evaluation and social auditing organizations develop and are accepted by business managements as a means of establishing, verifying, and validating corporate social accounts by social audits. It seems most probable that a combination of the two will occur. Currently in the United States several major accounting firms are beginning to advertise their capability for conducting corporate social performance evaluations and audits, while at the same time some major companies have engaged private research firms to aid them in establishing social accounts and conducting social audits.

Social Audits Required by Law?

Prospects for the legal implementation of social audits vary from country to country, depending primarily on public opinion and on government pressures for improved corporate social performance, balanced by the initiative that private industry takes to maintain its freedom of action and to preempt such public concerns.

In the United States, legal implementation of social audits has proceeded in piecemeal fashion, with current legal requirements being limited primarily to equal employment opportunity, occupational health and safety, environmental impact, and consumer product safety. It is currently a legal requirement for the American corporation to file annual equal employment opportunity reports that state its current practice in terms of minority and female employment and, if this is inequitable, what steps are being taken to improve equality of job opportunity. The requirements are for quantitative, numerical measures of both the current status and trends (changes) in that status, although the monetized social worth of these is not yet required to be stated.

Environmental impact statements are required by the federal government for major facilities. The legal requirement is for a qualitative audit, with some estimated impacts quantified, but usually in terms of variables which are incommensurable. Again there is no requirement for a statement of the monetized market worth of social costs and benefits resulting from corporate actions.

The prospect for legal implementation of more comprehensive social audits depends not only on public and government opinion but also on the degree to which government officials and legislators regard the idea with favor. In the United States, a significant number of highly influential congressmen and senators have actively supported the concept and have introduced legislation in support of it. While serving as a Senator of Minnesota, for example, Vice President Walter Mondale introduced a bill that would require the government to create and publish an annual national social performance report and would also require large organizational units to publish their social performance information annually. Early in 1970, Congressman Thomas P. O'Neill, Jr., at that time the Democratic majority leader of the House of Representatives, introduced the Abt social audit concept into the *Congressional Record* with a statement in its support.

These favorable indications from influential American legislators concerning legal implementation of social audit legislation should not be taken to mean that legal implementation is likely to be comprehensive in the very near future—say before 1980. First of all, the Equal Employment Opportunity legislation, environmental impact legislation, and consumer product safety legislation have already responded to the most immediate public and reformist demands for improved corporate social responsibility and social performance measurement. Secondly, the pressure for comprehensive social accounts and social audits has also been somewhat distracted or deferred by the current economic recession, the energy crisis, and industrial shortages. In such times as these, public opinion tends to favor making whatever changes are needed to increase production and employment.

On the other hand, it can be argued that energy and other resource shortages will hasten the prospects for legal implementation of social audits: Government authorities may need to find a way to justify to public opinion, consumer groups, and industry reformers the essential public worth of building additional facilities (such as nuclear power plants to minimize oil imports) and even of occasional temporary relaxation of environmental pollution controls. As energy shortage forces U.S. power companies to use higher-pollutant fuels such as coal, the conflict between industries concerned with growth and prices on the one hand and environmentalist and community groups on the other must and will become sharper. In the inevitable rush of new plant construction and conversion to different sources of energy, the government may feel it necessary to intervene with legislation requiring companies to explain how their overall social performance will be increased by such actions. Corporations supplying essential public products and services such as electric power, steel, and oil may then be more inclined—and might indeed be legally required—to publish corporate social performance statements employing social accounts and social audits, as a way of demonstrating to the public that the actions taken were substantially in the public interest and that alternative actions would have been less effective in supporting the public interest.

The prospects for legal implementation of corporate social accounts and social audits will also be influenced by the advances in the techniques of social accounting and social auditing and the effectiveness with which such advances and the feasibility of their implementation are communicated to both business and government leaders. In the past, the cries for corporate social responsibility from various reformers have met a mixed response from industry and government leaders. The demands for corporate social performance were not always treated with great seriousness or respect. To the ex-

tent that social accounting and social audits remain relatively un-
known to many businessmen and government officials and to the extent that social audits become mistakenly associated with demands
for social reform that are uninformed by the realities of business
practice, to that extent the legal implementation of social audits will
not be as rapid as it might otherwise be. On the other hand, if the
developers and practitioners of social accounting and social audits
not only grow as a group in size and effectiveness, but also succeed
in presenting their ideas more clearly and in convincing business
managements, government officials, and the general public that they
are offering a much improved method for achieving higher overall
social efficiency, to that extent the prospects for legal implementation of social accounts and social audits will be accelerated.

How Shall We Allocate Our Social Evaluation Research?

Some ecological chains and social impact chains are very long
and have very remote effects. How do we know which to investigate
and how much effort to allocate to their investigation? Should we
stop at primary, secondary, tertiary, or quaternary effects? Should
we evaluate only primary effects for some types of social impacts,
while going to secondary and tertiary effects for others? Is this to be
decided by some common social measure of total effect that we wish
to maximize? If one of the most important results of social cost/bene-
fit analysis has been gradually and increasingly to influence project
generation by requiring new social programs to be more sophisticated in their development and estimation of impacts, how shall we
allocate such analyses?

Is the return on research investment concerning evaluation of
social impacts greatest at the institutional level, the government
level, or the corporate enterprise level? At the regional level, the sectorial level, or the national level? (For example, do we get more
policy-useful social impact data from social audits of corporations
and communities, or from social indicators of national social trends,
or from some mix of the two?) Obviously in answering this one can
point out that there is more detailed information for the social impact evaluation of the smaller socioeconomic unit, but there is also
greater danger of distortion because the sample is drawn selectively
rather than at random and probably overrepresents socially benevo-

lent and socially malevolent organizations, while these effects are canceled out at the national level of aggregation.

In allocating the efforts in evaluation research, categories of various kinds can be used. At one end of the scale, the allocations can be completely random. At the other, they can be highly selective, sometimes well chosen for optimization of goals, sometimes inappropriately biased. Lacking a particular rationale, it would seem that a uniform application of evaluation research resources to government social policies and programs would be most appropriate, provided that sufficient resources are available for a competent evaluation of all programs. If such resources are not available—and there is reason to believe that we lack them, not so much in money as in human skills and in data—the next best strategy would appear to be a completely randomized application of resources in evaluation research.

Now, however, the programs to which evaluation research resources tend to be applied are those that are most current and salient politically (although not necessarily most important politically in the long run), those that are under the heaviest political attack, those that are most critical to the survival of the programs of a particular government or other institution, and those that tend to demonstrate most effectively the strengths and capabilities of a particular discipline or intellectual resource.

Another consideration in the allocation of research evaluating social programs is the optimum level of application: national, regional, or local, institutional or programmatic. For example, at the national level, school dropout data are as good as unrelated to race, but on a local school district basis the relationship between dropout rate and race is very high. Thus, at a national level of evaluation, one would tend to miss a major causal factor that could be easily identified at a local level. Similarly, unemployment statistics on a national basis provide only macroeconomic clues—no microeconomic, socioeconomic, or regional clues—as to how unemployment can be reduced; while at a microeconomic, local, or institutional level, the factors often completely dominate the macroeconomic considerations, such as the level of government spending or monetary policy.

Criteria for Allocation

Offered below are some general criteria for selection of the type and level of social impact evaluation to measure the social performance of a program or organization. Different types and levels of social programs will require different evaluation designs, but the criteria given below are believed to be relevant to all of them.

1. Resources should be allocated to both formative and summative evaluations.* If only formative evaluations are employed, there will not be available an undistorted assessment of the total benefits and costs of a program on the basis of which overall program selection can be made. If only summative evaluations are employed, much corrective information which might have been fed back to the program to help realize its full potential will not be available until it is too late to be useful.

The best mix of formative and summative evaluations depends on the uses which decision makers intend for the evaluation. If the decision aid sought concerns the choice of overall programs and there is time to make such a choice after summative evaluations of alternative programs, then most of the effort should be allocated to summative evaluations, but with enough formative evaluation distributed among competing projects to ensure that each realizes its potential and is unhampered by unevenly distributed externalities.

If the decision aid sought concerns a choice of intraprogram instrumentalities, and these choices can be most effectively made without waiting for a summative evaluation, then the bulk of the evaluation effort should be allocated to formative evaluation.

Consider an example at both the national and the local organizational level. At the national level, what would be the best mix of evaluations for a health insurance program? Assume that the major policy variables are costs, quality of service to patients, and acceptability to physicians. Here the evaluation mix would emphasize summative evaluation of experimental pilot plant alternatives because the alternative costs and other factors must be reliably and precisely determined or very costly policy mistakes can ensue.

Now consider the same program at the community or organization level. Here there is neither the time nor the resources to experiment with alternatives, and the major question for decision makers is not so much the "optimizing" one ("Which program is best?") as the "satisficing" one ("Is the program good enough to do the job, and if not, what internal aspects of it must be changed to make it good enough?"). Thus in the local application of the same social program,

* Formative evaluations accompany a project with constructive criticism as it proceeds. Summative evaluations consider the *results* of a program and (in order to minimize risks of contamination) have very little contact with its operations.

emphasis on formative evaluation may be more relevant to decision needs.

2. Evaluations of *impact* as well as *output* should be made. The two are often confused. Output evaluations compare program outputs to inputs, yielding measures of internal *process efficiency*. Impact evaluations compare impacts to goals for overall *program efficiency*. "Process efficiency" is an intervening variable on the way to "program efficiency" and is included in it.

The need for the distinction may be illustrated by an example. A health program may have high *process* efficiency if the number of patient-hours per dollar is comparatively high. However, if the goal of the program is better health but the patient-hours are devoted to the wrong health problems, the success of the *program* in achieving its goals will not be adequate, and its efficiency will be low. Distinguishing the goal makes it possible to correct the problem by attending to the error of application rather than wasting time correcting an inefficient subprocess.

Similarly, if the program is directed to the right problem but is not being operated efficiently, the two measurements make it possible to correct the process rather than offering the misleading result that the entire program direction is mistaken.

3. *Process* evaluation should be included as well as output and impact evaluations. Done correctly, these are merely subordinate output evaluations of subprograms; where no other means are available they can simply be observations of critical subprocesses made by participants. Without such process evaluation, subprocesses intervening between program inputs and outputs may damage or distort the overall results without being identified for correction.

Such process evaluation is a part of most formative evaluations, but unfortunately it is frequently absent in retrospective summative evaluations. Without it, because of the confusion of many interacting effects, the sometimes inconclusive findings of summative evaluations cannot be broken down to yield information which is useful in modifying programs.

4. Evaluation efforts should be allocated in proportion to the *estimated criticality of the findings*. This means evaluating first, and with the most resources, those programs having the highest costs and largest or most essential benefits. Since estimates of costs and benefits made prior to evaluation are sometimes wide of the mark, this process should be an iterative one, with a thin layer of "quick and

dirty" evaluations first, followed by more concentrated efforts based on estimates of criticality developed from the first cycle of evaluations. In a sense, this amounts to nothing more complicated than a general reconnaissance for the best evaluation target, followed by a detailed assessment of the evaluation targets thus identified.

5. *Stratified random selection of evaluation targets* might be tried when estimates of program criticality cannot be made because of urgency or lack of information, and there are insufficient evaluation resources to provide a minimum competency assessment of all programs. The stratification can be by type of program goal, or by type of approach, or by whatever dimension seems most critical for social policy choice.

Random selection will provide some protection against biased selection of programs for evaluation on either a defensive or a hostile basis. Since not all programs—and perhaps not all types of programs—will be evaluated, the best allocation of resources among programs will not be possible on this basis. What will be possible is the establishment of a general minimum level of program quality, effectiveness, or efficiency, within the limits of the statistical confidence afforded by the sample size and the variance in the program characteristics which are of interest.

6. Since without agreement on program criticality, evaluation research effort allocation is likely to continue to be a somewhat arbitrary, politically biased, scattered, and uncertain effort, steps should be taken to ensure a *minimum of program impact evaluation of all social actions programs.* Though such a policy reduces the average amount of resources available for any particular evaluation effort, a minimum level of self-evaluation of all programs, externally corroborated, can be enforced by requiring perhaps 5 percent of the budget of all new social impact programs to be devoted to external and internal formative and summative evaluation. (Standardization of such impact evaluation processes and procedures would also improve their efficiency.)

7. There should be *two levels of decision making in the allocation of evaluation research.* Impact evaluation research should not be done by the organizations responsible for implementing the programs. If it is, the greatest effort is then likely to be allocated to those programs that most need to be defended, and not necessarily to the most productive or strategically critical programs. A higher agency con-

cerned with the overall efficiency of the government, such as the OMB or the GAO, needs its own independent evaluation research budget so that it may allocate impact evaluation research activities on the basis of critical choices at the national policy level, independent of the agencies responsible for the development and execution of particular programs.

Within an agency or an enterprise, impact research should be shared by the policy level and the implementation level to assure results relevant both to choice of program and to alternatives in the implementation of programs.

The Coming Quantification of Social Impacts: Why, Where, When, and How?

There are different routes up the mountain of quantification:

GOAL	APPROACH
Corporate social responsibility	Social accountability
Optimized resource allocation	Social production functions
Response to social needs	Market surveys of perceived worths

Why quantify? Why will managements quantify social impacts sooner or later? Because without quantification there is no basis for accurate comparisons among programs, years of performance, or organizations. Without quantification managers and investors and voters and employees cannot make well-informed decisions. Without quantification it is difficult to prevent organizations from making misleading claims, listing many small virtues to obscure enormous vices. Without quantification the defense of corporations against charges of not contributing to society can be unpersuasive. Without quantification the assertions of social reformers that some enterprises are consuming more public goods than they are producing may go unproved. Without quantification there will be no data base to stimulate and support research—and without research, progress is slow.

Where should quantification of social impacts begin? Wherever it seems urgent and feasible—that is, where major decisions are being urged by corporate constituencies, and where enough data already exist to provide some basis for measurement.

When should quantification begin? As soon as the need for it is understood well enough to elicit the necessary support. In most organizations, this will be when external pressures require a scientific basis for socially significant decisions rather than simple judgment.

How should social impacts be quantified? By expressing them in terms of their market worth, perceived or imputed, as measured by opinion surveys or direct observation.

Appendix A

Forced Compliance with Public Standards

AMERICAN TELEPHONE & TELEGRAPH CO., New York, New York, is a holding company in the communications field, with annual sales of nearly $24 billion.

In January 1973, AT&T agreed to pay "massive wage boosts for women and minorities in settling U.S. job bias case." This settlement gave $45 million to nonmanagement employees as compensation.

In May 1974, AT&T agreed to pay an additional $30 million to managerial employees to settle charges of sex discrimination. This settlement consisted of $7 million to be paid to 7,000 employees, plus an adjustment of wages by $23 million during the next year to compensate for pay discrimination.

SOURCE: *The Wall Street Journal,* January 19, 1973, and May 17, 1974.

CARBORUNDUM COMPANY of Niagara Falls, New York, manufactures machinery, air and water pollution control equipment, electronic resistors, crystal, and china, with annual sales of $349 million.

In May 1974, Carborundum announced that it settled a two-year sex-discrimination suit out of court for $43,000.

SOURCE: *The Wall Street Journal,* May 28, 1974.

DETROIT EDISON CO. of Detroit, Michigan, is an electric utility with annual sales of $599 million.

In September 1973, the utility was fined $1,500, settling three cases brought by the U.S. Coast Guard for water pollution due to accidental oil spills.

One month later, a federal court ordered Detroit Edison to pay $4 million as punitive damages, compensating for alleged loss of wages by black employees who were denied promotion, black applicants who were denied employment, and blacks who were deterred from seeking employment because of Detroit Edison's "reputation in the black community."

Detroit Edison is appealing the case.

SOURCE: 1973 annual report.

B. F. GOODRICH CO. of Akron, Ohio, is a manufacturer of natural and synthetic rubber, chemicals, and plastics and a retailer of tires. Its annual sales are over $1.5 billion.

B. F. Goodrich agreed in June 1974 to add 260 women to its management ranks by 1979. The agreement was a result of charges of sex bias brought by a former trainee through the EEOC.

SOURCE: *The Wall Street Journal,* June 7, 1974.

STANDARD OIL CO. OF CALIFORNIA, San Francisco, California, is a producer and refiner of wholesale and retail petroleum products and a holding company with annual sales of $6.5 billion.

In May 1974, Standard Oil settled a United States action charging it with age bias. Standard Oil agreed to pay $2 million in back wages to 160 discharged employees and to rehire 120 of them. The employees in question were between the ages of 40 and 65.

SOURCE: *The Wall Street Journal,* May 16, 1974.

VOLKSWAGEN corporation is a wholesale importer of automobiles and equipment with annual sales of $1 billion.

In March 1974, Volkswagen agreed to pay $120,000 to settle a complaint brought by the U.S. Environmental Protection Agency. The EPA charged that Volkswagen failed to adequately report the installation of devices modifying pollution-control systems on four models of 1973 cars, thus violating the 1970 Clean Air Act and EPA regulations.

SOURCE: *The Wall Street Journal,* March 13, 1974.

In March 1974, the U.S. Environmental Protection Agency refused to permit the marketing of up to 22 million chickens contaminated with a pesticide known to cause cancer on prolonged exposure. The chicken producers and the Mississippi congressional delegation had asked the EPA for an exemption from this standard.

SOURCE: *The Wall Street Journal,* March 25, 1974.

Appendix B

Improved Corporate Social Performance

GENERAL TIRE & RUBBER CO. based in Akron, Ohio, with annual sales of $1.37 billion, awarded $171,202 to 6,860 employees as a reward for suggestions which resulted in savings to the company of more than $856,000. Employee suggestions which result in saving energy and materials receive special bonuses, "as an incentive to gain wider awareness of the energy crisis."

SOURCE: 1973 annual report.

MOBIL OIL CORP. of New York, New York, with annual sales of more than $12.7 billion, is a producer and distributor of petroleum products.

Mobil has assisted some 1,000 U.S. employees to enroll in accredited courses through an "educational refund plan." In 1973, Mobil recruited new employees at 29 traditionally black universities. Mobil has supported several minority-oriented college programs for the past six years and has sponsored a one-week orientation to Mobil for black students from 20 colleges. Black executives serve as visiting lecturers at these schools. Mobil's programs to promote the hiring and upgrading of qualified women employees was instituted at the recommendation of its task force. The matching gifts program encourages employee gifts to schools and hospitals. Mobil has sponsored various programs on educational TV and underwrites "Operation Sound Search"—a "project to uncover and develop musical talent in depressed areas of New York and Los Angeles."

SOURCE: 1974, 1975 annual reports.

PHILLIPS VAN HEUSEN CORP. of New York, New York, with annual sales of $300 million, is a manufacturer of men's and boys' clothing.

In 1972, Phillips Van Heusen set up the "Committee on Corporate Account-ability" and the "Committee on Environmental Policies." Each committee is composed of eight members of the company's divisions, with the objective of advising top management with respect to the social responsibility and con-duct of the company, its suppliers, and companies whose securities are held by Van Heusen's pension and retirement funds.

The Dreyfus Third Century Fund rated Phillips Van Heusen 100 percent with respect to demographics of plant communities, number of minority and female employees in the top two Equal Employment Opportunity cat-egories, and the yearly rate of change in the above statistics.

Its 1973 Annual Report describes its educational assistance plan, which aids minorities, schools featuring apparel education, and employees and their children.

Note: The 24-person executive committee lacks both women and minority members.

SOURCE: 1972, 1973 annual reports.

POLAROID CORP. of Cambridge, Massachusetts, manufactures cameras, films, polarizing filters, and sunglass lenses. Its annual sales are $571 million.

In 1973, 23 percent of Polaroid's employees used its training/education pro-grams. More than 1,000 employees received tuition refunds.

Polaroid's equal opportunity program sets annual goals and maintains spe-cific hiring programs for blacks, women, non-English-speaking, and hand-icapped. Its "Inner City, Inc.," program has a 75 percent success ratio in training the previously "unhirable." Its "10/75" plan sought 10 percent black representation at all levels by 1975. (In 1973, 16.7 percent were in produc-tion, 7.2 percent salaried.) Its woman's action plan seeks equal represen-tation of women in all phases. Its community relations programs include an ex-prisoner placement (99 percent successful). Four million dollars would be spent for environmental concerns in 1974, as estimated in the 1973 annual report.

SOURCE: 1973, 1974 annual reports.

THE QUAKER OATS CO. of Chicago, Illinois, is a manufacturer of foods, pet foods, toys, art needlecraft, and chemicals, with annual sales of $771 million.

Its 1971 Annual Report described its "Social Progress Plan." Some high-lights:

Deposits in minority-owned banks.
Support of youth programs.

Nutrition education for low-income housewives.

Environmental quality committee.

Hiring of 241 disadvantaged unemployed.

Volunteer tutoring program by employees for children with reading problems.

Sponsorship of *Sesame Street*, an educational television program, in the amount of $100,000.

Donation to charity of $500,000 in 1971 by Quaker Oats Foundation.

Extensive employee involvements in community activities.

In 1973, Quaker Oats formed a six-person "Public Responsibility Committee," including three outside directors.

SOURCE: 1971, 1972, 1973 annual reports.

RCA CORPORATION is based in New York, New York, and has annual sales of nearly $3.9 billion. RCA Corporation disclosed its social activities in its 1973 Annual Report. Some highlights:

Corporate energy planning and conservation committee (to help RCA save consumption of fuel).

Breakdown of percentage of minority and female employment at various employment levels.

Two intercompany awards for antipollution and ecological activity.

Concert which raised $60,000 for Martin Luther King Center for Social Change.

Renovation of more than 500 houses in six years for sale to low-income families.

Project to beautify railroad overpasses in Harrison and Kearny, New Jersey.

More than $850,000 to education, and $1.4 million to health and youth programs.

Payment of $483,000 to employees for suggestions which saved RCA $3 million.

SOURCE: 1973 Annual Report

SEARS, ROEBUCK & Co., Chicago, Illinois, is a retail and catalog sales company of general merchandise, with annual sales of $10.5 billion.

In its 1973 Annual Report, Sears, Roebuck disclosed the breakdown of its employees from 1969–1973, showing the number of women and minorities at each level.

SOURCE: *Business and Society Review/Innovation*, No. 10 (Summer 1974), p. 99.

Appendix C

Bodega Bay

IN May 1958, the Pacific Gas & Electric Company initiated negotiations to purchase land at Bodega Bay, 50 miles north of San Francisco. The location was part of a state recreation area where the University of California operated a marine study facility. Classes had been held there in the summers of 1956 and 1957. The events in the following historical summary were set in motion by the rumors that the plant would be nuclear and that the University of California faculty would fight the company.*

1959
—Site shifted to tip of headland to get away from San Andreas fault zone (earthquake danger).
—Family owners allegedly intimidated into selling land to PG&E against their wishes after being in family over 100 years.
—Local government grants PG&E use permit for power lines over local park without public hearing, despite opposing petition carrying 1,300 signatures. PG&E refuses to put lines underground, citing this as "uneconomical."

1960
—Local government grants company permit to build plant without public hearing and submission of plans on grounds this would "impose a hardship on the company."
—Faculty Committee concludes: "We agreed unanimously that there was not a single one of these sites that was equal to Bodega Head as it now stands. Bluntly stated, a unique Class A site for a marine facility is being exploited for power production."

* Information taken from *Up Against the Corporation Wall*, S. Prakash Sethi, ed. (Englewood Cliffs, N.J.: Prentice-Hall, 1971).

1961

—PG&E announces intention to build a *nuclear* plant for first time, raising public safety as a new major issue, in addition to research and recreation alternate uses of the land at issue. The three main new problems raised are:
  1. Geological instability of the area and reactor proximity to an earthquake zone.
  2. Location of a nuclear reactor near a major city.
  3. Problems of radioactive waste discharge.
—Local government approves access road following tidelands around bay, over university's objections that it would disturb the ecology of the area essential to marine research.

1962

—Public hearings: bitter conflict between county officials seeking power plant tax benefits and local fishermen and university marine biologists seeking to preserve local marine ecology.
—Public opinion grows in opposition to the plant, partly because of PG&E's refusal to hold further public hearings and make reports on the earthquake danger public.
—Public Utilities Commission receives over 2,500 protest letters, reopening hearings.
—Despite public opposition, Public Utilities Commission grants permission to build.

1963

—Opposition lobby applies for rehearing with AEC, is denied. Widespread public opposition mobilized by opposition lobby. Naval seismologist testifies that site is dangerous for a reactor. The company experts are in disagreement about the danger.

1964

—Company revises plant design to compensate for earthquake danger. Mounting negative public opinion begins to influence AEC, which advises company that "Bodega Head is not a suitable location for the proposed nuclear power plant at the present state of our knowledge."
—PG&E announces it is abandoning the project after investing several million dollars and seven years of controversy. PG&E president states that PG&E has made provisions for adequate electrical generating capacity elsewhere, and that the company has spent $4 million at the site.

Appendix D

Selected Questions and Answers

Harvard Business School

The author was invited to give a lecture on corporate social responsibility and social audits at the Harvard Business School. Following a presentation of how social costs and benefits can be measured, these questions were asked.

QUESTION You cited asking people whether they prefer having clean water as opposed to, let's say, a bowling alley. What happens in the case where you do go out and ask people and they do prefer to have a bowling alley as opposed to clean water? How do you deal with the perceptions of those who believe something to be in their interest which as a point of fact in the long run may not be?

RESPONSE I think that's a matter of an education effort. If the managers of a company feel that the employees want something that is truly not as good for them, in terms of the employees' ultimate objectives, as something else the management has proposed, then the management ought to launch an education effort. And I don't mean brainwashing, I mean an objective outside education effort explaining why good water is essential to child health, which some employees may not understand. Then if employees persist in wanting something that isn't as socially productive as something else is, I think the management has to make some compromise with that, and that's a joint decision—probably by management and representatives of the staff together—about how they want to compromise that trade-off.

QUESTION   How realistic is it to expect a company—I was speaking in terms of a community rather than employees of a company—how realistic is it to operate on the hypothesis that a company is not going to minimize the cash outflow of the social benefit programs but rather to try to get the maximum social utility per dollar invested? It would seem to me that precisely this sort of situation might arise and it would be more in the company's interest to kind of dupe people, as it were, or at least go along with their perceptions if those perceptions represented a minimum cash outlay to a company.

RESPONSE   That hasn't been my experience. Let me give you an example. A few years ago we instituted a disability insurance that is very expensive. We did this because one of our staff was crippled in an automobile accident. We did not have a disability insurance at that time and we felt we owed it to that individual to keep supporting him. That was very costly to the company, but it would have been insufferably costly to the individual if we hadn't done so. So we decided to put in long-term disability insurance at a significant cost to profit-sharing bonuses. We explained it to the staff, saying that if there are great objections to this, we'll reconsider, but we would like to do it because it puts the company in a very unfortunate moral bind if somebody is permanently disabled and we have to make the choice between losing money or losing the confidence of the individual. We don't want to have to be put in that position, so we want to ensure against that and we think it is worth it. We were able to convince our staff that it was worth it and after some discussion we were agreed on it. My own feeling is that most employers—at least in companies that have employees of a fairly high educational level, and even in those that don't, where the company is willing to make educational efforts—will find some consonance of rational self-interest with its employees. In other words, I think this is a slightly unreal problem; or putting it another way, there are so many other problems standing in line to be solved ahead of rational self-interest problems, that I think it's a little bit of an academic issue.

QUESTION   Is that in reply to the question about this community at large as well?

RESPONSE   Well, the problem with the community is issue aggregation. That's a political process problem because there are many different groups wanting different things. Usually the company can play a supportive role in getting a community to organize itself so that it can set its own priorities, whatever they are. It's usually wisest for the company to supply information and education but not the direct leadership of the community groups.

QUESTION   Why do you not think that committing the social audit of a firm's activities to financial terms, in some sense, lessens the firm's credibility, since many of the assumptions necessary to convert social impact to financial terms are arbitrary and would not be accepted as reasonable by many in the community?

RESPONSE   Well, if I understand your question, first of all I can't agree that the conversion to financial terms is arbitrary or at least any more arbitrary than the conversion to financial terms of the worth of an inventory, the depreciation rate of buildings, inventories assessed in a way that often bears little relation to their real market value, and so on. And all we're trying to do with social benefits in measuring their dollar worth is to establish their equivalent market values, so I don't feel that is any more arbitrary— and in some cases, it is less arbitrary—than financial accounting. But I'm sorry, I don't believe that completely answers the first part of your question. Would you care to restate it?

QUESTION   Yes, of course. It seems to me that to commit a firm's social impact to financial terms at this stage, mainly when no one else is doing it, runs the danger of lessening the firm's credibility in a community because you will then have every special interest group criticizing the conversion terms instead of criticizing the fundamental issues which are: What are your priorities? Do you want clean water or bowling alleys?

RESPONSE   I think that discussion is likely to make more salient the issues you are concerned with. A company which publishes an annual report that attempts, however badly or mistakenly or even misleadingly, to define its social contributions will raise the saliency of those issues to people who are reading the report, will increase the accessibility of facts about its social performance to people who are interested, and will subject itself to arguments about both the comprehensiveness and accuracy of those measures of social performance which can't help but engage the issues that you're concerned about. So I think that is all to the good. Now credibility of the company can be an objective that may or may not suffer. I think that would be a temporary thing. Which company would be more credible—a company which says nothing about its social performance, does only classical financial reporting but obviously has major social impact, or a company that does a social audit blunderingly, incompletely, partly inaccurately, apparently sincerely, and with a lot of problems in it, but tries to reveal its own perceptions of its own social performance? Which has the greater credibility? In the eyes of a financial analyst, the former may have the greater credibility unless he's a financial analyst working for the Third Century Fund or the Pax Fund, or one of the several other funds that are interested in corporate social responsibility, or unless he's a financial analyst working for a foundation, or unless he's a financial analyst working for a major insurance group that's interested in corporate social responsibility. Unless he's a community representative who wants to get at the issues in the corporations and finds the conventional annual report completely impervious to inspection of those issues.

QUESTION   I have a question about implementation. Given that you take a look at the various possible social investments that are open to you to decide what's best, I think that your system would work very well in a case of a whole new social investment. But where you have existing programs, it seems that it doesn't take into account the resistance to the elimination of those programs. In other words, if it's a lot better to clean up the water, as you kind of determined it through the criterion you talked about, you are going to have a very angry bowling team and this, I think, is going to cause a lot of trouble in the kind of overturning of one thing and then having the company say this new system is actually more efficient in terms of social utility.

RESPONSE   Well, there will always be groups who are dissatisfied as long as not everybody agrees on what's wanted. All that we're trying to implement with the social audit process concerned with employee benefits is that normal democratic processes be followed for deciding what most people want most. There will always be people who like unusual things, who will not be satisfied, and the decision process about that isn't unique to the social audit. That's a question of how the majority of the people involved want to decide. They may feel rich enough to give everybody a little bit of what he wants, no matter how bizarre, and then to allocate the remainder of their resources in proportion to popular demand. They may decide on a more rigid system of allocation to what the majority decides, where the majority gets all the resources and minority interests are not at all satisfied. That's up to the individual group and that's not a particular characteristic of the social audit. What's characteristic of the social audit is that it attempts to measure the consumer response and to do this in quantitative terms.

QUESTION   I think that your answer is right for considering a lot of new programs. My question is really that existing programs tend to take on a rather greater value in the minds of the relevant group, be it the staff or the community. And that's a real problem. You try to decide an ideal system somehow, taking into account what you've said, but doesn't it become very hard to get rid of the existing programs if they are not as efficient? In other words, you could perhaps arbitrarily tack on a 50 percent surcharge because they are already there and people are already experiencing them.

RESPONSE   That hasn't been my experience. We've dropped some programs. I think the main objection people have to programs being changed is not so much the change (as a matter of fact there's usually a kind of Hawthorne effect to any change) but to the fact that they're not in on the decision; that's what they really resent. And if they're allowed to be involved in the decision, and they're encouraged to participate in the decision, they'll find the decision much more acceptable.

QUESTION   I find your answer somewhat inadequate to the previous question in that I don't think your organization is all that typical of the sort of thing he was referring to. Do you have any experience in that line, other than in your own organization?

RESPONSE   As a matter of fact, yes, I do. I can recall some changes in benefits in a large corporation in which I used to be employed. And it went by without any great hubbub; in fact, most people weren't even aware of the benefit which was being changed. Now you can always think of examples that prove the point either way. I merely suggest that this isn't the particular characteristic of the social audit one way or the other, and to the extent that people resent not having access to the decision and access to the issues, the social audit reduces that resentment by providing transparency in its way of measuring relative costs and benefits. If the decision-making style is autocratic and arrogant, social audits won't fix that.

QUESTION   I'm interested in how you initially got credibility in terms of how your function is performed, how you maintained your credibility. Because it seems to me that what could very easily happen is that your company could become a tool for the government and companies that just rationalize gradual change . . . and in fact, this seems to be what you have been saying, but kind of incongruent with what I read last night.

RESPONSE   First of all, I have to confess to you that we don't have credibility.

QUESTION   You have a lot of business, apparently.

RESPONSE   We do have credibility with the federal government in doing program evaluation; we don't have credibility with industry doing social audits. We've only done one and that wasn't very happily received, so I'm still seeking credibility, enough credibility to do the job, but I don't think we have it. Now as to our being corrupted and co-opted into making bad things look good, I think the history of measurement of social phenomena just generally shows that the more attention given to precise quantitative measurement of a phenomenon—this has a way of taking off on its own and escaping from whatever purpose anybody wants to put it to. In other words, it raises the level of discussion to a more scientific one, yet it can't be as easily controlled by the people using it as they would like. For example, look at what happened in social statistics or macroeconomic statistics. Theoreticians disagree, ideologists disagree about the interpretations. But there are a hell of a lot more facts available to anybody who wants to make reforms. It is easier to make reforms now, or to identify feasible reforms, than it was 100 years ago, when the data were not there and there was no means of measurement.

QUESTION   Isn't that exactly what is happening, though, in terms of your evaluation processes for government spending?

RESPONSE   We criticize a lot of programs.

QUESTION A lot of governments and businesses are saying that their backup is pretty good. It's difficult for me to see why they take the position of credibility.

RESPONSE You are assuming that the only reason the government gives business to firms like ours is that we tell the government what it wants to hear and whitewash their programs. I have to ask you to believe that there are a great many actors in government who are a little more farsighted than that and believe the success of their programs depends on real, objective response to social needs, and they want to know if their programs are being sufficiently responsive to those needs. They don't want to publicize it, but they want to know what's wrong so that they can fix it before they develop a very bad reputation or a political response to their own failure.

QUESTION How would you calculate the change in your social balance sheet as a result of the meeting today and your being here?

RESPONSE We thought about that. And the whole idea of the question was: Do we generate a social benefit by providing educational services? And do we take a social benefit for that? In other words, right now, for example, for every article published or for major lectures by anyone on the staff, we assume that those are worth, I think, on the average of $200 apiece in terms of contribution to knowledge. That's a very conservative computation if the thing is worth anything. And I have no idea if that's a reasonable number. We want to attribute some worth to education, and that's a financial cost to the company: a short-term financial cost, a short-term social benefit. It may be a long-term financial benefit if some of you go out to work in companies and are convinced that the idea is worthwhile and begin to generate social audit requirements and maybe involve us in doing social audits. I have no idea. That would be a possible long-term financial benefit and a possible social benefit.

QUESTION My question was about the meeting today, not your policy regarding qualifications. What's this meeting worth here?

RESPONSE Same thing. We aggregate lectures and publications.

QUESTION The value is what I was asking—$200?

RESPONSE I would say it was $200, which is a conservative market estimation. I can't prove that it's worth more than $200. I could probably prove, if I wanted to charge for it, that it would cost Harvard $200 to get it. And that's the bottom estimate. Now a much more generous estimate would be to estimate some probability of change of individuals in the audience as a consequence of what they hear and then the economic and social impact of the difference in their behavior and so on, but that gets very fuzzy. We've limited ourselves to first-order market effects only, and we think that's a conservative estimate. Now if you are all unanimous in feeling at the end of your discussion that this was worthless, then there's no social benefit. Because no matter what effort I make, if you all agree that it's worthless, there's no social benefit accruing to a futile effort. And in the same way, in our contract work, if we merely provide information we feel that a conservative estimate of social worth is what was paid for the work. That's the market worth of it. If the client says, as he sometimes does, either "This is garbage" or "A great job was done but it's on the wrong problem," or "Fine piece of research but we can't use it for various political reasons," or whatever, then we consider it a social debit. That is, the cost of the work is the opportunity cost of not doing something else with those resources, and that's a social deficit. If, on the other hand, there's a multiplier effect, and as a result of our work, our information, our training, or our technical assistance, or whatever, an organization is able to mobilize additional resources or is able to generate efficiencies in its operation that have economic multiplier effects, we take some credit for the net social benefit of those effects to the degree that we believe that we are responsible for them.

QUESTION In evaluating different social programs, how do you evaluate groups that have different intensification of feelings? For example, if everyone is fairly happy about the breakfast program, but not really overjoyed, although a much smaller group is really angry to the point of throwing balls, how would you measure those differences?

RESPONSE I don't know, my inclination would be to give one man one vote, not to give extra credit for anger.

QUESTION However, in the paper you read, you mentioned the heart fund problem—that someone with a heart disease might feel very strongly about it, whereas someone who might be going to the lake for recreational reasons might not. So I thought that you had considered this before, the one man, one vote.

RESPONSE Yes. Well, I would send it back to the group and say, "Do you want to recognize the superior intensity of feeling of this small minority of individuals and give in to their objectives because of the intensity of their feelings, despite their being in the minority of the group?" And that's up to the majority to decide. But that's not a social audit issue; that's an issue of political process and decision making.

QUESTION Well, can't you just ask the people involved how much it is worth to them, so that it is consistent with your idea of true value and kind of equalizing the pursuit of value?

RESPONSE That works when people have comparable resources. And if they have comparable resources, you can ask them to put an attributed value on the alternative decision.

QUESTION What do you mean by comparable resources?

RESPONSE Let's say that they didn't all have the same income—that a dollar is not worth the same to a poor man as it is to a rich man—and so you have to correct for the differences in disposable income and perceived worth of the money unit, which I think makes it very difficult to measure the relative worth of a service or an object or benefit across highly different income groups. That has to be corrected for.

QUESTION   To what extent could management be getting itself into a harder stance by taking the survey of employee priorities and raising interest in having those needs solved?

RESPONSE   It is a fair question and there is a risk. I think it's the lesser risk, but there's no question that dissatisfactions will surface if they are solicited. However, I think that's a healthier process than suppressing dissatisfactions and pretending they don't exist and then either having them expressed neurotically (by neurotically, I mean expressed not about the thing that is the real source of dissatisfaction but by transference to an artificial reason that is much more difficult to deal with) or having them boil over in a sudden crisis. I think there is that risk, but it is the lesser risk.

QUESTION   I see. This is the way you would explain it to a corporate manager who is not used to thinking in these terms?

RESPONSE   That's right. Now I have to confess to you I haven't been very persuasive.

QUESTION   I'm interested in knowing your feelings as to the future potential of the system throughout the United States. Specifically, at what point would a firm capitalize its social assets in the terminology of the financial assets on its balance sheet?

RESPONSE   It's my hope that social audits will be as prevalent as financial audits in about ten years and that they will be carried out in at least three ways: internal audits conducted by social auditors in every significant corporation, who will be comparable to the financial-controller staff; external audits by independent social auditors, who will be comparable to independent public accountants, and who will work in teams usually consisting of economists, cost accountants, and social scientists; and government audits of government contractors, much like those the Defense Contracts Audits Agency now conducts to establish proper overhead rates, developed into a regularly established and relatively standardized procedure. It may be optimistic to hope that the procedure will be standardized within a decade.

As to the second question, when could the company hope to capitalize the social benefits in financial terms, the theory is of course not yet complete in many respects, particularly in the integration of the social and the financial balance sheets. I'm a little surprised none of you caught it or mentioned it, but one of the problems in our own social audit is that we don't have neatly logical, exhaustive, and mutually exclusive categories; we have an overlap between the social and the financial balance sheets. So, if I can draw a little Venn diagram here, the social audit and the financial audit overlap. For example, in the income statement, there are some financial items that are exclusive to the financial statement; there are some social items that are exclusive to the social statement (for example, benefits to the staff from increased market value as a result of promotion and professional development); and there are some that are in both places (for example, insurance benefits to staff). That's a money overhead cost in the financial statement and it is a social benefit to staff in the social statement. This is a problem that needs to be addressed by an integration of these two forms of measurement. We didn't do so this time because, first of all, we have not fully developed the theory and, secondly, we wanted to satisfy our conservative audience that we were not mucking up the financial statement because we were trying to hide something. So we felt it was very important to make an absolutely conventional financial statement and put the social audit in in addition. It is my own view that ultimately these two have to be combined. And next year, we hope to provide the traditional financial statement (again for the conservatives who don't want it confused), the separate social audit, and then an integrated version. In that integrated version, we hope to eliminate some of the redundancies and some of the overlaps of social benefits and social costs, so that we will reduce all social and financial costs and benefits to a common financial dollar basis.

The question of when we capitalize social benefits has two components. The first question is, When do you capitalize a cost? And the accounting answer to that is you can capitalize a cost when there is a future earnings stream associated with it. The second issue concerns capitalizing social benefits. That depends on our future explanation of them.

Kansai Electric Power Company, Osaka

The following questions were asked of the author by executives of a major Japanese utility in the course of a workshop on social performance measurement.

QUESTION For an electric power company, what constitutes social responsibilities?

RESPONSE Whatever owners, operators, consumers, and the general public think they are. From company reports it can be gathered that the company believes its social responsibilities are to supply power reliably and economically without damage to the environment.

QUESTION Doesn't the ability to supply adequate, good-quality electricity at stable rates in itself represent the accomplishment of social responsibilities?

RESPONSE Yes, but not *all* social responsibilities.

QUESTION Since the electric rates are determined by the operating costs, cost increases attendant on social activities raise the rates. Don't the execution of social responsibilities and the rate increase contradict each other?

RESPONSE No, for two possible reasons. First, social investments often have financial payoffs too, so costs sometimes are decreased. Second, consumers may prefer a small cost increase to a large increase in pollution.

QUESTION At present, we and other power companies are forced into the situation where we are unable to build for growth even though we comply with the environmental regulations and standards set by the Japanese government—because of opposition by our constituencies. How effective are social audits in helping corporations (in this case, utilities) to survive?

RESPONSE It is too early to tell since social audits have not yet been used by utilities. However, it is believed that they will help utilities and other corporations survive by helping them to respond effectively and economically to constituent pressures.

QUESTION During supply shortages, Kansai Electric must interrupt services to certain consumers based on the degree of importance of services to them. Can social audits be applied to prioritize consumers' needs?

RESPONSE Certainly. For example, the social cost of interrupting power to hospitals and schools is measurably greater than that of interrupting power to amusement parks.

QUESTION How do you evaluate the social cost of blackouts or reduced services?

RESPONSE By estimating the cost in lost services powered by electricity, or the cost of replacement, plus the social costs of the reduction in the rate of economic growth.

QUESTION If a corporation endeavors to economize natural resources, to stop inflation, and to restrain speculative enterprises, should these items be included in the scope of corporate social responsibilities?

RESPONSE Yes, if their social benefits can be estimated in terms of the results of company actions (not attempts).

QUESTION Where do you place the limit of social responsibilities for a corporation which is operating in the red?

RESPONSE To obey the law, and become self-supporting again as soon as possible by sound business management. Bankruptcy is generally socially costly in terms of lost employment, career costs, and so forth.

QUESTION Wouldn't the provision of social benefits to one group in the constituency, in order to appease the criticism of the constituency as a whole, contradict the principle of fair and equal treatment to all consumers?

RESPONSE Yes, it would.

QUESTION Is your concept of social responsibilities based on economic theories, such as welfare economics?

RESPONSE In part only. More specifically, it is based on the liberal capitalist concept that business flourishes best when it responds to mass consumer markets. There *is* today a mass market for social responsibility.

QUESTION As value changes continuously, so does the degree of agreement as to what constitutes corporate social responsibilities. How do you adjust to these changes?

RESPONSE The changes are slow enough to permit companies to adjust to them. For example in the United States equality of opportunity has been a major social issue for over a decade. Environmental protection has been a major issue for almost a decade.

QUESTION In terms of measuring corporate social accomplishments, do you believe that your method of presenting a social audit in the form of a balance sheet and income statement will be widely adapted?

RESPONSE I am still very uncertain. I believe that some similar form, if not exactly this one, will be widely used.

QUESTION What would your feeling be as to some indication of the penetration ratio so many years hence, and in what types of business?

RESPONSE It may penetrate socially sensitive industries (power, paper, chemicals, labor-intensive industries) 20 percent to 60 percent in the next decade, and 50 percent to 90 percent in 20 years, because by that time a better way of presenting company social and financial performance will have been developed.

QUESTION It is imperative that an objective method of measuring social costs and benefits be established in order to avoid subjectivity. However, how does one go about obtaining a consensus from the business community and the general public?

RESPONSE By continuous, dedicated efforts to communicate honestly one's own assumptions about social costs and benefits, and welcoming of critical feedback and correction; by involving industry colleagues and representatives of all constituencies in the criteria-setting process. This last can be done with sample surveys of consumer preference.

QUESTION How do you handle those social benefits which cannot be translated into monetary terms, such as the degrees of, first, environmental improvement due to pollution abatement measures; second, accident prevention due to safety measures; third, improvement of services to the consumer and constituency; and fourth, environmental beautification due to tree planting?

RESPONSE All these can be translated into monetary terms. Environmental improvements are worth as a minimum what they cost, or the costs of unimproved environment which they avoid. Accident prevention is worth the money equivalent of lost man-hours, plus the cost of medical care saved. Improved services are worth their market (shadow) price. Tree planting is worth its cost or the cost of an equivalent environment.

QUESTION How do you feel about the use of indicators in addition to the monetary terms?

RESPONSE A useful preliminary step to monetization, helping to indicate the specific areas sensitive enough to be worth quantifying in detail.

QUESTION What is the prospect of developing a measuring method for inter-sector comparison?

RESPONSE It will take a long time because the relative inter-sector social utilities will have to be estimated first, and there is little agreement on this.

QUESTION How do you accrue stocks (inventories) such as social assets and social liabilities from a flow?

RESPONSE Social assets can be accumulated as goodwill or distributed annually to all constituencies. This remains a theoretical problem.

QUESTION How do you arrive at a consolidated valuation of a corporation when it shows a high social valuation in the social audit on one hand and a low financial valuation in the financial statement on the other hand?

RESPONSE By monetizing both, converting to the same present-value dollars, and adding the values.

QUESTION What measures are available to raise the financial valuation?

RESPONSE Showing the present value of future financial returns from current social investments.

QUESTION Please give concrete examples of the "social discount rate."

RESPONSE There are only implicit rates to date, expressed by social investment decisions in such long-term prospects as basic medical research, early child care, and education.

QUESTION How did you apply the shadow pricing method in preparing your social balance sheet and social income statement?

RESPONSE By determining the equivalent "price" to potential consumers of such social benefits as equality of opportunity and by determining the potential or actual price paid for an equivalent benefit.

QUESTION If you consider the cost of pollution abatement equipment as the cost of social contributions, can one also include the cost of staff engaged in antipollution activities?

RESPONSE Yes, definitely. The total amount of time they spend on antipollution work, multiplied by their salary rates, yields the monetized social contribution.

QUESTION You treat staff promotions as social benefits. In the case of Japan, where labor mobility is low, a corporation that provides a lot of staff benefits will be putting undue pressure on other corporations; hence, I feel, no social benefits result. What is your thought on this?

RESPONSE The social benefits to the staff must be balanced against the social costs and benefits of the pressure put on other corporations. This is a complex "benefits market" analysis.

QUESTION When do you account for externalities?

RESPONSE Whenever they are identified, measured, and can be internalized.

QUESTION Isn't there a slight difference when you compare the results of individual project evaluations and the total picture shown in a social audit?

RESPONSE Yes, there is, from unresolved imperfections in the internal consistency of the method. Theoretically, there should be no such difference.

QUESTION Which project should a corporation undertake—the one which promises to produce a great deal of social benefit or another which promises a great deal of long-term return on investment for the corporation? Does a social audit clarify the selection mechanism?

RESPONSE The same projects might maximize both social and financial return. Only in some cases are social and financial long-term goals in conflict. More often, the conflict is between short-term and long-term goals, not social and financial. In any case, the social audit clarifies the choice by estimating the social benefits and costs to be added to the financial ones of the candidate projects, thus reflecting a more complete view of total return.

QUESTION Please indicate, based on the following examples, how you compute social benefits and costs and corporate benefits and costs.

RESPONSE The two overlap. The corporation can enjoy a social benefit as well as society, and vice versa. Of course, some social benefits, such as those to employees, benefit the corporation more than society in general, while others, such as pollution abatement, do the reverse.

QUESTION Investment in pollution abatement equipment?

RESPONSE This is mainly a social benefit and a corporate cost except where profit is improved by recovery of valuable chemicals such as sulphur.

QUESTION Regarding the legal environmental standards and regulations, how do you define a pollution-related investment as necessary or required as compared with being a social contribution? Where do you draw a line?

RESPONSE Legally required antipollution investments, however involuntary, are still counted as a social contribution because we are concerned only with accounting for concrete acts, not their motivations.

QUESTION How do you deal with a welfare-oriented electric generating plant, the construction plan of which includes the cost of establishing social assets for the constituency, for example, a meeting place, roads, and recreational facilities?

RESPONSE All the investments in social assets for the constituency count as social benefits as well as corporate financial ones. In the integrated balance sheet, double counting is avoided by proper allocation or estimation of multiplier benefits exceeding investment value.

QUESTION A public relations building next to a generating plant?

RESPONSE A public relations building may or may not be a social benefit, depending on how it is used. It would be a social benefit if the noncompany community had good reasons for believing it brought real benefits, rather than mere company propaganda.

QUESTION Laying urban service wires underground? (*Japan is lagging behind the West in underground transmission, owing to the cost, the hazards of water damage, and so on. Even in Osaka, the underground transmission accounts for only about 30 percent of total service wires.*)

RESPONSE This is definitely a social benefit to the community in terms of added safety, reliability of service, and preservation of visual aesthetics —all offsetting the higher financial cost.

QUESTION The municipal property tax on a generating plant represents a revenue for the local self-governing body; however, the central government deducts this amount from the local tax allocation, and therefore the erection of a generating plant does not benefit the local government financially.

RESPONSE It might benefit the local government financially in other ways, such as providing more local taxable income and possibly cheaper municipal power.

Appendix E

The Social Audit
of Abt Associates Inc.

THE 1975 Abt Social Audit, conducted by Dr. Clark C. Abt, Dr. Donald Muse, and Mr. Neal S. Perry, is the fifth one made by Abt Associates of its operations and reported to the public in its annual report. The Abt Social Audit was the first comprehensive and quantitative social audit completed by a private corporation and presented to the public with other required financial reporting statements. The measures of social responsibility developed by Abt Associates have been used by management to improve decision making concerning social benefits and costs to consumers and suppliers of social resources.

The notes referred to in the Social and Financial Balance Sheet can be found at the end of the appendix.

Appendix E

FINANCIAL STATEMENTS

Abt Associates Inc. Balance Sheets
December 31, 1975 and 1974

Assets	1975	1974
Current assets:		
Cash	$ 102,302	26,962
Accounts receivable, contracts, less allowance for doubtful accounts $20,000 ($44,000 in 1974)	1,654,763	1,567,203
Unbilled contract costs and fees	2,137,743	1,885,405
Other current assets	156,731	137,304
Total current assets	4,051,539	3,616,874
Property and equipment, at cost:		
Land and land improvements	508,248	467,442
Buildings	3,504,036	3,492,447
Building improvements	319,610	262,138
Equipment, furniture and fixtures	485,727	430,364
	4,817,621	4,652,391
Less accumulated depreciation	495,844	335,915
Net property and equipment	4,321,777	4,316,476
Other assets	43,634	37,988
	$ 8,416,950	7,971,338

Liabilities and Shareholders' Equity	1975	1974
Current liabilities:		
Notes payable	$ 105,565	405,565
Accounts payable	1,120,200	788,240
Accrued expenses:		
Payroll and accrued vacation pay	644,079	628,651
Other	421,318	430,504
Total accrued expenses	1,065,397	1,059,155
Federal income taxes	6,011	24,273
Total current liabilities	2,297,173	2,277,233
Deferred Federal income taxes	167,200	98,000
Long-term liabilities:		
Notes payable	2,191,690	2,300,485
Leasehold interest in property	130,695	129,566
Total long-term liabilities	2,322,385	2,430,051
Shareholders' equity:		
Common stock, $1.00 par value per share. Authorized 1,000,000 shares; issued 195,384 Series A, and 99,700 Series B shares	295,084	295,084
Additional paid-in capital	1,490,684	1,490,684
Retained earnings	1,844,424	1,380,286
Total shareholders' equity	3,630,192	3,166,054
	$ 8,416,950	7,971,338

Abt Associates Inc.   Social and Financial Balance Sheet

SOCIAL ASSETS

are resources which promise to provide future social and economic benefits and are a social asset to the company valued at their present worth.

Suppliers of Social Resources

	Notes	1975	1974
Staff Available Within One Year	1	$ 8,225,000	$ 7,555,000
Staff Available After One Year	2	16,276,000	14,895,000
Training Investment	3	3,752,000	2,986,000
		28,253,000	25,436,000
Less Accumulated Training Obsolescence	4	1,526,000	1,422,000
Total Staff Assets		**$26,727,000**	**$24,014,000**

Staff (Note 44) appears at left.

	Notes	1975	1974
Creation and Development of Organization	6	$ 911,000	$ 554,000
Child Care Development	7	51,000	25,000
Social Audit Development	8	50,000	46,000
Total Organizational Assets		**$ 1,012,000**	**$ 625,000**

Organization at left.

	Notes	1975	1974
Public Services Paid For Through Taxes (Net of Consumption)	10	$ 940,000	$ 641,000

General Public and Community

	Notes	1975	1974
Total Public and Community Assets		$ 940,000	$ 641,000
Cash	13	$ 102,000	$ 27,000
Accounts Receivable Less Allowance For Doubtful Accounts	13	1,655,000	1,567,000
Unbilled Contract Cost and Fees	13	2,137,000	1,886,000
Other Current Financial Assets	13 & 14	157,000	137,000
Other Assets	13 & 14	44,000	38,000
Total Current Assets		**$ 4,095,000**	**$ 3,655,000**
Physical Assets:			
Recreation Center	13	$ 106,000	$ 106,000
Land and Improvements	13	508,000	467,000
Buildings and Improvements	13	3,718,000	3,649,000
Equipment, Furniture, and Fixtures	13	486,000	430,000
Total Physical Assets		4,818,000	4,652,000
Less Accumulated Depreciation	13	496,000	336,000
Total Net Physical Assets		**$ 4,322,000**	**$ 4,316,000**

Stockholders at left.

	Notes	1975	1974
Total Stockholders' Assets		$ 8,417,000	$ 7,971,000
TOTAL	15	**$37,096,000**	**$33,251,000**

SOCIAL LIABILITIES

are future sources of economic or social cost and are valued at their present economic worth.

	Notes	1975	1974
Staff Wages Payable	5	$26,727,000	$24,014,000
Total Staff Liabilities		$26,727,000	$24,014,000
Organizational Financing Requirements	9	$ 1,189,000	$ 1,056,000
Total Organization Liabilities		$ 1,189,000	$ 1,056,000
Accumulated Pollution To The Environment Caused By Company Operations:			
Electricity Generation	11	$ 168,000	$ 113,000
Staff Commuting	11	77,000	58,000
Paper Consumed	11	25,000	18,000
Total Public and Community Liabilities		$ 270,000	$ 189,000
Notes Payable	13	$ 106,000	$ 406,000
Accounts Payable and Accrued Expenses	13	1,120,000	788,000
Accrued Expenses	13	1,065,000	1,059,000
Federal Income Taxes	13	6,000	24,000
Deferred Federal Income Taxes	13	167,000	$ 98,000
Notes Payable (Long-Term)	13	2,192,000	2,300,000
Leasehold Interest In Property	13	131,000	130,000
Total Stockholders Liabilities		$ 4,787,000	$ 4,805,000
		$32,973,000	$30,064,000

SOCIAL EQUITY

or society's investment in the company is created by recognizing the difference between the net increase in value of social assets and social liabilities.

	1975	1974
See statement below for financial equity that is not a social asset or liability.		
Total Staff Equity	0	0
Total Organizational Equity	$ (177,000)	$ (431,000)
Total General Public and Community Equity *(Note 12)*	$ 670,000	$ 452,000
Staff Stockholders' Equity		
Common Stock	$ 93,000	$ 95,000
Additional Paid-In Capital	469,000	480,000
Retained Earnings	580,000	444,000
Total	$ 1,142,000	$ 1,019,000
Non-Staff Stockholders' Equity:		
Common Stock	202,000	200,000
Additional Paid-In Capital	1,022,000	1,011,000
Retained Earnings	1,264,000	936,000
Total	$ 2,488,000	$ 2,147,000
Total Stockholders' Equity	$ 3,630,000	$ 3,166,000
(Note 16)	$ 4,123,000	$ 3,187,000

Abt Associates Inc. Social and Financial Income Statement

	SOCIAL BENEFITS			
Suppliers of Social Resources	*are social or economic resources that are generated by company operations and have a positive impact or add to society's resources.*			
		Notes	1975	1974
	Contract Revenue	17	$15,806,000	$16,423,000
	Federal Services Consumed	18	253,000	262,000
	State Services Consumed	19	95,000	104,000
	Local Services Consumed	20	42,000	40,000
	Pollution to the Environment Caused by Company Operations:	21		
	Generation of Electricity	22	55,000	37,000
	Staff Commuting	23	19,000	21,000
	Paper Consumed	24	7,000	7,000
	Dividends	25	74,000	59,000
Company/Stockholders	Total Company/ Stockholder Benefits		$16,351,000	$16,953,000
	Salaries Paid for Time Worked	45	$ 6,473,000	$ 6,231,000
	Career Advancement	46	758,000	700,000
	Vacation and Holidays	47	763,000	719,000
	Health, Dental and Life Insurance	48	454,000	461,000
	Sick Leave	49	185,000	185,000
	Retirement Income Plan	50	118,000	50,000
Staff *(Note 44)*	Employee Stock Ownership Plan	51	30,000	0
	Staff Food Service	52	73,000	67,000
	Parking	53	121,000	95,000
	Quality of Work Space	54	122,000	134,000
	Tuition Reimbursement	55	23,000	15,000
	Child Care Facility	56	26,000	18,000
	Credit Union	57	16,000	11,000
	Recreation Center	58	35,000	27,000
	Total Staff Benefits		$ 9,197,000	$ 8,713,000
	Value of Contract Research	65	$15,806,000	$16,423,000
	Staff Overtime Worked But Not Paid	66	1,036,000	1,184,000
Clients/General Public	Federal Taxes Paid	67	462,000	474,000
	State and Federal Tax Worth of Net Jobs Created	68	25,000	96,000
	State Taxes Paid	67	109,000	130,000
	Contribution to Knowledge	69	72,000	60,000
	Total Client Benefits		$17,510,000	$18,367,000
	Local Taxes Paid	73	$ 118,000	$ 78,000
	Local Tax Worth of Net Jobs Created	74	4,000	16,000
Community	Environmental Improvements	75	29,000	36,000
	Reduced Parking Area	76	0	29,000
	Total Community Benefits		$ 151,000	$ 159,000
	Total	79	$43,209,000	$44,192,000

SOCIAL COSTS

are social or economic resources that are consumed by company operations and are a cost, sacrifice or detriment to society.

NET SOCIAL INCOME

or social profit is the social gain or loss to society resources that result from company operations.

	Notes	1975	1974		1975	1974
Salaries Paid (Exclusive of Training Investment and Fringe Benefits	26	$ 5,707,000	$ 5,296,000	Net social income is a social dividend paid out to company/stockholders, and it does not accrue the net social worth on the balance sheet.		
Training Investment in Staff	27	766,000	935,000			
Direct Contract Cost	28	4,298,000	5,529,000			
Overhead/General Administrative Expenditures Not Itemized	29	1,823,000	1,796,000			
Vacation and Holidays	30	763,000	719,000			
Improvements in Space and Environment	31	127,000	137,000			
Federal Taxes Paid	32	462,000	474,000			
State Taxes Paid	32	109,000	130,000			
Local Taxes Paid	32	118,000	78,000			
Health, Dental and Life Insurance	33	252,000	256,000			
Sick Leave	34	185,000	185,000			
Staff Food Service	35	73,000	67,000			
Child Care Facilities	36	26,000	18,000			
Tuition Reimbursement	37	23,000	15,000			
Employee Stock Ownership Plan	38	30,000	0			
Interest Payments	39	267,000	197,000			
Income Foregone on Paid-In Capital	40	306,000	265,000			
Social Audit Development	41	4,000	14,000			
Retirement Income Plan	42	118,000	50,000	Total Company/ Stockholders		
Total Company/ Stockholders Equity		$15,457,000	$16,161,000	Equity *(Note 43)*	$ 894,000	$ 792,000
Opportunity Cost of Total Time Worked	59	$ 7,509,000	$ 7,540,000	Net social income is a social dividend paid out to staff, and it does not accrue to the net social worth on the balance sheet.		
Absence of Retirement Income Plan	60	0	1,000			
Layoffs and Involuntary Terminations	61	115,000	77,000			
Inequality of Opportunity	62	1,000	1,000			
Uncompensated Losses Through Theft	63	1,000	1,000			
Reduced Parking Area	64	0	29,000			
Total Staff Cost		$ 7,626,000	$ 7,649,000	Total Staff Equity	$ 1,571,000	$ 1,064,000
Cost of Contract Work to Clients	70	$15,806,000	$16,423,000	Net social income is a social dividend paid out to clients/general public,and it does not accrue to the social net worth on the balance sheet.		
Federal Services Consumed	71	253,000	262,000			
State Services Consumed	71	95,000	104,000			
Pollution to the Environment Caused by Company Operations:	72					
Generation of Electricity	22	55,000	37,000			
Staff Commuting	23	19,000	21,000			
Paper Consumed	24	7,000	7,000	Total Client		
Total Cost to Clients		$16,235,000	$16,854,000	Equity	$ 1,275,000	$ 1,513,000
Increased Parking Area	77	$ 3,000	$ 0	Net social income is a social dividend paid out to the community, and it does not accrue to the social net worth on the balance sheet.		
Local Services Consumed	78	42,000	40,000			
				Total Community		
Total Cost to Community		$ 45,000	$ 40,000	Equity	$ 106,000	$ 119,000
Total		$39,363,000	$40,704,000	Total *(Note 80)*	$ 3,846,000	$ 3,488,000

Technical Notes for the 1975
Social Audit of Abt Associates Inc.

Social and Financial Balance Sheet:

Note 1: Valuation of staff assets available within one year is based on year end payroll (1975: $8,414,000 and 1974: $7,777,000) discounted to present value using (1975: .9776 and 1974: .9715), the discount rate being a function of mean staff tenure (1975: 2.29 years and 1974: 2.96 years) and using table for the present value of $1.*

*Source: Jerome Brachen and Charles J. Christerson, Tables for Use in Analyzing Business Decision, (Homewood, Ill.: Richard D. Erwin, Inc. 1965).

Note 2: Valuation of staff assets after one year is based on year end payroll (note 1) discounted to present value using (1975: 1.9345 and 1974: 1.9153), the discount rate being a function of mean staff tenure (note 1) and using table for the present value of $1 received annually. Source see note 1.

Note 3: Staff training investment is estimated from a staff survey that indicated average training in 1975 was 9.1 percent and in 1974 was 15 percent of year end payroll (note 1).

Note 4: Valuation of accumulated training obsolence is based on a straight-line depreciation of training investment (note 3) over the mean staff tenure (note 1).

Note 5: Valuation of staff wages payable is equal to total staff assets. This amount does not constitute a current legal liability to the staff but is contingent upon future staff performance on contract work.

Note 6: Creation and development of organization is computed by weighting the capital stock and paid-in capital account (1975 and 1974: $1,786,000) from 1965 (the year of the company's founding) to the present by the deflator for Gross Private Fixed Investment (1975: 132.6, 1974: 112.6 and 1973: 106).

Note 7: Child care development accumulates by the amount of the company's investment in related research each year (1975: $26,000 and 1974: $18,000).

Note 8: Social audit development accumulates by the amount of the company's investment in related research each year (1975: $4,000 and 1974: $14,000).

Note 9: Valuation of organizational financing requirements is based on the accumulation of the difference between mean borrowing during the year (1975: $3,773,000 and 1974: $3,148 $3,148,000) and year-end borrowing (1975: $3,906,000 and 1974: $3,641,000). Borrowing includes accounts payable, accrued expenses, federal income taxes, deferred federal income tax and notes payable.

Note 10: Valuation of public services paid for through taxes is equal to the difference between the value of public services consumed (1975: $390,000 and 1974: $406,000) and total taxes paid (1975: $689,000 and 1974: $682,000). The amount of 1974 public services paid for through taxes has been revalued to $641,000 because of an accounting error that overstated services not consumed by $198,000.

Note 11: Accumulated pollution to the environment causes by the company operation is considered a cumulative social liability. Paper consumed (1975: $7,000 and 1974: $7,000), electricity used (1975: $55,000 and 1974: $37,000) and staff commuting (1975: $19,000 and 1974: $21,000). See notes 21, 22, 23 and 24.

Note 12: The 1974 general public and community equity has been adjusted from $650,000 to $452,000 (note 10).

Note 13: Financial and physical assets, financial liabilities and stockholders' equity are items conventionally accounted for on the Financial Balance Sheet. Individual line items are the same or rearranged and rounded off for integration into the social balance sheet.

Note 14: These accounts were reclassified by the auditors in their annual audit which resulted in changes in the dollar amounts shown for 1974.

Note 15: Total social assets for 1974 has been decreased from $33,449,000 (note 10).

Note 16: Total social equity for 1974 has been decreased from $3,385,000 (notes 10, 12 and 15).

Social and Financial Income Statement:

Note 17: Valuation of contract revenue is based upon the total revenue from the 1975 and 1974 income statements.

Note 18: Federal services consumed by the company are calculated by multiplying the ratio of company revenues to total U.S. corporate revenue times the total U.S. corporate tax collections. Federal services consumed average about 1.59 percent of total company revenue over the past four years. Source: Survey of Current Business, U.S. Dept. of Commerce.

Note 19: State services consumed by the company are calculated by multiplying the ratio of company revenue to the State of Mass. corporate revenue times the total State of Mass. corporate tax collections. State services consumed average about 0.6 percent of the company's revenue over the past five years.

Note 20: The company's share of local services consumed is computed by multiplying the ratio of the average daily work force of the company to the local population by total local taxes collected and subtracting the percentage of the local community budget going to education. Local services consumed average about 0.65 percent of total salaries paid for time worked (note 45).

Note 21: In its operations, the company contributes to the degradation of environmental resources through pollution. The cost of pollution abatement is treated as a benefit to the company and a cost to society.

Note 22: The company consumed 2,731,000 kWH of electric power in 1975 and 1,831,000 kWH in 1974. The cost of abatement of air pollution created by the production of this power is estimated at $.02 per kWH.

Note 23: The company generated 1,894,464 commuting trip miles in 1975 and 2,079,450 miles in 1974 (4,784 and 4,037 per staff member). The cost of abatement of air pollution caused by automobile commuting is estimated at $.01 per mile.

Note 24: The company used 212 tons of paper in 1975 and 200 tons in 1974. The cost of abatement of water pollution created by the manufacture of this paper is estimated at $35 per ton.

Note 25: The company paid dividends of $74,000 in 1975 and $59,000 in 1974 which are treated as benefit to the stockholders and added for the first time this year.

Note 26: Salaries paid exclusive of training investment and fringe benefits are valued at total salaries earned by staff (1975: $6,473,000 and 1974: $6,231,000) less training investment (note 27).

Note 27: Training investment in staff is a social cost to the company and stockholders because time spent in training is not billable to contracts and results in less profit per staff member. The staff survey (note 3) indicates the amount of time staff spent in training and these percentages have been applied to total salaries for time worked (note 26) to delineate training investment.

Note 28: Figures taken from 1975 and 1974 financial income statement.

Note 29: Figures taken from 1975 and 1974 financial income statement and adjusted for itemized expenditures. The 1974 amount shown on the 1974 statement has been changed from $1,860,000 to $1,796,000 because social audit development and retirement income plan are now shown as itemized expenditures (notes 41 and 42).

Note 30: Vacation and holiday is part of the annual payroll for time worked and is valued at its cost to the company.

Note 31: Actual expenditures on building maintenance are a social and economic cost to the company and stockholders.

Note 32: Federal, state and local taxes paid by the company represent social and economic cost because they result in a direct loss of funds to the company. Valuation is based upon cost to the company.

Note 33: The cost of health, dental and life insurance purchased for staff is assumed to be equal to its cost to the company.

Note 34: Sick leave is part of the annual payroll for time worked and its cost is assumed to be equal to its cost to the company.

Note 35: Valuation of staff food service is assumed to be equal to its cost to the company of $47,000 for food and coffee provided and $26,000 for the value of space given up to provide eating facilities (4,000 sq. ft. at $6.50).

Note 36: Valuation of child care facility is based on its cost to the company of $26,000 for food and other miscellaneous services.

Note 37: Valuation of tuition reimbursement is equal to its cost to the company.

Note 38: Valuation of employee stock ownership plan is assumed to be equal to its cost to the company of $30,000 in 1975.

Note 39: Interest payments are a social and economic cost to the company and stockholders because the amount spent to borrow money cannot be used for other purposes. Social cost is equal to the amount actually spent during the year.

Note 40: Income foregone on paid-in capital is the opportunity cost to stockholders of having equity (beginning 1975: $3,166,000 and beginning 1974: $2,698,000) tied up in the company. The opportunity cost is equivalent to the expected return on investment in a medium-risk venture (estimated at 12 percent) less dividends paid during the year (1975: $74,000 and 1974: $59,000).

Note 41: Valuation of social audit development is equal to its cost to the company during the year.

Note 42: Employee retirement income plan was started as a new staff benefit in 1974. Its social cost to the company is equal to amounts spent on the plan by the company each year.

Note 43: The 1974 net benefits for stockholders was restated because of the addition of dividends to stockholders (note 25).

Note 44: Total number of employees increased from 519 in 1974 to 536 in 1975 and these numbers are reflected in the totals reported in the social and financial income statements.

Note 45: Salaries paid for time worked is valued at the total amount of pay staff receive for time worked during the year. Average salary per employee was $12,076 in 1975 and $12,005 in 1974.

Note 46: Career advancement is equated to the added earning power from salary increases for merit or promotion. The annualized salary increases (monthly amount times 12) was $758,000 in 1975 and $700,000 in 1974. Average increase per employee was $1,414 in 1975 and $1,348 in 1974.

Note 47: Vacation and holidays is a social benefit to the staff valued at its dollar cost to the company which resulted in a benefit per employee of $1,423 in 1975 and $1,385 in 1974.

Note 48: The value of health, dental and life insurance provided by the company is assumed to be equal to the cost of purchasing comparable coverage individually by full-time staff. For each dollar spent, the company generates $1.80 of benefits per employee. Benefits per employee amounted to $847 in 1975 and $888 in 1974.

Note 49: Sick leave is a social benefit to the staff assumed to be equal to its cost to the company. Benefits per employee were $345 in 1975 and $356 in 1974.

Note 50: The value of the retirement income plan is equal to the cost of purchasing the plan by the company. Benefits per employee were $220 in 1975 and $192 in 1974.

Note 51: The employee stock ownership plan is a new benefit to staff which is valued at its cost to the company.

Note 52: Staff food service is a social benefit to the staff valued at its cost to the company (note 35). Benefits per employee were $136 in 1975 and $129 in 1974.

Note 53: Free parking is offered to all employees and is a social benefit to staff valued at the estimated savings in terms of alternative locations. Free parking privileges are assumed to be worth $30 per month and the number of parking spaces increased from 150 in 1974 to 222 in 1975. Benefits per employee were $225 in 1975 and $183 in 1974.

Note 54: The value of the quality of work space the company provides employees is estimated to be the amount of floor space per staff (125 sq. ft. in 1975 and 130 sq. ft. in 1974) exceeding industry standards (average of 90 sq. ft. per employee). The value of actual square footage in excess of industry standards is estimated at $6.50/sq. ft. As a result of company employment growth, the average benefit per employee has decreased from $258 in 1974 to $227 in 1975.

Note 55: Valuation of tuition reimbursement as a benefit to staff is based on the cost to the company (note 37). Average benefits per employee were $42 in 1975 and $28 in 1974.

Note 56: The value of social benefits the child care center provides to the staff is equal to the cost to the company (note 36). Average benefits per employee were $48 in 1975 and $34 in 1974.

Note 57: The value of social benefits the credit union provides to the staff (in the form of lower interest rates for loans and higher dividends for deposits) is measured at its cost to the company for resources contributed such as staff salaries (1975: $15,000 and 1974: $10,000) and floor space and other services (1975: $1,000 and 1974: $1,000).

Note 58: Recreation center membership is offered to all employees and is a social benefit to the staff valued at the estimated saving members receive in terms of alternative membership in swimming and tennis clubs. Saving per member is estimated to be $225 per year. In 1975 there were 157 staff memberships compared to 120 in 1974.

Note 59: Opportunity cost of total time worked is a social cost to the staff because it represents total time given up by the staff while working for the company. The value of this cost to society is equal to the total salaries received for regular working hours (1975: $6,473,000 and 1974: $6,231,000) plus the value of overtime worked but not paid (1975: $1,036,000 and 1974: $1,184,000). Average cost per employee was $14,009 in 1975 and $14,527 in 1974.

Note 60: Absence of retirement plan is a social cost to the four employees who would have had a vested interest (present value of benefits is estimated to be $1,000), but terminated before the retirement plan began on 1 July 1974.

Note 61: Layoffs and involuntary terminations are social costs to the staff. A survey of terminees indicates that 45 percent were still unemployed after 60 days, therefore the social cost is estimated to be one month's salary at time of termination (1975: $1,140 and 1974: $736) for the terminees who found employment within 60 days (1975: 39 and 1974: 40) and two month's salary for the terminees who found work after 60 days (1975: 31 and 1974: 32). The average cost per staff was $213 in 1975 and $148 in 1974.

Note 62: Inequality of opportunity is a social cost to the staff valued at the cost to individuals of the income loss equal to the difference between what the minority individual or female earns and what a non-minority or male individual doing the same job with the same qualifications earns. The social cost of inequality of opportunity has remained constant at $1,000 in 1975 and 1974.

Note 63: Uncompensated loss through theft of staff personal property is a social cost to the staff because of the loss suffered for which they were not reimbursed. The loss has remained constant at $1,000 in 1975 and 1974 after the establishment of security measures.

Note 64: Reducation in parking area in 1974 was a cost to the staff valued at $30 a month for the 80 parking spaces no longer available for staff usage. Parking was increased in 1975 so that the cost to the staff was reduced to zero.

Note 65: Contract research is a benefit to the client and society because it is the primary output of company operations. The value of the benefit is assumed to be equal to the price that the client paid to have the work done (1975: $15,806,000 and 1974: $16,423,000) since this represents the fair market value or cost of the research. A survey of clients indicated that the evaluation of contract values at cost to the client understates the true value to the public of the work performed by the company. However, the available data is not reliable enough to be used to estimate the actual value of the research.

Note 66: The total value of overtime worked and not paid for is a social benefit provided to the client and the general public by the company staff. The 1975 staff survey showed a decrease of overtime to 16 percent of regular working hours ($6,473,000) from 19 percent of regular working hours ($6,231,000) in 1974.

Note 67: Federal and state taxes paid by the company are a social and economic benefit to the general public and their benefit is valued at their cost to the company.

Note 68: Federal and state tax worth of net jobs created are a social benefit to the general public because each new job will create additional tax revenue. Expansion of the company has created 17 net new jobs in 1975 as compared to 67 in 1974. The tax value of these additional jobs for the federal and state government is computed as 20 percent of the average starting salary of $12,000 weighted by the proportion of a full year that these net new jobs have been effective (.62).

Note 69: Contribution to knowledge is a social benefit to the general public because publications by the company staff constitute additions to the stock of knowledge. These publications are valued at the average market rate for similar publications which is estimated to be $4,000 for the 18 technical publications in 1975.

Note 70: Cost of contract research is a social cost to the client (federal and state governments) because payment to the company reduces the amount of money available for other purposes and therefore represents a direct cost to society. It is valued at the amount paid to the company (1975: $15,806,000 and 1974: $16,423,000).

Note 71: Federal and state services consumed are social cost to the general public and society because of the company's use of public services that flow from the federal and state governments. See notes 18 and 19 for method of measurement for services consumed.

Note 72: Pollution to the environment caused by the company's operation is a social cost to the general public and society caused by the company operation and not paid for. Valuation of these costs to the client can be found in notes 21, 22 and 23.

Note 73: Local taxes paid by the company are a social benefit to the local community which are valued at their cost to the company.

Note 74: Local tax worth of net jobs created are a social benefit to the local community because each new job will create additional tax revenue. Expansion of the company has created 17 net new jobs in 1975, a decrease from 67 in 1974. Additional revenue to the local community are in terms of sales taxes, excise taxes and real estate taxes estimated to be 3.2 percent of the average starting salary of $12,000, weighted by the proportion of the years that the jobs have been in effect (.62).

Note 75: Environmental improvements are a direct, visible social benefit to the local community that are valued at their cost to the company. In 1975 the company spent $29,000 on landscaping, a decrease from $36,000 in 1974.

Note 76: Reduction in parking area in 1974 was a social benefit to the local community because it reduced pollution, traffic and other social problems associated with automobiles. However, the parking area was increased during 1975 so that there was no social benefit to the community in 1975.

Note 77: Increase in parking area in 1975 (72 spaces) was a social cost to the local community because of increased automobile usage during the year. The value of this cost is estimated at the amount of pollution caused by 72 automobiles commuting an average of 18.4 miles per day and the cost of abatement of air pollution estimated at $.01 per mile (1975: $3,000).

Note 78: Local services consumed are a social cost to the local community because use of these services by the company reduces the amount of services available for others in the community. See note 20 for details on the calculation of this cost to the local community.

Note 79: Total social benefit for 1974 has been increased from $44,133,000 (note 25).

Note 80: Total net social benefit for 1974 has been increased from $3,429,000 (notes 25, 43 and 79).

Selected Readings

Anshen, Melvin, ed. *Managing the Socially Responsible Corporation.* New York: The Macmillan Co., 1974.

Becker, Gary S. *Human Capital: A Theoretical and Empirical Analysis, with Special Reference to Education.* New York: National Bureau of Economic Research, distributed by Columbia University Press, 1964.

Biderman, Albert D., and Thomas F. Drury, eds. *Measuring Work Quality for Social Reporting.* New York: John Wiley and Sons, 1976.

Bradshaw, Thornton F., ed. *Participation: The Social Responsibilities Report of Atlantic Richfield Company.* Los Angeles: Atlantic Richfield Company, 1975.

Clearinghouse on Corporate Social Responsibility. *1975 Social Reporting. Program of the Life and Health Insurance Business.* New York, 1975.

Commission on Private Philanthropy and Public Needs. *Giving in America: Toward a Stronger Voluntary Sector.* 1975.

Dierkes, Meinolf, and R. A. Bauer, eds. *Corporate Social Accounting.* New York: Praeger Publishers, 1973.

Dorfman, Robert, and Nancy S. Dorfman. *Economics of the Environment.* New York: W. W. Norton and Company, 1972.

Fitzsimmons, Stephen J., Lorrie Stuart, and Peter Wolff. *Social Assessment Manual.* Cambridge, Mass.: Abt Associates Inc., 1975.

Hansen, W. Lee, ed. *Education, Income, and Human Capital.* New York: Columbia University Press, 1970.

Humble, John. *The Responsible Multinational Enterprise.* London: Foundation for Business Responsibilities, 1975.

McKie, James W., ed. *Social Responsibility and the Business Predicament.* Washington, D.C.: The Brookings Institution, 1974.

Public Interest Research Centre Ltd. "Social Audit on the Avon Rubber Co. Ltd." London, 1976.

Seidler, Lee J., and Lynn L. Seidler. *Social Accounting: Theory, Issues, and Cases.* Los Angeles: Melville Publishing Company, 1975.

Sethi, S. Prakash, ed. *The Unstable Ground: Corporate Social Policy in a Dynamic Society.* Los Angeles: Melville Publishing Company, 1974.

Sethi, S. Prakash. *Up Against the Corporate Wall*. Englewood Cliffs, N.J.: Prentice-Hall, 1971.

Sorkin, Alan L. *Health Economics*. Lexington, Mass.: Lexington Books, D. C. Heath and Company, 1976.

Tufte, Edward R., ed. *The Quantitative Analysis of Social Problems*. Reading, Mass.: Addison-Wesley Publishing Company, 1970.

U.S. Office of Management and Budget. "Social Indicators." Washington, D.C.: Social and Economic Statistics Administration, U.S. Department of Commerce, 1973.

Wagner, Harvey M. *Principles of Operations Research with Applications to Managerial Decisions*. Englewood Cliffs, N.J.: Prentice-Hall, 1969.

Webb, Eugene J., D. T. Campbell, R. D. Schwartz, and L. Séchrest. *Unobtrusive Measures: Nonreactive Research in the Social Sciences*. Chicago: Rand McNally College Publishing Company, 1966.

Index

s s

research and development, in technology utilization, 161–164
residents, *see* community
resources, in financial accounting, 47
responsibility, social, *see* social responsibility
responsiveness in social measurements, 36
retirement plans, 173, 200–201
revenue realization, in accounting theory, 190
R.G. Barry Corporation, 130–132
Rickover, Hyman, 209
risk/benefit analyses, 41–43

safety, in quality of life, 167
San Juan Bautista, California, 70
satisficing, 49*n*.
schools
 corporate commitment to, 95–96, 98–99
 in corporate responsibilities, 16, 18
 see also education
Schuhmacher, E.F., 122*n*.
scientific methods, in management of corporate social programs, 105–107
Scovill Manufacturing Company, 138–148
Sears, Roebuck & Company, 237
Securities and Exchange Commission, 124
security, in quality of life, 167
Sethi, S. Prakash, 238*n*.
shadow prices, 23, 111–112
 in social efficiency of technology, 170
shareholders
 responsibilities to, 2, 12
 social measurements useful to, 35
Sheldon, Eleanor, 10
Smith, Adam, 28, 156
Smith, Adam (pseudonym), 105*n*

sociability, in quality of life, 167
social accounts
 financial accounts compared with, 45–47, 111, 192–198, 242
 financial accounts integrated with, 39, 41, 52–58, 247–248
Social Audit, 129
social audits
 of Abt Associates, 254–264
 accounting theory in, 188–193
 antecedents of, 217
 in corporate responsibilities, 9–13
 corporations' use of, 91–96
 costs and time required for, 111–116
 criticisms of, 181–206
 data bases for, 215–216
 examples of, 130–150
 future of, 216–219, 247–248
 by government, 117–129, 247
 implementation of, 87–110
 interdisciplinary approach in, 218
 in legal requirements, 223–226
 in management decisions, 60–86
 methods and criteria in, 20–43
 problems involved in, 220–223
social balance sheets, 44–59, 205–206
social bankruptcy, 58–59
social change
 costs of, 109–110
 technology in, 161–171
social credit, 59
social evaluation research, 226–231
social experiments, companies as, 152–154
social ideology, 152
social income, 45–47, 50
social income statements, 45
social indicators, 5–6, 126*n*.
 see also social measurement
social investments, 48
socialism, 2, 3
social measurement, 7
 corporations' use of, 91–96

DATE DUE			
APR 25 '88			
JUL 07 1994			